Sea...

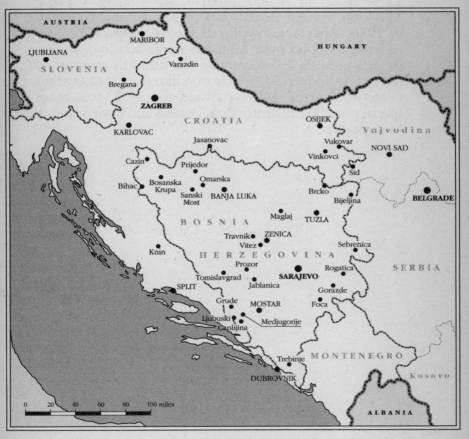

Croatia and Bosnia-Herzegovina

Ed Vulliamy was born and grew up in Notting Hill, London, and was educated at Oxford University. He trained with the Mirror Group and was a journalist with Granada TV's 'World in Action' programme, winning a Royal Television Society Award, before joining the *Guardian* in 1986. After a fellowship at the *Washington Post*, he returned to report from Romania, Berlin and Iraq, and on the Italian Mafia and corruption scandals. His coverage of the wars in former Yugoslavia won him Granada's Foreign Correspondent of the Year Award for 1992, plus other special prizes in the British Press Awards and from Amnesty International.

Seasons in Hell

Understanding Bosnia's War

Ed Vulliamy

SIMON & SCHUSTER

LONDON·SYDNEY·NEW YORK·TOKYO·SINGAPORE·TORONTO

First published in Great Britain by Simon & Schuster Ltd, 1994
A Paramount Communications Company

Copyright © Ed Vulliamy, 1994

The right of Ed Vulliamy to be identified as author of this
work has been asserted in accordance with sections 77 and 78
of the Copyright, Designs and Patents Act 1988.

Simon & Schuster Ltd
West Garden Place
Kendal Street
London W2 2AQ

Simon & Schuster of Australia Pty Ltd
Sydney

A CIP catalogue record for this book is available
from the British Library.

ISBN 0-671-71345-0

Typeset in Galliard by
Hewer Text Composition Services, Edinburgh
Printed and bound in Great Britain by
Harper*Collins* Manufacturing, Glasgow

To Emir, Fahro, Nadja and Fikret

Contents

List of Maps

Acknowledgements

No single journalist could honestly say that he or she had 'covered' the war in Bosnia-Herzegovina. It would have been physically impossible, too dangerous and emotionally crippling. Besides, there were two wars, really: the phenomenon and torture of the Sarajevo seige, and the war of 'ethnic cleansing' in the rural hinterland. Oddly, they rarely overlapped. A group of us, however, tried to cover as much of this carnage as we could for the duration of the war and the earlier war in Croatia.

I do believe that in that enterprise, new standards were set by some of the best people I have ever had the good fortune to meet, whom I am now proud to count among my friends, and to thank in this book, an attempt to recount what we have seen. Warm thanks must go to Andrej Gustinčić, with whom I went through the most unforgettable moments of the war; thanks for endless chats in cars and cold barracks, for taking very seriously what was going on around us, but for being able to laugh nonetheless. Many thanks, also, for the splendid companionship on the road of: Michael Montgomery, Alec Russell, Maud S. Beelman, Cathy Jenkins, Robert Fox, Kate Adie, Alan Hayman, John Pomfret, Patrick Bishop, Tony Smith, Tim Judah, John Landay, Tamara Levak, Richard Beeston, Marc Champion, Jeremy Cooke, Jeremy Stigter, Penny Marshall, Erica Zlomislić and Ian Williams.

This book inevitably focuses on those few episodes of the war that I witnessed. To attempt anything like a comprehensive picture, I have had to rely on the eyes, ears and work of these colleagues and friends, to become a sort of master of ceremonies and in places to introduce and quote them. Most of us thought we could make a difference, at first. It seemed incredible that the world could watch, read and hear about what was happening to the victim people of this war, and yet do nothing – and worse. As it turned out, we went unheeded by the diplomats and on occasions were even cursed by political leaders, notably Douglas Hurd. But we were heeded by our reading, listening and viewing public, which was at least part of the object of the excercise. Bosnia's tragedy would have gone unseen and unheard of, were it not for the courage and commitment of the following:

From the *Guardian*, my colleagues Ian Traynor, Maggie O'Kane and Yigal Chazan. From Reuters, Andrej Gustincic, Kurt Schork, Mark Heinrich, Richard Meares, Meriel Beattie and Hugh Paine. From the *Daily Telegraph*, Robert Fox, Mike Montgomery, Patrick Bishop and Alec Russell. From the BBC, Martin Bell, Kate Adie, Alan Little, Jeremy Bowen, Misha Glenny, John Simpson, Cathy Jenkins, Jeremy Cooke and Martin Dawes. From the *Washington Post*, Blane Harden and John Pomfret, and from the *New York Times*, John Burns and Chuck Sudetic. From *Newsday*, Roy Gutman and from National Public Radio, Tom Gjetlen. From the Associated Press, Tony Smith and Maud S. Beelman, and from UPI John Landay. From *The Times*, Tim Judah and Richard Beeston; and from *The Independent*, Robert Fisk, Marc Champion and Marcus Tanner. From the *Observer*, Colin Smith, John Sweeney and Victoria Clark; and from *The Sunday Times*, Janine di Giovanni and Andrew Hogg. From ITN, Penny Marshall and Ian Williams and from ABC Tony Birtley. From *Libération* Didier François, from *El Mundo* Alfonso Rojo and from *El País* Hermann Tersch. Then there were the photographers: Steve Connors, Corrine Dufka, Chris Helgren, Ron Haviv, Jon Jones, Jeremy Stigter, and many others, of the highest quality and determination. Forty-two reporters and photographers were killed while covering this war – more than in Vietnam and Lebanon put together; there is a special homage due to them.

In Sarajevo, special thanks to Senada Krešo and Bojan Zec for their resilience, to the staff of the Holiday Inn and to all at *Oslobodjenje* and Radio Zid. Thanks to the BBC's encampments in central Bosnia for tea bags, proper beer and

Cadbury's chocolate. Among the soldiers of the 1st Battalion 22 Cheshire Regiment, thanks to Colonel Bob Stewart for his late night 'Sit. Reps' and outspoken principles, and to Captains Martin Forgrave, Simon Ellis, Mark Cooper and Bob Ryan for their decency and high spirits. Thanks for the unsung labours of the interpreters and fixers, who take all the risks without getting the bylines, notably Tamara Levak, and Erica Zlomislić to whom I am indebted for translating on the road and from documents and videos for this book. Thanks also to Fedja Dalagija, Sanja Kovačević and Dina Stojpović for their help on the manuscript.

I owe a debt of gratitude to Peter Preston, Jonathan Fenby, Paul Webster, Peter Murtagh and everyone on the Foreign Desk at the *Guardian* who decided at the outset that the atrocity of Bosnia should be given the attention that they rightly gave it. My thanks to Nick Richmond for his assiduous surveys of the picture archives, to Paul Blake for his essential help with computers, and to Finbarr Sheehy for drawing the maps. Many thanks also to my editor Carol O'Brien, and to Jessica Cuthbert-Smith and Sian Parkhouse for producing the book.

Most of us were at some point accused – and this book will be accused – of being 'pro-Muslim', whatever that means. For some reason, the instinct to stand by democratic Europe's basic principles was to be considered 'pro-Muslim' in Bosnia, and the principles were sunk beneath what people shrugged off as 'the realities on the ground' or some bizarre requirement that we remain 'objective' over the most appalling racialist violence. There is no attempt here to be objective towards the perpetrators of Bosnia's ethnic carnage or those who appeased them. My gratitude to the public figures who refused to be 'objective' in this cynical, cowardly way: Lady Thatcher, Paddy Ashdown and Michael Meacher, and to George Kenney and Marshall Harris of the US State Department for resigning in disgust at their government's whimsical caprice.

Finally, no thanks to the staff of Croatia Airways who must have made a lot of money by stealing flak jackets, helmets and

Swiss army knives out of our baggage with such depressing regularity.

War is a curious, many-sided thing, and the courage and optimism of the good people is often as heartening as the downward spiral of barbarism and betrayal is demoralising. Each time I leave Bosnia, relieved to be safely out again, part of me always yearns to be back there, where values are raw.

Note: The day after the discovery of the Serbian camp at Omarska, I gave the ridiculous number of fifty-four television and radio interviews. There were newspaper headlines that day like 'Belsen 1992'. The reaction was so tumultuous that, to my annoyance, I was obliged to spend more time emphasising that Omarska was not Belsen or Auschwitz than detailing the abomination of what we had found. At the time, I declined to use the term 'concentration camp', because of its resonance since the Nazi Holocaust. On reflection, however, I have decided that 'concentration camp' is exactly the right term. That is precisely what Omarska and some of the other camps operated by the Serbs and later the Croatians were: places in which populations were concentrated prior to enforced deportation and meanwhile tortured, beaten and murdered in large numbers. I use the term in its pre-1939 meaning.

Although several thousand people were undoubtedly murdered in the more infamous of the camps, it would be wrong to say they were 'Extermination Camps' or 'Death Camps', which are the proper descriptions of the Nazi camps alone. I insist that Omarska and others, including the worst Croatian camps at Dretelj and elsewhere, warrant the strict definition of 'concentration camp', but there is no intention to draw parallels with the scale of the Nazi Holocaust, or to belittle that outrage, nor is any disrespect intended to its survivors or the memory of its victims. That there are political resonances common to both the Nazi project and the present Balkan persecutions is, however, a fundamental theme of this book.

Dramatis Personae

The Presidents

Slobodan Milošević: president of Serbia

Franjo Tudjman: president of Croatia

Alija Izetbegović: president of Bosnia-Herzegovina

Milan Panić
Dobrica Cosić } presidents of the rump Yugoslavia (Serbia and Montenegro)

Breakaway Presidents within Bosnia

Radovan Karadžić: president of the Serbian Republic of Bosnia-Herzegovina

Mate Boban: president of the Croatian Union of Herzeg-Bosna

Others

General Ratko Mladić: commander, Bosnian-Serbian forces

General Sefer Halilović: commander, Army of Bosnia-Herzegovina

Ejup Ganic: deputy president of Bosnia-Herzegovina

Stjepan Kljuić: ousted Croatian member of the Bosnian presidency, loyal to the government

Organisations

Military:

HVO: army of the Bosnian Croats

HV: army of Croatia proper

Armija: (mixed mainly Muslim) Government Army of the Republic of Bosnia-Herzegovina

MOS: Muslim Armed Forces or 7th Muslim Brigade (fundamentalist Brigade in the Armija)

HOS: Croatian Defence Association (Fascist Croat Militia)

Political

SDS: Serbian Democratic Party (Serbs in Bosnia)

SDA: Democratic Action Party (Muslims in Bosnia)

HDZ: Croatian Democratic Union (Croats in Croatia proper and in Bosnia)

International

EC: European Community

NATO: North Atlantic Treaty Organisation

WEU: Western European Union

UN: United Nations

UNHCR: United Nations High Commission for Refugees

UNPROFOR: United Nations Protection Force

Introduction

The War of Maps

August 1992

The sun sank disloyally behind the mountain ridge, so that a heavy indigo dusk hung from the sky, and still we had no idea where we were. Columns of soldiers were moving in and out of the woods above the fields that ran along the otherwise lonely track, and the first shots of the evening echoed across the valley, some of them just above our heads. 'Go to Allah!' shouted one of the Serbian soldiers, in mockery. 'Butcher them!', they had shrieked from the wayside, soldiers and children alike.

Our ramshackle procession of old cars, heaving trucks and buses had spent the day being herded over the mountains by gunmen and lynch mobs, through an extended gauntlet of hatred and humiliation. The 1,600 Muslims who packed the lurching convoy had been kicked and bullied out of their homes that morning. 'Ethnic cleansing' it was called in the world out there, but here and now its name was bewildered, desolate fear. And now we had been stopped again, by more soldiers, then moved on, then stopped again. Each time, more kicking, more spitting, more checking, and before long, the last of the twilight was lost to unwelcome night. They were cocking their guns, heard but unseen in the bushes by the road, and still we had no idea where we were.

At the next roadblock, the soldiers started taking the cars,

one by one. The people were silent and submissive as the
guards yanked them out of the seats with one hand, while
sticking the barrel of a machine gun at their chests with the
other. Slowly and carefully, the refugees took out what they
thought they might be able to manage on foot, to wherever
we were going. And when the cars were gone and buses had
belched out their passengers and turned back, we were cast
out along the road like some great phantom parade: the
old, the crippled, the weary and the very young. Ahead,
the bright fire of the rockets was slicing the dark sky, each
time in a perfect arc, and crashing onto the road. The battle
was starting. Further along, fresh blood was sprayed across
the asphalt in places. It was sticky underfoot and there were
worse things to tread on: human pieces, ripped flesh strewn
here and there along the lane. Slowly they shuffled forward
the only direction the cast-out refugee knows. Even the little
children were dumb with fear and resolve.

Bosnia's war unfolded in modern Europe, at the birth of the
New World Order, although it often looked like a war
from another time. Europe was luxuriating in her union
of economies and had barely completed celebrating the
triumph of Western democracy in the newly expanded,
post-communist continent, when it was confronted from
Bosnia by the first serious test of its political and moral
fibre and of its new military role.

The war has baffled that new world. It has been errone-
ously portrayed as too complicated to understand. In reality,
although it is being fought in the labyrinthine cauldron of
Balkan history, Bosnia's war is cruelly simple. It is the result
of the resurrection in our time of the dreams and aggrieved
historical quests of two great Balkan powers of medieval
origin, Serbia and Croatia, and the attempt to re-establish
their ancient frontiers with modern weaponry in the chaos
of post-communist eastern Europe. Where the frontiers of
these two dreams overlap or do not fit together, there is
either war or compromise. Either way, there exists a third

people who do not fit, who do not belong to either Serbia or Croatia, and whose homeland is a third, ethnically mixed, country which emerged between the two great Balkan powers, called Bosnia. Bosnia is shared between Serbs, Croats and the third people, Slavic Muslims.

The Bosnian war is above all the War of Maps and the War of the '*narod*'. '*Narod*' is the slavonic word for 'people' in a sense that resembles the German '*das Volk*'; it means 'people' and 'nation' at the same time. You hear it everywhere in former Yugoslavia nowadays, every tap-room philosopher, television broadcaster, toothless soldier, is always on about the '*narod*': the *Hrvatski narod*, the Croatian people; the *Srpski narod*, the Serbian people; and also the *Bosanski narod*, the Bosnian people, which means something much more complicated; and of late, the *Musulmanski narod*, the Muslim people, too.

The Serbs and the Croats have, in the past few years, re-discovered assertive and deep-rooted identities as *narods* in this race-conscious way. Both are south Slav peoples (or 'Jugo-slav'; *jug* means south) but derive very different identities from their respective and rival traditions. In the War of Maps and of the *narod*, there is no such thing as objective history, and no consensus over the maps that delineate the rightful frontiers of this *narod* or that. With what becomes either an irksome or terrifying tedium, history dominates every interview in the Bosnian war. The answer to a question about an artillery attack yesterday will begin in the year 925, invariably illustrated with maps. Eventually you realise that what is so important to the participants in the war has to be important to any understanding of it.

Christianity moved in two convergent directions across the south Slav lands during the awakening from the dark ages: from the west, eastwards, came Charlemagne's armies of the Roman Catholic Frankish empire. From the east, westwards, came those of the Orthodox Byzantine emperors. The original southern Slav people had arrived in the Balkans from what is now Poland and Russia as marauders of the Roman empire, but had settled and now began to convert to Christianity – but convert to two separate churches. Dalmatia and Croatia came within Charlemagne's domain, and under the cloak of the Roman faith, while Serbia and Macedonia came within the Byzantine empire and their creed was Orthodoxy.

The principality of Serbia emerged under the tutelage of Byzantium, but by the twelfth century it had become a powerful independent kingdom. From a territory called Raška, King Nemanja began the building of a Balkan power which reached its zenith in the mid-1300s under the Emperor Dusan, who proclaimed himself 'Czar of the Serbs and Greeks' in 1346. Within a century, it had been buried under the Turkish advance, but the last years of Serbia's empire were marked by a vigorous cultural nationalism which has since refused to die.

The Croatian Slavs had accepted the suzerainty of Emperor Charlemagne early in the ninth century, but his Holy Roman empire was pushed back by Byzantium within a generation. In 924, however, the Croatian King Tomislav led a remarkable expansion, free of both Frankish and Byzantine influence, all the way from Istria in the west, north to the present Hungarian border and as far east as the river Drina, where it faced what was then Serbian Raška and is now Serbia. Some old Croatian maps, re-produced during the Croatian war of 1991, have the disputed frontiers of Tomislav's kingdom stretching all the way to the Zemun river, near Belgrade. The kingdom's frontiers lasted three years before being eroded, and Croatia absorbed within Hungarian rule.

Croatia's awkward horseshoe shape reflects the eastern frontier of Charlemagne's empire, and the later western extremity of the Ottoman empire, both circumstances firing the Croats' conviction that they are the gatekeepers of western Christendom against the Byzantine perversion and Ottoman infidelity. The inside curve of the horseshoe is the belt called the 'Krajina', which means 'military frontier'. But the horseshoe, which is the frontier of the state that won its independence from Yugoslavia in 1992, is not enough for the Croats, and the Drina is not enough for the Serbs, for each has *narod* caught outside those boundaries.

All this history seems of little import to the outsider. But suffice it to say that one of the first things the Croats in Bosnia did after independence from Yugoslavia in 1992 was to rename the place of King Tomislav's coronation, Duvno, Tomislavgrad. But Tomislavgrad does not lie within the horseshoe frontier, it is within the frontiers of the third country, Bosnia-Herzegovina. And suffice it to say that the event carefully chosen for the launch of 'Greater Serbia' as a serious political project in 1989 was a vast drunken rally, addressed by Serbian President Slobodan Milošević, on the field of the battle of Kosovo Polje, where in 1389 the Serbian army was finally defeated by the oncoming Turks – an event revived as the emblematic focus for the avenging memory of the Serbian *narod*. On the eve of Yugoslavia's present war, both sides became involved in the cult of digging up rotting bodies: Serbian victims of fascist Croatia, Croat victims of communist partisans, all subject to obsessive television coverage.

Since medieval times, the Serbian and Croatian '*narods*' have been variously subjugated by Hungarians, Turks, Hapsburgs or – as they saw it – communists, and have staged fiery political rebellions, each drawing upon the inspiration of some perceived Golden Age before the Ottoman empire. Both have risen against their overlords and each other, and both have enjoyed brief periods of sometimes terrifying power before being held in check by the canny wit of Marshall Josip Broz Tito's soft communist dictatorship.

The general revival of nationalism in Europe that followed the fall of the Berlin Wall in 1989 found its most pernicious and robust expression in the War of Maps already nascent between the Serbs and Croats during the 1980s. The context was the surge of popular revolutions against communist tyranny, which generated a re-emergence of old maps and *narods*: Russians, Ukrainians, Georgians, Armenians, Moldavians, Slovaks, Czechs and others. There was the revival of nationalism in Germany, Poland and Hungary, and separatist movements sprouted in northern Italy and Spain, all charting their new maps by resurrecting old ones.

But nowhere were the new maps so ubiquitous as in former Yugoslavia, and nowhere were their frontiers so charged with historical emotion. They were on the walls of barracks, in the soldiers' handbooks, pinned up in cafés and framed above the hearth.

Milan Kovačević, the big, impervious and haunted deputy mayor of the now Serbian-controlled town of Prijedor – and the man responsible for the delivery of Muslim prisoners to the Omarska concentration camp – precedes a visit to the camp in August 1992 that he does not want to happen with a study session over a series of maps drawn up by Stefan Moljević and Nikola Kalabić, founders of the modern 'Greater Serbia' project, in 1941. The maps show a 'future Yugoslavia' in which Serbia encompasses all of Bosnia-Herzegovina and all southern Croatia, leaving behind a rump around Zagreb and Osijek and what looks like a vassal Dalmatia. The bearish Mr Kovačević runs his rugged finger along a line of text atop the map with careful deliberation: 'The first and main duty imposed on Serbs today,' he reads, 'is to create and organise a homogenous Serbia to encompass the whole ethnic region in which the Serbs live, and to provide and ensure necessary strategic and traffic lines in order to afford a free economic, political and cultural life, for ever.' Moustachioed, fair-haired Mr Kovačević looks up with a message in his eyes of both solemnity and mischief. We must understand, he says, that wherever there are Serbs, there is Serbia, and that Serbs cannot be 'free from persecution' until Kalabić's and Moljević's frontiers are 'secured from all the enemies of the Serbian *narod*'. With that, he arches his back, raises his chin defiantly, folds up the map slowly and deliberately and puts it away in his neat leather file. 'You are lucky enough to be witnessing a great moment in the history of the Serbian nation,' he says, rolling his eyes in a slightly feverish way. Kovačević was born in a Croatian concentration camp during the Second World War. Outside the window of his office, Muslim women are queuing at the police station for news of their menfolk, whom they have not seen since they were taken away to Kovačević's camps two months ago.

Just as menacing, many months later, is the vituperative Colonel Joko Šiljeg, commander of the Bosnian–Croat army in wintry Tomislavgrad, with forest-like eyebrows and a curiously deadpan expression in his dark eyes which seems at odds with the way he grinds the tabletop with his hairy fists as he speaks, slowly and loudly. He produces a series of twelve maps on the same windswept October evening that his men return for a boozy night on the town, having been to Prozor about thirty miles up the road. In Prozor, Colonel Šiljeg's militias have just given the Muslim civilians a good nights' pounding with tank and artillery fire before going in with machine guns at dawn today to 'flush them out'; the first, sudden wave of Croatian 'ethnic cleansing' against their erstwhile allies. Five thousand unarmed Muslim civilians are tonight looking for mountain caves in which to hide.

The Colonel takes two hours to justify this action by meticulous explanation of all twelve maps. They begin with Croatia's 'rightful' frontiers of 925–28, in this instance extending across all of Bosnia-Herzegovina. Then Croatia shrinks, across nine maps, as upstart countries such as Bosnia emerge, and with successive invasions of the Balkans. Colonel Šiljeg feels the pain of this process, and finally accepts a glass of wine to calm himself. In 1939, something resembling modern Croatia is recognised as an autonomous province, says Colonel Šiljeg, building up to a crescendo, and suddenly in 1941 her frontiers burst free to their former glory of a millennium ago. Colonel Šiljeg pours another glass of wine, but this latest 'Independent State of Croatia' was formed under Nazi tutelage and, as a former professional soldier in the communist Yugoslav army, Colonel Šiljeg adds that 'maybe the Nazi element was not commendable, but the national and territorial aspect, yes. This is our cause.' The penultimate map is the 'horseshoe' republic recognised in 1992, and the last one, number 12, is entitled 'Future Croatian Federation'. It shows a Croatia that envelops all of Bosnia-Herzegovina, which ceases to exist. The maps were devised in South America by Croatian emigrants. There is gunfire outside in the streets of Tomislavgrad; nothing to worry about, says Colonel Šiljeg with a disagreeable smile, only 'night games'. The lads are celebrating their victory over the Muslim civilians of Prozor.

In the middle of the War of Maps is Bosnia-Herzegovina. Over this country, the frontiers of Serbia or Croatia, and the wayward dreams of each, interweave, overlap and retreat down the centuries and into the proposed future. Like some unfortunate buffer between *narods*, Bosnia-Herzegovina is usually there in some mutated form, also enjoying its own golden ages of ample territory. But frequently, it disappears altogether in the grand designs of the *narods*. Bosnia-Herzegovina has always been a mixed country made up of all the south Slav peoples. In 1992, Bosnia voted for its independence from Yugoslavia and won international recognition as a sovereign, multi-ethnic state based on the principles of modern Western democracy. The biggest ethnic group was Muslim, followed by Serbs and then Croats. But there was no place for a shared country in the War of Maps that was already under way behind the scenes. The Serbs and the Croats opposed but understood each other as they resurrected their ancient dreams and set out to fulfil their historical missions and regain their frontiers. For those dreams to be realised, or a compromise between them found, the Muslims of Bosnia would have to be dealt with.

But before they could turn their attention to Bosnia and the Muslims, the armies of the two *narods* faced each other on the plains of Croatia.

Prelude

The War in Croatia

November 1991

'So you see, life can begin under some pretty strange circumstances,' says Branka, the ruddy-faced young midwife whose smile is a ready one but which requires a lot of effort these days. The poky, subterranean room in which she has lived and worked for a month is now the maternity ward of what was the Vinkovci General Hospital, entirely decamped into the cellars. Five storeys of wards and offices have been reduced to a gutted skeleton of concrete and broken glass standing on the exposed edges of town, 300 yards from the Serbian front line at Mirkovci, across the river. Every few minutes, the coughing of rusty heating pipes in the little 'maternity ward' is interrupted by a rough, loud thud on the ground above, as another rocket lands in the courtyard. Branka ducks instinctively but pointlessly. Just the day before, little Anna Miljenko was born; she sleeps though the artillery attack above. 'No, you do not get used to it,' says Branka. In the 'ward' next door, the next baby waits to be born; beside the mother lies the naked body of a man who has just died, his face covered with a cloth.

During the past month, 1,300 wounded people have been brought down into this Hades. And there is a sudden commotion: three more are about to be added to the list. Men rush down the stairway, clearing a way for the bearers of three stretchers, carrying men who were trying to defuse a mine which blew up. One of them is moaning horribly, with cuts to his legs, body and face; the second is unconscious but alive and twitching, and has been transformed from a human being into something resembling a piece of meat in a butcher's shop window. The third is limp, his arms folded over his shredded body. They are wheeled into another claustrophobic corner of the basement, the 'intensive care unit'.

Josip Dolanski took over as director of one of the best hospitals in the region last year. 'I have no real recollection what it was like then,' he says, 'I cannot really imagine it any more. Nor can I imagine any future peace either. Some of us go out every now and then to get some air, but come back down pretty fast. This is our home, really, it's like being in a space ship or submarine; but then you make your best friends in a submarine.'

Vinkovci was the last Croatian-held town before the city of Vukovar up the road, under ferocious and infamous siege by the Serbs. Not the last Croatian outpost, however: that was Nustar, where not a single house remained standing on the main street. We drove cautiously through what had been a hamlet teeming with Croatian troops two days beforehand, but which was now deserted apart from a dead pig lying in the road. Suddenly, the explanation came: a mortar twenty yards ahead crashed into the remains of a nearby house, and sent us scurrying into the ditch, face-down. Nustar was now no man's land, another minor adjustment to the dirt-track war, in which there is no front line, just a jigsaw of meandering battlelines across cornfields, ditches and village squares and which shift from day to day.

It is hard to say when the war between Croatia and what was politely called Yugoslavia began. What is certain was that both sides were eager to fight it. Slovenia had, by the skin of her teeth, spirited herself away from the Yugoslav federation with relative ease in summer 1991, after a low-key conflict in which the Yugoslav army put up only a token

resistance. At the time no one quite understood the significance of the Slovene rebellion, least of all the occupants of
an unexpected, beat-up grey Toyota which came chugging
up the track towards a bridge over the motorway at Bregana
in eastern Slovenia, where a crowd had gathered to inspect
the unwelcome overnight arrival of six Yugoslav tanks,
barrels trained on the village and its church spire. Inside
the incongruously British-registered car was the bewildered
Tahir Ghani from Satley, Birmingham, his bearded father
Abdul, aged sixty-two, plus uncle Karim smiling away in
the back amid a load of old kettles, vegetable ghee and
powdered milk. The Ghanis, originally from Kashmir, were
returning home to the West Midlands from their *Hadj* to
Mecca, via Jordan, Syria, Turkey and Yugoslavia. They had
been turned off the main road by the army and were now
lost. 'Why are there so many tanks around?' asked Tahir
in a denim jacket (who supported Birmingham City, he
said, not Aston Villa). 'Because there's a civil war on.'
'Oh. Who's it between?' 'Slovenia and Yugoslavia.' 'Oh,'
said Tahir, adding profuse thanks for the enlightenment,
accepting an adapted map of (so far) war-free routes and
chugging off again, stirring dust off the road, with old uncle
Karim waving out of the back window above the kettles and
vegetable ghee. The Ghanis' confusion at what was going on
was shared by most of their fellow inhabitants of the planet.
Nevertheless, in Slovenia the bloody break-up of Yugoslavia
had begun, and so had Serbia's war.

For the Serbs in the federal capital of Belgrade, Croatia's
referendum and declaration of independence in 1990 had
to be handled differently from Slovenia's. Croatia could
not be left to go its own way, for there was a sizeable
Serbian community in Croatia, and Croatia came within
Serbia's orbit in the War of Maps. Moreover, that Serbian
community was under threat. Provocative legislation by the
Croatian President Franjo Tudjman had required an oath
of loyalty to the new republic 'of the Croatian people', and
some Serbs were already losing their jobs. Even before

the world's baffled attention turned to Slovenia, Serbian vigilantes in their bastion village of Borovo Selo, just inside Croatia, ambushed and killed twelve Croatian policemen. From then on, it was a matter of watching the first War of Maps unfold along all Croatia's frontiers.

'You know what the score is around here this week?' asked the rugged young Serb grinning and brandishing his Kalashnikov in the driving rain at yet another roadblock in eastern Croatia. 'Serbs 3, Croatian police 2. We're winning.' He searched the vehicle roughly and thoroughly, asked a few questions and ushered the car through onto the otherwise deserted road. This was early July 1992, and probably one of the last days on which one could drive with any safety between the patches of territory that were being staked out by the stubborn mobilisations of both sides. There were guns everywhere, and family homes were empty or emptying as people left the land, the Croats for the main body of their republic, the Serbs across the border.

The previous night, the moderate Croatian police chief of Osijek had been murdered by hardliners from his own side in the suburban village of Tenja. At the northern end of Tenja, Croatian lads were taking over the porches and front rooms, muttering into walkie-talkie sets and training their guns down the silent main street. At first they let our car through into the wet, abandoned village, but a youth then followed us, running: 'Don't! Come back, they'll shoot!' Round the corner were the Serbs, controlling the old centre, where just a few old people had stayed on. This boy was Ljuban, who was supposed to be taking his chemistry exams in Zagreb. 'My mother said I should go, but I think I've blown it for this year. If I leave, who will defend the village?' Skirting Tenja, the road was blocked by a parked tractor. Three men appeared from a farmyard in waterproof capes, gumboots and carrying machine guns. As they checked our papers, other armed men emerged to peer from the barns and outbuildings. They wore no insignia but it was soon clear who they

were: the land around Tenja was now Serbian, and these
were its guardians.

A roadblock of uniformed Croatians announced the next
zone, then the Yugoslav army, then more Croats, then the
army again, this time guarding the entrance to the most
bitterly divided village of all: Borovo. 'Keep driving straight
and whatever you do don't turn off', advised the army officer
at the edge of Borovo Selo, the Serbian end, where automatic pistols and telescopic sights were being passed around
and inspected at the Red Star Pizzeria. Then on past another
army check, and next a gaggle of ruffians thirty yards on; it
was anybody's guess whose side they were on. 'You been
in Borovo Selo?' said one with an old rifle and a hare-lip.
'Notice anything funny going on?' These were Croats; the
official welcome to Borovo Naselje, their end of the village.
Beyond that, Vukovar, where you could still have lunch
before meeting up with the motorway and deciding whether
to follow signs for Belgrade or Zagreb. Within days, such a
drive would be unthinkable, probably suicidal.

Two days later, the road from Borovo Naselje to Borovo
Selo was closed. Any car coming up from Vukovar was
flagged down by what were now groups of raucous
Croatians in paramilitary fatigues, camped in a civic building and equipped with two-way radios and a cassette
player spewing banal disco music. The Serbs, who could
be reached by crossing and re-crossing the border, now
offered two hours of unpleasant 'protective detention' in a
barn, taking passports for inspection. Amongst the cattlefeed
was an awesome arsenal of weaponry.

Eight weeks later, the War of the *narod* was raging.
Croatian Osijek was under daily and nightly bombardment.
In the shopping centre-turned-shelter beneath the main
square, people gathered to sleep in makeshift bunk beds,
and as the weeks went by their faces wore down, gaunt
with fear and exhuastion. One terrible evening, during a
glorious sunset, the first bombs were dropped from the air.
Even the zoo was fair game. Suzanna the elephant would

stomp to and fro across her compound while the crack and thud of machine gun and mortar fire filled the air around her. She was lucky enough to be booked in for a transfer to Hungary, but luck failed to protect Mato Barišin, who had been minding the zoo entrance when a mortar landed five yards from his ticket booth, ripping his legs off and wounding his jaw. Mato's blood was still splattered across the gateway when the elephant expert Zoltan Takač arrived from Budapest to befriend the wondrous Suzanna and prepare her for the journey. Ante Pradić, Suzanna's keeper for twenty-five years, was finding it hard to keep a dry eye. 'What can I say? I doubt I will ever see her again. She was in a circus in Czechoslovakia for twelve years, but she didn't obey orders, so she came here. She has been quite good, apart from eating ladies' handbags in the hope of finding candy inside. When the shells come at night she wakes up and charges around in a circle, trumpeting with fear. The kangaroos are still here, and they jump around when the fighting starts; Zita the giraffe also runs and screams.' Zita was the unfortunate one: she was too tall to fit under the bridge across the safe road to Budapest, and would soon be the zoo's lone occupant. The local newpaper ran a story that Rex the Tiger had escaped and was roaming the countryside. 'Actually, it was made up,' admits Mr Pradić, 'to scare the Chetniks'; he cheers up a little. In the goat pound, among the skittish kids, there is a new dugout of Croatian troops, cleaning their weapons in the morning sunshine and firing out at the Serbian lines beyond the fence.

Meanwhile in Zagreb, the war was fought as a piece of high melodrama. A dreadful, sugary ditty was written called 'Stop the War in Croatia' and was played, in English, at every bar and on every radio station without cease until a tune even more heavily laden with syrup was released by a combo of leading artistes calling itself 'Croatia Band Aid', which went something like 'Let Croatia be one of Europe's stars . . .' Twenty miles down the road in Karlovac, the war was accompanied by a squalid violence.

On the driveway beside the morgue at Karlovac hospital, there were piles of maggots, some wriggling, some dead and drying out in the sun, brushed off the flesh on which they had bred and fed during the ten days it could take to get bodies across the battlefields. During one week in October, fifty-four bodies were brought in, mostly civilian. A recent arrival was Nada Tomać, aged thirty-seven, lying on a table in a small room stinking of stale death, wearing a pristine white shirt, a smart two-piece suit and a white lace handkerchief sticking out of her breast pocket. Her shoes were polished and her hair was neatly done. She stared at the ceiling and had two red holes in her pale, lifeless forehead. The certificate compiled by Dr Boris Lović, the pathologist, said: '*Vulnus sclopetarium capitis*' – gunshot wounds to the head – but that did not tell the whole story.

Mrs Tomać had gone to answer her front door and had sensibly looked through the peephole to see who was there. She would have seen nothing, because two shots blasted through the lens. The rest is mystery; her killer could have been a gunman from a Serbian fifth column operating in town, or maybe she was believed by the Croat militias to be a fifth columnist herself. Ten days previously, Dr Lović used to file detailed notes and photographs of the victims. 'But now we have people without heads, or whose stomachs are missing or who have just been torn apart. There isn't enough time, anyway. How can you identify someone without a head? I used to practise medicine here, but this isn't medicine any more.'

Meanwhile, the Croatian army was trying to make soldiers out of people like Dragutin Spoljar, who was guarding its headquarters in Karlovac that day. 'They've hit the brewery and it has broken my heart,' he lamented, swigging from a can of locally brewed Karlovačka Pivo beer, his machine gun slung over his shoulder. 'I would rather they had killed me.' There were twenty empty bottles arranged in a row along the wall of the guardhouse: 'The very last, the very last,' sighed Dragutin, brandishing his can. He was trying

to deal as best he could with a retired textile worker, Lucija
Žganec, whose eyes were as red with tears as Dragutin's
were with drink. She had come by bus, a hundred miles
from Varaždin, to try and find out whether her son Željko
was still alive. A Croat, he had joined up to do his Yugoslav
army national service at Karlovac barracks, recently target of
fierce Croatian fire. He had phoned home every night for
ten months, until a few days ago, when he had suddenly
stopped. 'He was very scared because of the fighting, and
his dad told him to try and run away,' she choked as she
spoke. 'The last phone call he made he didn't know what
was happening in the war, he was just so terrified, and that
was all we heard.' Dragutin steadied himself and wandered
in to see if the guards could make an enquiry after Željko,
but was told no; if they did put in a word, it would only
put the boy at risk. Mrs Žganec left to catch the bus back
to Varaždin.

The chaotic Croatian army trained itself quickly into a
force able to beat back the young Serbian, Albanian and
Macedonian conscripts in hand-to-hand fighting through
which some villages and towns were held against the might
of the Serbs' firepower, though others, like the lovely but
decimated Petrinja, were lost. Croatian soldiers tended to
stay in their home towns, however, and the only mobile
units moving around the country were a division calling
themselves the Tigers, plus a plethora of freelance 'special'
militias, the main one called HOS, which fought with
reckless courage fired by fascistic politics. In some places,
all the militias would come under the tutelage of a single
warlord, such as a psychopathic militarist called Branimir
Glavaš in Osijek, straight out of a video nasty with a stare
that could shatter glass.

The Croats' enemy was made up of the regular Yugoslav
army, volunteer freelancers from Serbia and the 'territorials'
in parts of Croatia where the population was predominantly
Serbian. Among the regular army officers were the last of
the old Yugoslavs, like Major Slavko Milovanov, trapped

inside Marshall Tito barracks in Zagreb under siege by the Croatians. 'We have the Croats who call us an army of occupation and attack us. We have the people in Belgrade who insist that we fight. The political leaders are to blame, weighed down by their own nationalism. If you divide the country up into people calling themselves this nationality or that, you open a hornets' nest, because the borders don't accord with the nationalities. I've always thought of myself as a Yugoslav and I was a communist, which is difficult in the real world. If I ever got to heaven, I'd be a communist again.'

Milovanov was one of a dying breed. Down at the other end of Croatia, a new generation of army officers was bringing the tanks of his army thundering across the border bridges with the red star on their sides painted out and flying the flags not of Yugoslavia but of Serbia. Their drivers greeted the cheering crowds that lined the village streets with the salute of the old Serbian Royalist Chetnik movement: a two-fingered victory sign, plus a raised thumb. (The Orthdox Christians cross themselves with those two fingers and a thumb, closed together, to represent the Trinity.)

The regular troopers were in the main terrified and uncommitted, drawn from all parts of Yugoslavia. Armoured personnel carriers would advance against Croatian lines and the men would be told to 'de-bus' and fight on the terrain, but refused to do so, and carriers returned to ramshackle Šid, safely inside Serbia, where the army was based. But the volunteer units from Serbia or its ally Montenegro and the 'territorials' from Serbian-held Croatia were a rowdier bunch, boozy at their best, wild and sadistic at their worst. It was the 'territorials' who massacred twenty-seven Croatian civilians at Dalj, near Borovo Selo, and it was they who opened fire on Red Cross volunteers as they tried to evacuate the inmates of a lunatic asylum at Pakrac in September 1991 during the army's bombardment of the town. What the Croats could not counter was the Yugoslav army's artillery, and it was the overwhelming superiority of its firepower which enabled the Serbs, despite crippling casualties, to finally crush the symbol of Croatia's resistance, Vukovar. Vukovar was a foretaste of the nightmares to come in Sarajevo and east Mostar: 12,000 people were trapped for six months in what became a city of rubble.

By late September, Borovo Naselje had become the northern outpost of Vukovar, and Borovo Selo one of the besieging front lines. Our road between the hamlets from three months back had ceased to exist. We drove along what was left of it one day, as far as three mines spread in front of us, only to find it a concrete savannah of shell craters and the remains of houses. The last road out of Vukovar until early that month had been a path cut through a cornfield towards Vinkovci. My farewell journey out of that lovely baroque town on the Danube was along that corridor between walls of unharvested corn, early one bright morning when we had been assured that the Serb gunmen at Marinci would be sleeping off their hangovers. Along the way were peasants and townsfolk heading for anywhere that was not Vukovar.

After that, the closest you could get to Vukovar was on the Serbian line at Trpinja, at the end of another maze of cornfield tracks, this time leading from Borovo Selo. At the back of the dank dugout, Dragan, a good-looking young man, was talking to his radio. He was, his mates explained, the best ham in the area. Dragan was joking and laughing and exchanging friendly insults; we wrongly assumed he was bantering with his men on the lines. He was talking into Vukovar; the translation went something like this: 'Is that you, Davor, you Ustasha bastard, you all OK there?' 'Fine, Chetnik scumbag. When did you last see a bar of soap?' 'Your wife still stuck in there? Good! Here's one for her,' and he puts down the receiver and goes out to the little huddle around the mortar, who duly load their weapon, push their fingers in their ears and fire. 'Didn't even hear it,' comes the crackly voice from Vukovar some time later, 'You're useless.' They knew each other from the local shoe factory, in which they had worked as packagers until six months previously.

The successive attempts by the European Community to get a convoy of medical supplies into Vukovar, and to evacuate wounded civilians, dominated the autumn of 1991. The first convoy was attacked in Nustar by a loud mocking crack which sent us diving into people's cellars, and was then turned back after the Yugoslavs found arms smuggled into the Croat deliveries. A second convoy was also forced back, having reached the outskirts of town, after the Serbs had tried to get the defences to lift a minefield and fire corridor to allow the vehicles through; the defence command had put their military priorities first and refused. The failure left one of the convoy's tough organisers, Miljenko Mlinarić from Zagreb, on the brink of tears: 'Nobody trusts anybody any more. Neither side respects the rules, they're trying to use the convoy to lay a trap for the other. It is just a big, big game.'

The third attempt, by the French charity, *Médecins Sans Frontières*, breached the siege and came back out with 109 wounded people, after a journey during which their convoy was booby-trapped by Serbian guerillas and dragged for twelve hours through rain and a mire of mud by the delaying tactics of the Yugoslav army. The convoy returned in the dead of night, driving rain and bitter cold at the Croatian town of Djakovo. The wounded had travelled by tarpaulin-covered goods truck, and their unloading in the yard of a field hospital looked like something out of Hieronymus Bosch: aboard the trucks was a mess of bloodied humanity, packed four deep, lying in two inches of icy water that had soaked through the canvas. They wore strange expressions of bewildered relief as hospital orderlies tried to unload them onto stretchers without hurting them further. One evacuated Croatian fighter, Drago Skoko, said: 'The city is living underground, in cellars. The Serbs' system is this: send in rockets, then stop for half an hour, and people come out onto the streets because the cellars are wet and stinking. Then send in more rockets when they are outside; that is how most of the civilians are killed or wounded. The usual quota is about 3,000 projectiles a day.' Doctors reported that citizens were unable to gather the bodies of their dead.

Vukovar fell shortly before Christmas 1991. By taking the surrender as the pitiful defenders lined up to submit their weapons, the Serbs were assured of the lynchpin needed to consolidate their occupation of eastern Croatia. To the southwest, the Croatian Krajina region and the Serbian heartland town of Knin had been been easily held and a substantial chunk of the central front around Okučani was also retained by the Serbs; in fact, there were very few Serbs left in Croatia not under Serbian authority. But there was one further chapter to conclude before even a temporary peace could be signed, and that was the war on the coast. Out from the drab, maize-covered plains to the glorious, wild shoreline of Dalmatia, with its mighty ports of the Venetian seaborne empire and its sheltered fishing harbours, the war seemed utterly incongruous. But the Serbs were shelling the jewels of Dalmatia and a Montenegrin advance up the south Dalmatian coast had laid waste Yugoslavia's most affluent settlements, and by October reached the resplendent port of Dubrovnik.

The only way in was by sea on the car ferry *Ljburnia*, engaged in what we later learned was an ammunition run. There was a tense game of cat-and-mouse through the islands with a Yugoslav navy frigate which followed us along the Sound of Mljet; from the deck, we watched the fires of burning houses on the hillsides as dusk fell. The captain hid us in the restaurant when the guards boarded for a cursory and unsuccessful search for weapons, and we docked in harbour during the pitch dark of an enforced blackout and under a star-filled night. Now in port, the total dark only served to highlight a burst of tracer fire which came suddenly out of nowhere, through the ship's masts and into the sea.

Next morning, there was the Pearl of the Adriatic in all its glory; but shells were landing on the splendid Stradun main street, until so recently thronging with tourists. The city was full of refugees and the great east gate to the Venetian republic, built of pale stone and rising above the drawbridge, was guarded by two lads called Teo and Srečko with a brace of submachine guns and dressed in their jeans and sneakers.

Neither side won or lost the first War of Maps. Dubrovnik and other cities were saved by a military stalemate and the imposition of a United Nations plan drawn up by special envoy Cyrus Vance. It was an auspicious start to the international community's role in ex-Yugoslavia. The battle lines were frozen, and an uneasy peace enforced leaving one third of Croatia under Serbian control and UN tutelage. The war was put on hold.

The most emotive patch of ground in Croatia is the site of the Jasenovac concentration camp, near the Bosnian border. It was here that hundreds of thousands of Serbs, Jews, Muslims, gypsies and dissident Croats were exterminated by the Croatian Ustasha, rulers of the Nazi puppet state from 1941 to 1945. No one is certain how many died here: the highest Serbian estimates are 1.1 million; historians tend to converge on a figure around 600,000. Croatian academics have played a tasteless revisionist game of trying to prove lower figures. President Tudjman joined in the game with a heinous essay, inaccurately republished by the Serbs, that purported to show that the numbers had been exaggerated and that Jews had managed the camp. There were no gas chambers. Most of the killing was done with bullets, axes and knives. There is a famous snapshot of three smiling, uniformed Ustasha militants posing with a chainsaw against the throat of a Serb they have in a vice-grip, just prior to decapitating him.

It is today a silent, awesome and evil place, with the last train to bring in its load sitting, a reluctant witness, on its tracks. The railway leads into a grassy field, in the midst of which is a mound pregnant with death and a clumsy monument called the 'Flower of Life'. It is almost impossible to imagine what happened here, even with the help of the gunfire booming through an otherwise tranquil October afternoon in 1991.

For a while, the Croats allowed the keeper of the Jasenovac museum to stay on and protect his exhibits from the fighting around him. Of all the people in these wars seeped in history, it is Jovan Mirković's job never to forget. For him, the present war revived a language of forty-five years ago, in an exchange of racial odium disguised as a new democracy on the Croatian side, and the lust for conquest and bloodthirsty revenge on the other. He is what Western media called a 'moderate Serb'. 'I am one of the lucky ones,' he says. 'My grandfather was blind and killed by the Ustasha in his bed, with a knife. But they never found us, a group hiding in the shed. The people said to my mother that she should throttle me, because if I cried they would kill us all. But it seems I was a good baby.'

'What is happening in Yugoslavia?' he asks back, 'I have enough difficulty explaining it to myself. The Serbian and Croatian governments are throwing nationalist time bombs. People looking for a role in history: Milošević to unite the Serbs, Tudjman to found the independent Croatia. The result: total brainwashing by war. They talk about democracy, but they couldn't even spell the word. We have a saying in Serbia,' he smiles, '"Never put two donkeys in the same field because they'll eat all the grass." We're short of grass in Yugoslavia these days, but there are plenty of donkeys.'

Two Croatian guards arrive and brusquely stomp into the museum. Two weeks later it had been closed down. 'I've been sitting here in this museum,' Dr Mirković had said, 'and I hoped it had all become enshrined in these exhibits as a lesson, so that it would never happen again. I thought it had been overcome. I was wrong, and I cannot stand it, this appropriation of the residue of history. It is part of some global thing, the revival of Naziism. In the West you seem to have marginalised it, but here I fear that it will become very important indeed, in the very near future.'

The museum was overrun again by the Serbs. By then Dr Mirković had disappeared and the beginnings of the next war were stirring in Bosnia-Herzegovina, just a few hundred yards away. There was a joke going round Bosnia at the time: 'Why is there still no war in Bosnia-Herzegovina?' Answer: 'Because we in Bosnia are going straight for the play-offs.'

Part One
A View of History from Hell

Chapter One

What is Bosnia-Herzegovina?

Irfan Ljubljankić is a composer of music and a surgeon at the hospital in Bihać, a town surrounded and besieged by Serbian guns since April 1992, the beginning of the Bosnian war. He is a restrained man, now treating men and women ripped open by shrapnel and children caught by snipers' bullets, and he describes his country thus: 'Bosnia has always been the home of heretics, for centuries. Now, by wishing something simple like our own independence, and to live with each other without persecution, we are still heretics to many of our compatriots and heretics to you all.'

Bosnia-Herzegovina is a much-invaded, much trodden-upon country which has emerged, been submerged and re-emerged over a millennium. It has never had the national-racial identity of Serbia or Croatia, and has been variously claimed and overrun by both. Its people are southern Slavs, some of whom call themselves Croats, some Serbs, some Muslims and some just 'Bosnians'. Bosnia has always been populated by a minestrone of ethnic groups, and this has been its identity: a crossroads between east and west, and a special case in the stereotypical Balkan mess. It has a double-barrelled name, having usually been made up of two different components, Bosnia in the north and Herzegovina in the south. The medieval kindgom of Bosnia annexed the region of Hum (Herzegovina) from Serbia. The single word 'Bosnia' is a permissible shorthand for the whole country.

The territory that is now Bosnia had been variously

trampled by Illyrians, Romans and Hungarians when the first mention of 'Bosnae' appeared in a mid-tenth-century text called the *De Administrando Imperio*, according to which it was a constituent part of Serbia. By 1100, Bosnia was politically independent, the bases of state and government established under the authority of a 'Ban', or secular Duke. But the fledgling nation was engulfed by wars between Hungary and Byzantium, and a robust independent country bearing the name of Bosnia did not emerge until the assertive leadership of the 'Great Ban' Kulin, in the late twelfth century.

Already the Bosnians had set themselves curiously apart from the ethnic and religious antagonism between Catholic Rome and Orthodox Byzantium. The territory of Bosnia was the nest for a mystical heresy against both Catholicism and Orthodoxy called the Bogomil movement, founded by a Bulgarian priest of that name. 'Bogomir' means roughly 'God's Peace'. The heresy is believed to have been the first European expression of a Manichean belief traced back to Mesopotamia, which later erupted in the French city of Albi during the thirteenth century, sparking off a bloody religious war. It was an ascetic, puritanical revolt which challenged the edifice of High Christian theology with an alternative division of the universe in which God and Satan had exactly equal power. For the Bogomils, two contending sets of dynamic forces had propelled the universe since the moment of creation: God versus Devil, Spirit versus Matter, Soul versus Body, Light versus Dark. The purpose of spiritual life was to liberate soul from body, light from dark, God from matter.[1] Bogomilism rejected the crucifixion, refused to concede the holiness of the Mother of Christ, defied organised religious hierarchies and the entire liturgy with the exception of the Lord's Prayer, since it had been spoken by Jesus himself.

Like all ascetic or apocalyptic sects in pre-Protestant Europe, the Bogomil heresy became synonomous with political revolution. The preacher Bogomil exhorted Macedonian peasants to rise under the banner of his faith against the rule of Constantinople. In Bosnia, Great Ban Kulin proclaimed himself a convert to the heresy, and Bosnians adopted it in tandem with their assertion of political independence. Both Byzantium and Rome anxiously deployed their respective Serbian, Croatian and Hungarian followers to combat such spiritual and political impudence. The papacy launched a series of Hungarian-led crusades against Ban Kulin (who recanted on his deathbed in order to avert a crusader war against his country) and his successors, who were either converted themselves, or too weak to resist the infectious appeal of popular Bogomilism.

Papal legates were despatched to Bosnia to prepare for Holy War, and the Hungarian Archbishop of Kalosca urged a crusade which would 'rouse the faithful against the infidel'. The war began in 1235, and after thirty years Hungarian overlords brought the Bosnians to heel by force of arms and by sending in columns of Dominican and Franciscan monks. But the heresy defied persecution, and in 1322, another of its followers, Stjepan II Kotromanić, was elected Ban, revived the Bosnian movement and energetically extended her frontiers once more. There followed a prosperous age, based upon the mining of precious minerals, and Stjepan crowned his son Tvrtko the 'King of Bosnia, Serbia and the Western lands' in 1353, ruler of a vast Balkan territory extending into Serbia and to the coast.

But the suffocation of the heresy by both Christian churches intensified and the Bogomils, fearing for their existence, turned to greet an approaching force which seemed both compatible with their mystical theology, and also had the potential to protect them: the Islam of the Ottoman empire, whose armies conquered Serbia in 1453 and moved into Bosnia a decade later. For fifty years, Bosnia remained a battleground between the Hungarians and Ottomans. Meanwhile, the Bogomils were quietly taking on the religion of their eastern, not western, invader.

Today's Bosnian Muslims are direct decendants of the

Bogomil heretics. The salute of the Bosnian Government Army is a hand held out to show a full palm and all five fingers splayed, taken from a motif common to carvings on Bogomil tombs which show strange figures holding out their disproportionately huge, fully open hands. The conversion to Islam was a rapid one. By the middle of the sixteenth century, half the population of Bosnia was Muslim, and all of the city of Sarajevo. As a reward for their spiritual loyalty, the Bosnian Muslims became a favoured social stratum under Ottoman rule. Apart from the relative theological ease of the passage from Bogomilism to Islam, there were more worldly incentives to convert, like exemption from the special '*dzizja*' tax imposed on Christians.

The Ottoman empire was a centralised institution; the Sultan himself owned vast estates and in theory all the lands under his domain. The converted Bosnians inserted themselves within this disciplined feudalism as landowners (strictly speaking, land managers), bureaucratic administrators and merchants. They built wondrous mosques, libraries and schools, they kept detailed records of demography, property ownership and the affairs of state, and were sent to manage Turkish interests in Hungary as the empire's frontiers expanded. The Balkan Christians, Serbian Orthodox and Croatian Catholic, were generally left to worship freely provided they fulfilled the onerous financial obligations to their overlords. But the Christian peasantry was nevertheless firmly under the governorship of the now Muslim Bosnian middle and upper classes, giving rise to resentments and rancour that burst forth in surges of Serbian and Croatian nationalism during the last decades of Ottoman rule, and which are pivotal to the present war. As far back as the seventeenth century, there were attacks by marauding militias of anti-Muslim brigands calling themselves the '*Hajduks*'. (Modern Croatia's leading soccer team is called '*Hajduk Split*'.)

The Serbian Orthodox church worked more easily with

the Ottomans than the Catholics did, and was even authorised to collect tithes from Catholic worshippers. The Franciscans were the main resistance to this practice and from them the tradition of militant Catholicism spread among the Croatians of Bosnia. And around 1720, the tides began to turn against the Ottoman empire, announcing the start of two centuries of revolt against the Turks, and the first persecutions of the Bosnian heretics, now the Muslims.

The revenge against Bosnia's Muslims began in the 'Great Vienna War' of 1638–99, when the Ottomans lost territories in Hungary, Slavonia and Dalmatia. Muslims from these areas withdrew back into Bosnia, where rebel Croats were preparing to welcome the armies advancing from Catholic Austria–Hungary. The Serbs were similarly sponsored by the arrival of Russia as a power on the world stage, and the Czars as champions of the Orthodox faith. The affinities of Croats and Serbs in the present partition of Bosnia have barely changed since then: Croatians still look to the Germanic axis, while Russia and the Ukraine have unashamedly backed the Serbs.

The first serious Serbian rebellions against the Turks came at the beginning of the eighteenth century. They were accompanied by attacks on 'the converts to Islam', given weight by a text of justification from the Orthodox Bishop Petar Njegoš called *The Mountain Wreath*, which has since become a cornerstone of Serbian nationalist literature. A second Serbian revolt of 1804 was based in just those areas which have witnessed savage violence in the present war: the Bosnian 'Krajina' or 'military frontier' around Banja Luka, and the Drina valley, Bosnia's present border with Serbia. The rebellion entailed what the Serbian historian Stojan Novakovic found to be 'a general extermination of the Turks [i.e. Muslims]'.

In 1812, Sultan Mahmud II was forced by treaty to concede six administrative territories to Serbia, and in 1830 the Sultan declared Serbia a principality within the empire. Achieved largely under Russian patronage, the autonomous Serbian nation, in vassal form, was re-born. There followed an expulsion of Muslims from Belgrade and a migration of Balkan Muslims back into Bosnia. The now besieged Ottoman authorities were obliged to bring Serbs into the administrative and commercial life of Bosnia, and the ludicrous 'Christian Tax' was abolished. But the concessions were insufficient to douse the now ubiquitous Christian revolts across the empire.

By the end of the nineteenth century the Balkans were the cockpit of a wider crisis as Russia and Austria led Europe into a struggle for the power vacuum left by the ailing Turkish empire, a tumult which A.J.P. Taylor baptised 'the Great Eastern Crisis,' and which led ultimately to the outbreak of the First World War. The Austrian Hapsburgs, anxious to stop Serbia and Russia from reaping exessive gain from the imminent collapse of the empire, occupied Bosnia-Herzegovina in 1878 and annexed it thirty years later. Austria overcame Muslim and Serbian resistance, and was able to steal a march on the Croats, whose own Slav nationalism Vienna was anxious to curb, but also to deploy in their own's interests. Herzegovinian Croats had been instrumental in the most turbulent anti-Turkish rebellions around Mostar. The Hapsburg occupation precipitated another migration of Muslims, this time out of Bosnia, to Turkey, America and the mainly Muslim Sandzak region of Serbia.

Something resembling modern political and economic activity evolved in Bosnia under Hapsburg tutelage, but each religious group formed its own political parties, the Muslim Progressive party, the Serbian National Organisation and the Croat National Community – ancestors of the parties which steered the newborn republic of 1991 headlong into war. The only non-religious political grouping were the social democrats, who later became the communists.

The freshly defiant Serbs were now fighting on all fronts: against Austrians to the west, and in alliance with Greece against Bulgarians to the east. Within four years of Austria's annexation of Bosnia, the Balkans were ablaze with violence, and the first Balkan War erupted in 1912, bringing the world to the edge of the Great War with the infamous murder in 1914 of the Austrian Archduke Ferdinand at Sarajevo. The assassin was a freelance Serbian nationalist, Gavrilo Princip.

Out of the cyclone of the First World War and the Hapsburgs' defeat, the first unified Yugoslavia was forged: the 'Kingdom of Serbs, Croats and Slovenes', under a Serbian King and Serbian supremacy. The Bosnians' status was clear from the title: they did not exist. The loyal Ottoman province was now the kingdom's leper, the Muslims disgraced. The new Yugoslavia was divided into administrative districts and Bosnia dismembered between three of them, so that Muslims would be a minority in each. A wave of violence was unleashed against Muslims in the early 1920s. Three thousand extrajudicial murders were chronicled in 1924 in eastern Herzegovina alone, 600 of them during the massacre of two villages, Šahovići and Pavino Polje. But more methodical and far-reaching changes underpinned this violence during the inter-war years: a series of land reforms enacted by the Serbian royal authorities.

The Austrians had introduced measures to break up feudalism at the end of the nineteenth century, creating a partially independent peasantry. A detailed land census of 1910 paints an enlightening portrait of Bosnia: of 10,463 landowners with serfs, 9,537 were Muslims, 633 were Orthodox and 267 were Catholics. Among the new, so-called 'free peasants', 77,518 were Muslim, 35,414 were Orthodox and 22,916 were Catholic. Among retained serfs, there were 3,653 Muslims, 58,895 Orthodox and 17,116 Catholic. The social landscape is clear: a Muslim landowning class employing non-Muslim serfs, with Muslim peasants tending to take advantage of the Austrian scheme for 'voluntary redemption' from serfdom, while Serbs stayed within the medieval structure. The purpose of the reforms was to break that pattern and transfer landownership away from the Muslim class which had managed the empire, to the Serbs.

The inter-war reforms now offered compensation for compulsarily purchased land marked for redistribution to the 'population of the less developed regions of Bosnia', plus some war veterans. It has been one of the more pointless labours of modern Muslim historians to try to calculate how little of the compensation was actually paid. In theory, some landowners should still have been receiving their repayments as late as 1971, by which time rather too much had happened to ensure their continuation. About twenty-five per cent of compensation was paid by 1939, and some 1,175,000 hectares of land, just over half the registered acreage, had been redistributed to 250,000 new owners. In ninety per cent of cases, the new landowners were Serbs, many from outside Bosnia.[2]

There was a reorganisation of the kingdom in 1939, the so-called Banovina plan. Under pressure from Croatian nationalists, the king agreed to a straight division of Bosnia between Serbia and a newly constituted Croatia, known as 'Banovina Croatia'. The frontiers of this particular treaty were to prove highly relevant to the present war, a model for the Serbo–Croat carve-up of the Bosnian republic born in 1992. But first time round, the Banovina borders were swept aside as Nazi Germany invaded Yugoslavia, and fascist Croatia cut a swathe through the entire country, and above all its Serbian population. One in ten Bosnian Muslims would also lose their lives, victims to both sides; the Croats too would suffer before the tide of revenge. Bosnia was again divided in 1941, between the German and Italian occupying authorities, before being submerged completely within the Nazi client regime, the Independent State of Croatia. According to the Ustasha ('Rebellion') Party at the helm of that state, Bosnians were 'Croatians of Muslim faith', thinking which has steered Croatian rhetoric ever since.

All the main players in the cruel history of the Second World War in Yugoslavia were at their most ferocious in Bosnia. The Ustasha founded its most sadistic columns among the militant nationalists of Herzegovina. The rabid command of the Serbian Royalist Chetnik militias were based in Bosnia when the German troops advanced. Tito's partisans dealt out some of their most brutal reprisals in Bosnia, and the embryonic Socialist Yugoslav Federation was founded near the now flattened central Bosnian town of Jajce in 1943.

The war in Bosnia was a miasma of contorted alliances and re-alliances along ethnic or ideological gounds. For patriotic reasons, the fascistic Serbian Chetniks fought with Tito's Partisans at first, but then more logically with the Italians against the communists, all the while inflicting their bloodiest savagery on the Muslims. In response, a Muslim Ustasha column was formed to join the Croats' war against the Chetniks. More typical, however, were the 'Muslim Brigades' within Tito's ethnically mixed partisans. Tito himself was a Croat. The mass extermination of Serbs by the Croatian Ustasha began in 1941 with that of the small Serbian middle class. By late 1942, it had reached monstrous proportions, victims for the most part taken to Jasenovac. Ironically, Serbs going to the camp were assembled at Mount Kozara, just inside Bosnia and only a few miles from the camps that the Serbs established for Muslims in the present war.

On 6 April 1945, the partisan Third Corps paraded as liberators through Sarajevo. But behind the rhetoric of proletarian unity, there was confusion over what to do with Bosnia-Herzegovina in the new republic. Various options were discussed: to incorporate it into Serbia or Croatia, partition it, or to let it stand alone. Tito ruled that a return to the pre-royalist frontiers of a federated Bosnia was the appropriate outcome, and the meeting which founded that republic in 1943 declared: 'The steadfast decision of all nations and nationalities to live firmly united in brotherhood, unity and freedom in the Federal Republic of Bosnia-Herzegovina'. Bosnia would be 'neither Serbian, Croatian not Muslim, but Serbian, Croatian and Muslim'.

Tito was required by the labyrinth of Balkan *narod* to perform some remarkable political acrobatics. From the royalist period, he inherited three *narods* – Serbs, Croats and Slovenes – to which he added another two, Montenegrins and Macedonians. Then he endorsed a number of 'national minorities' – not *narods*, but still granted certain rights: Bosnian Muslims, Hungarians, Albanians, etc. Tito's task was made all the more difficult by the fact that the borders of the federated republics did not match those of the *narods*. There were Serbs in Croatia, whose protection alarmed the Croatians; there were the Albanians in Kosovo, whose new 'national minority' status upset the Serbs. Within Serbia, Tito created two 'autonomous provinces': Vojvodina in the north, where Hungarians were concentrated, and Albanian Kosovo. It was the text-book illustration of Abraham Lincoln's dictum that you cannot please all of the people all of the time. Titoism was a technique more than an ideology; one which managed to keep the bricks and mortar of Yugoslavia together with help from the secret police and stubborn neutrality in the Cold War. But the internal political and demographic borders were superimposed over and built on a dangerous network of seismic fault lines.

In the socialist republic of Bosnia-Herzegovina, where the three ethnic groups were intermingled, Serbs came to be over-represented in the party, and the notoriously corrupt state apparatus. The Muslim and Croat population was wary of this, and the Muslims unhappy at the fact that although they were the largest ethnic group, they were still a 'national minority'. On the other hand, Tito's federal apparatus gave them a shield against the claims of the other two *narods*. In 1964, to rectify the imbalance, Tito decared the Muslims a *narod* too. The contemptuous wrath of the Serbs and Croats, if there was any, did not yet surface.

There is a Bosnian identity and character which overrides

the differences between the *narods*. It is roguish, hospitable, set in its ways, fatalistic, suspicious and humorous. Bosnians are among the few people who make a point of laughing at themselves. The favourite Bosnian jokes are stories about two characters, Mujo and Suljo, whose adventures demonstrate the celebrated incapacity of the Bosnian brain, except that the jokes are driven by a barbed poke at pretentious sophistication, and celebrate the logic of the common man.

When Bosnians (usually Muslims, nowadays) tell you that all three people lived together without regard to ethnic group, they are by and large telling the truth. More than one in four marriages during the post-war period were mixed. But there was a rider to this optimism. While the towns and cities were nonchalant arenas for the practice of multi-ethnic Bosnia, everyday life in the countryside was one in which Muslims, Serbs and Croats were more insular. The Second World War in Bosnia had been driven by undercurrents of civil war and in the villages, peasants who had fought on all sides and in particular the Serbs, made sure to keep their weapons. For them, the war had not yet ended; it was a question of waiting for the right moment to re-commence it.

Two social and demographic themes, pertinent to the present disaster marked the 1950s and 1960s. First, the emergence of a secular Muslim intelligentsia within the already urbanised community, part of which was indigenous, part of which came from the gentry dispossessed by land reform. The landowners moved into the main population centres where their co-religionists were based. They were assimilated with relative ease and their children were early benificiaries of Tito's impressive, if ideologically straightjacketed, educational system. Then a second population movement followed: that of Serbian and Croatian peasants into the cities. Serbs from the rural Bosnian 'Krajina' flocked into Banja Luka, encouraged by industrialisation incentives and a series of natural disasters. Other rural Serbs converged on Sarajevo from the surrounding mountains and further afield, as new tower blocks spread to the feet of the hills. Croatians from the belligerent outback of Herzegovina came to Mostar, which had until 1950 been shared principally between Muslims and Serbs. There was an urbanisation of the rural culture of insularity within cities that had previously grown on relative tolerance.

These newcomers did not assimilate into the urban lifestyle, which was easy-going and either loyal to Tito's republic or apathetic towards both socialism and the *narod*. This was particularly true in Sarajevo. Before the present war, there were 150,000 Serbs in Sarajevo, of whom 90,000 remained behind in the capital to endure the siege and fight alongside the Muslims and Croats. Most of those who stayed have had families there for generations, but of those who left to join their blood brothers shelling the city, almost all were from families which had arrived only years before. There was a deep inferiority complex among the rural arrivals. The national pride of the village Serbs and Croats was blended with bitterness. Modern Bosnia has re-defined two old words to describe these two cultures, the urban and the rural: the old word *raja*, which characterised the usually non-Muslim peasantry in Ottoman times is now taken to mean the tolerant folk of the city, regardless of creed. The word *papak* describes the country folk among whom old hatreds are kept alive by aggressive nationalist sentimentality. People in Sarajevo will tell you this is a war between *raja* and *papak*.

In 1990, there were still those who called mixed Bosnia the 'little Yugoslavia' because it embodied the federal project in miniature. Others, conversely, preferred to call Yugoslavia 'big Bosnia' for the same reason. But by then the analogy was an unfortunate one, for Yugoslavia was falling apart. The leaders of Bosnia's majority Muslims and Croats did not wish to remain in a Serbian-dominated Yugoslavia from which Croatia and Slovenia were departing. The Bosnian Serbs, however, did not wish to be cut adrift from a Serbian-dominated Yugoslavia to become part of what they were told by Belgrade would be 'Muslim' Bosnia. The country went to the polls in November 1991, and rewarded all the ethnically rooted political parties. The language of formal party politics, at least, was now that of ethnic sectarianism.

Bosnia, according to the latest census, was forty-four per cent Muslim, thirty-four per cent Serb and seventeen per cent Croat. The Muslim Democratic Action Party, the SDA, became the biggest in parliament. Second was the Serbian Democratic Party, the SDS, a subsidiary of the Socialist Party of President Slobodan Milošević in Serbia proper; and the third was the Bosnian branch of President Franjo Tudjman's ruling Croatian Democratic Union, the HDZ, in Croatia. The leader of the SDA, Alija Izetbegovíc, duly became president of the republic, a man who had embraced the ethnicisation of politics as eagerly as any of his contemporaries, although with the idea of co-habitation, rather than war, as the premise upon which each *narod* might realise their respective cultures. It was to be a rotating collective presidency, made up of three Muslims, three Croats and three Serbs. Each president was to sit for two years as *primus inter pares*.

The Yugoslav federal army emitted a clear signal of its intentions by disarming Bosnia's part-time territorial reserve and re-distributing its weapons within the Serbian Democratic Party and its emerging paramilitary formations. Weapons and men were being brought back from the Croatian war, and were stopping in Bosnia. The war was in the starting stalls, but still no one believed that ethnic battle could be fought among three peoples whose lives were so closely entwined.

Chapter Two

Bosnia's End Game: The Players

'The myth of history is built on lies.'
— Miroslav Krleža, 1981

1. The Serbs

The revived symbol of the Greater Serbian project is a cross which has four Cs — one back-to-back in each of its corners. Of all the beloved heraldry in the Bosnian war, this emblem is the most striking and the most menacing. The Cs represent the saying, *Samo Sloga Srbina Spašava*, which means 'Only gathering can save the Serbs'. Apart from the mystical aura of Serbian nationalism, the persecution complex is its most manifest trait. At the height of the war in July 1993, with hundreds of thousands of Muslims dead, a party was held at the Bosnian–Serb 'capital' of Pale to launch a glossy booklet entitled 'Genocide against the Serbian People' at the hands of Bosnia's Muslims. Its authors said the Serbs were the Jews of modern times, and accused the world of failing to understand the analogy.

The Serbian *narod* is packaged as history's victim, overrun by Turks and Croats, humiliated by atheistic communism and now threatened by Islamic holy war at the heart of Europe. This time, however, the *narod* will avenge its martyrs and secure its future by binding together the

Serbs dispersed throughout Serbia, Bosnia and Croatia, and ensuring their physical as well as racial unity.

The experience of the Croatian Nazi regime has traumatised a generation of Serbs. The suffering re-planted the neurosis of threatened common identity upon which Serbian nationalism feeds, and transformed those sentiments into a now psychotic means of justifying violence. During their war against Croatia in 1991, the Serbs were fighting, they said, against a new Greater Germany piledriving its way to the Adriatic with the help of its wartime allies, the Ustasha. The Croats were indeed Serbia's enemy; Germany and Austria maybe. But in Bosnia, the Serbs' psychodramatic 'revenge' is being wreaked not upon her stronger Croatian opponents, but upon the one people the Serbs knew they could cut through like a knife through butter, the virtually unarmed Muslims, the progrom justified by the fabrication of the menace of an Islamic *jihad* about to engulf south-eastern Europe.

Serbs make good friends and awesome enemies. In September 1991, during the Croatian war, on the Serbian front line at Bjelo Brdo near Osijek, I was assigned a ribald, English-speaking bodyguard and interpreter. No one had asked to stay the night on this line before, and, oddly, it was considered a compliment by the jumble of rogues aged between seventeen and seventy crouching behind the houses on the edge of a field with the tanks and artillery of the Yugloslav army parked some way back in the village. My guide was Veljko, former manager of a video shop in Croatian-held Osijek. The enemy was half a field away, spread out in the darkness of unharvested corn. An almighty machine gun exchange was going on, a furious cacophony of fire from the men in the field and from Veljko's little band behind the house and in the attic above. During the lulls, Veljko and his mates swigged their šljivovic and fondled their weapons as they talked, over the muffled crackle of patriotic music on Radio Belgrade.

Dragan Šerić, an old fox, had moved his family out of

Bjelo Brdo two days before, expecting heavy fighting. 'We
had lost our jobs; employers were forcing people to kiss the
Croatian flag and we refused. The government said Croatia
was "for the Croatian people". I lost my work and money,
and I'm not going to lose my village too.' 'It's old, but
its good,' says the unrefined Milan Illić up in the attic,
patting the butt of his old Second World War weapon. 'I
was born downstairs, in 1926. We've seen all this before, the
Ustasha. In my family, only my father stayed alive. He had
four brothers, and they were all killed. Now it's all coming
round again, Germans, the Ustasha, always the same.'

'There is a fear,' said Veljko, too young to remember
much before Tito's death in 1980 let alone the Ustasha,
'lodged in this people, that what happened before could
happen again at any time. When the threat appears, we
realise our Serbianhood again.' It didn't seem like the right
place to argue that the 'Serbianhood' had been cranked up
long before the threat appeared, and that the Serbs had
fired first. In any case, a sudden deafening rattle from
the mounted machine gun in the attic announced the
resumption of fighting. After three more hours, I asked
Veljko if he would kindly direct me back to the schoolhouse
where I was to sleep; the whizzing of the bullets and their
ricochet off the buildings was getting closer. There was no
question about it: the commander ordered Veljko to escort
the visitor immediately to the relative safety of the school,
which he did, along the street where, he kindly informed
me, a man had been shot dead the previous night. We
darted from house to house, creeping across the empty
alleyways, past the huddles of regular soldiers and the dark
hulks of their tanks, past the groups of irregulars cleaning
their weapons around candles in the burned-out houses,
Veljko firing off a few covering rounds for good measure.
Now being ordered to sprint across the street and now to
hug the walls amid the cracking and whizzing of the shots,
and clinging onto the silences in between. 'No problem'
grinned Veljko as he delivered me to his own camp bed and

set off back through those uncomfortable streets, 'You are my guest, and shall be treated accordingly. See you in the morning.' The flag officially hoisted outside the school was that of Yugoslavia, with its red star. But the iconic symbols chalked upon the dormitory blackboard were the crossed Cs and two-headed eagle of royalist Serbia.

Down the road in Borovo Selo, Veljko's comrades were engaged in pounding, flattening and, as they put it, 'liberating' Vukovar. Virtually the headquarters for that siege and for the Serbian occupation of eastern Croatia was the Red Star Pizzeria in Borovo Selo, more to do with the Red Star Belgrade soccer team than with ideology. Irregular troops would gather for a smoke, coffee and a few glasses of šljivovic each morning before embarking on the day's activities. Here the proposals were a little less sophisticated than among Veljko's posse. The bearded man with crutches called Georgei poured himself a generous glassful, swallowed it in one and made a sweeping movement of his hand across the table, to illustrate obliteration. 'Osijek: vroom!'; and again: 'Zagreb: vroom!' and with a grimace of glee: 'All Serbia! Ha Ha!' And with that, he picked up his weapon and hobbled out towards a truck waiting to take him along the cornfield tracks down to the front line. Above, two Mig fighter-bombers of the Yugoslav air force cut gracefully across the sky, over poor Vukovar.

There was always this dichotomy within the Serbian military operation, especially when it progressed to the Bosnian campaign: between that hobbling, rasping gaffer and the clean, determined sweep of those jets. On the one hand there are the unkempt freebooting militiamen, recently in uniform, usually one over the eight and capable of extremes of cruelty – the Keystone Gestapo. On the other, there is the now better-oiled Serbian military machine and the Gucci-clad rhetoricians that direct it. This is a regular force of lavishly armed soldiers around which orbits a cluster of private armies and death squads. The regular troops shell and bludgeon their quarry until kingdom come from the safety of the hilltops while the hit squads either wade in as an avant-garde to terrorise and kill, or else do the 'mopping up' when a town or village surrenders, lobbing grenades into any cellars that may harbour signs of life.

Roadblock etiquette is essential to surviving the Bosnian war, and the Serbian checkpoints have changed over the past year, yielded by the Keystone Gestapo to what looks like a proper army. At the start of the war, these roadblocks were usually manned by some bog-trotter who would ostentatiously remove the safety catch on his Kalashnikov while pointing it at the driver's seat and, summoning his mates, wave you down. The checks were invariably decorated by some intimidatory item, like a mutilated shop dummy, and whether these clods scowled or grinned was simply a matter of chance. It was advisable to extinguish all cigarettes when winding the window down, since the guards' breath, blowing in at close range, was usually highly flammable.

Now it has changed. The toothless goons still patrol the streets of the 'cleansed' Muslim towns, but the roadblocks are manned with a dry, disagreeable neutrality intended to give the impression of efficiency: 'Dokument?' Instead of the initial Mexican bandolero look, the Serbs now wear new uniforms with the appropriate insignia. Many fighters still wear flowing hair and beards strewn with bits of old food, emblems of the Chetnik royalist militias, but those controlling the highways are of the newly confident, smarter variety. The change signifies victory, not over the Croatian army this time, but over a barely defended civilian people, the Muslims. And what a difference there is between the Serbian attitude to each. The Croats drive a mixture of fear, hatred and respect into the Serbs. Serbian fighters speak about bloody vengeance for Jasenovac, but in two years I never heard a single derogatory remark from a Serb about the Croats as people. Hatred, yes; contempt, never. But the Muslims are another matter, they are 'gypsies', 'filth', 'bitches', 'animals'. The Bosnian project did not entail seeing the Muslims as an enemy

– the threat of the *Jihad* was all hot air – so much as sub-humans.

Ratko Mladić, commander of the Bosnian-Serb army says: 'The Muslims? If you make way for one of them, he will come along with five wives and before you know what is happening, you have a village.' Mladić is a curious, fat man who wears an incongruous, simpering smile on his pasty face which contrasts with his monkey-wrench handshake. He appears to concentrate on a conversation, but his eyes are stone dead. He is a professional military servant of the Greater Serbian project, coming back to his native Bosnia from his role as commander of the Serbs at Knin in the Croatian Krajina. Mladić openly enjoys the adoration of his men, earned in gratitude for the violence they are encouraged to inflict on those they subjugate in an army that avoids any discipline of its soldiers' cruelty, and also for the way in which Mladić mocks, and is allowed to mock, the international community for its deliberate impotence in curbing these excesses. It was at the height of international tension over the future of Sarajevo that Mladić was merrily flying around his front lines by helicopter as though to say 'What kind of no-fly zone do you call this?'

Mladić's political superior, the leader of the Bosnian Serbs, is Radovan Karadžić, former psychiatrist now wanted for war crimes he has commissioned from his troops in between shaking hands with 'international mediators'. The portly Dr Karadžić buttons up his jacket as he waddles towards you as a gesture of feigned respect. He greets you with his troubled frown, forever casting a glance over his shoulder, in case there is someone else about needing similar attention. He runs his fingers through a dash of grey hair and invites you into his lair, a converted hotel in Pale, for coffee, French cognac and cheese. He has been here since the Bosnian Government Army stormed his headquarters in the Sarajevo Holiday Inn, where he was a reliable customer at the Casino. Karadžić writes bad, sentimental nationalist poetry and childrens' stories and rhymes. He speaks English and his tone is at once reasonable and decisive, but he fails to register any marked difference between truth and untruth. His rhetoric on the slaughter has barely changed, nor has the shrug that is intended to absolve him of responsibility for it. Like his puppet-master Milošević, Karadžić is a tin-pot dictator for all seasons, whom the West has taken seriously, and he cannot quite believe that he has got away with it. At first, the reports of concentration camps are 'lies' and 'Muslim propaganda'; then he purports to be shocked, saying he will seek out and punish the guilty, which somehow never happens. When the threat of military intervention is made, Dr Karadžić makes concessions, whatever sounds good on the day. Then when the threat subsides again, he sends his thugs, if he still controls them, back to business. He recalls Hannah Arendt's phrase, 'the banality of evil'.

Karadžić hails from the mountains of Montenegro, lured into the Bosnian capital by Tito's urbanisation programme. Karadžić was fifteen when he came to town, and found it hard to win acceptance within indigenous social circles. He studied medicine, specialising in psychiatry, married a fellow psychiatrist, was doctor to Sarajevo Football Club and was jailed for a fraudulent scam involving house-purchase loans. He says nowadays that he was incarcerated as a political dissident. In prison, he launched his career as a nationalist, and helped found the SDS in 1990. He began talking about the 'Historic ethnic struggle' and soon progressed to lying as second nature: for example, to *Le Figaro* in 1991, 'The Bosnian Serbs have no armed forces.' Then Karadžić latched on to the biggest lie of all: the imminent Islamic *jihad* in Bosnia. It was manifest rubbish, as any Serb who had lived with Bosnia's Muslims knew only too well. But our century tells us that the fabrication of giant conspiracies against a besieged race is a necessary prerequisite to unleashing the kind of violence that was to follow. And Karadžić turned that lie into a propaganda cocktail, with his speeches and reports of crucified Serbian babies supposedly cast into the river Drina with their eyes gouged out, the castration of virile Serbian men by the plotters of the *jamahirija* and 'evidence' of revolutionary Arabic texts seized in the homes of Bosnia's Muslims.

High above Sarajevo, on the hills commanding the city, there is a breathtaking view of the capital. Soon after the siege had begun in April 1992, Miloš and Radislav, soldiers from Karadžić's staff, took me on a drive over the ridge and into the Serbian quarter of Grbavica on the southern edge of town. We pulled off the road to look down at the city, the minarets of the mosques and the spires of the Orthodox and Catholic churches huddled together, the river winding through the damaged flats and the airport runways. It was my first view of Sarajevo. 'The only good Muslim,' said Miloš, 'is a dead Muslim. Their women are bitches and whores. They breed children like animals, more than ten per woman . . . Down there, they are fighting for a single land that will stretch from here to Tehran, where our women will wear shawls, where there is bigamy . . .'

Meanwhile, back in Belgrade, the architects of the latest incarnation of Greater Serbia were ready with all the artillery, tanks and 'mop-up' squads that their roughshod Bosnian blood brothers wanted for the realisation of their part in the 'historic ethnic struggle'. The crusade for the Greater Serbia has been most crudely implemented in Bosnia, but its cradle is Serbia proper. To that extent, Karadžić is no more than a stooge. The man who resurrected, manipulated and unleashed this quest was President Slobodan Milošević.

Milošević was born to a Montenegrin family, second son of an Orthodox priest, in 1941, year of the Nazi occupation. When little Slobodan was seven, his favourite uncle shot himself in the head. Fourteen years later, when he was settling into his first job at a lawyer's office, word came that Milošević's father had also blown his own head off on a remote mountainside. Ten years later, news arrived that his mother had now hanged herself in the family sitting room. By this time Milošević had a family of his own, married to the teenage sweetheart whose hand he took on walks down the high street of his home town of Požarevac. Like her husband, Mirjana Milošević never strayed from her career in the political apparatus; it was love at first sight, for each other, and for ambition.

Those who have known Milošević say that he is alternately angry and depressed, paranoid and a master schemer. He has severe diabetes and two passions besides politics: gardening and Scotch whisky. Having risen to power as the most publicly exhibited leader that nationalist Serbia has ever had, he now rules from within a political and physical bunker, surrounded by carefully appointed acolytes who might be discarded at any time, or the leaders of the Belgrade-based death squads from whom Milošević formally keeps his distance, but simultaneously patronises. Loyalty is not Milošević's guiding principle; indeed, his first victim was the very man who carried him to power.

Milošević's mentor during his climb through the apparatus was Ivan Stambulić, whom he replaced in every important office he ever held: president of the Technogas energy conglomerate, president of the powerful state bank, Beobank, head of the Belgrade communist party, and finally of the Serbian party. This last post Milošević could secure only by neutralising his patron, which he did by displaying for the first time his mastery of the mass media. Milošević invited television cameras to film the central committee meeting of 1987 at which he forced a showdown with Stambulić on the 'Serbian national question', publicly humiliating his mentor. Stambulić resigned, and Milošević purged the party of his supporters.

Yugoslavia's nationalists were not a force which swept aside the communist tyranny as in Poland, Russia or Hungary. Indeed, nationalism was embraced and institutionalised by the communists themselves to ensure their survival. Milošević and his political and military allies, enjoying the benefits of power as eagerly as any other rotten communist élite, saw which way the tide was turning in eastern Europe, and needed to devise a way of riding its waves rather than being drowned by them. So they performed a crude but convincing piece of ideological gymnastics, and facelifted their ambitions in order to embrace and lead – rather than fall victim to – the impatient tide of nationalist sentiment in the communist world. Milošević became a nationalist figurehead after an incident in Kosovo in April 1987. The centrepiece of Serbian historical legend, Kosovo was by now 90 per cent Albanian, to the chagrin of its Serbian minority. A demonstration was organised by that minority to protest against the erosion of its privileges, on the occasion of the visit by communist leader Milošević to Priština, Kosovo's capital. The marchers were faced by a cordon of police truncheons when Milošević suddenly emerged, remonstrated with the officers and strode bravely towards the demonstrators shouting: 'No one will beat the Serbs again!' His phrase resounded across the nation as the mantra of national pride and odium.

Milošević's next appointment in Kosovo was the turning point in the present Balkan nightmare, the Serbs' 'Nuremberg' Rally, significantly located at the adytum of Serbian nationalism, the field of the battle of Kosovo Polje. The date was 28 June 1989, day of the Serbian patron saint, St Vitus, and the six hundredth anniversary of defeat at the hands of the Turks, a battle lost but commemorated by the promise of revenge and resurrection. On this day, the *narod* – would make a pledge of honour to its past and to its future. Accounts of the rally describe crowds, flanked by Orthodox priests and a paramilitary phalanx, holding aloft two sets of icons: reproductions of the golden Byzantine kind, and the modern kind, portraits of Slobodan Milošević. Emerging from a helicopter, he took the podium from dancing maidens in traditional folk costume, and transported the crowd to heights of frenzied adoration with a simple message: never again would Islam subjugate the Serbs. Within six months, Milošević had secured the army; within a year, Albanian Kosovo was a police state; within two years, Serbia was at war. And yet the words 'Greater Serbia' had never once passed Milošević's lips.

That phrase had been revived in the army and by the nationalist Belgrade intelligentsia. Prominent figures at the Serbian Academy of Arts and Sciences published a celebrated memorandum in 1987 arguing for the expansion of Serbia's frontiers in order to take in the 'diaspora' of some two million Serbs scattered at the mercy of their enemies. The Academicians were gathered around the figure of Dobrica Ćosić, chief author of the memorandum and the man who would later become president of the rump Yugoslavia comprising Serbia and Montenegro. Next, the intelligentsia needed to steer the hate-hungry masses towards a more exciting narrative than their drab lives afforded, which was easy.

Milošević developed his own Keystone version of the Nazi mastery of propaganda technology. His takeover of communist television in a country where 35 per cent of people are illiterate turned the medium into a relentless deluge of crude broadcasting. Serbia's enemies were everywhere, and the antidote to one atrocity after another inflicted on the victim Serbs is the struggle of the Serbian soldiers and their leaders to 'liberate' the towns and villages they were blasting to smithereens. There was one particularly memorable political commercial during the Bosnian war. It showed a succession of luxurious images; sports cars, a fashion model on a catwalk, stereo systems and other consumer lootables, and then the slogan 'FOR THE GOOD LIFE: PARTITION AND SEPARATION'. Nebojša Popov, a Titoite communist, describes modern Serbia as 'a real Orwellian dictatorship of the proletariat. The masses feel they are involved. You can only compare the role of television here with that of Adolf Hitler's Germany; it reaches every level of Serbian society'.[1]

There is something suicidal about the cravings of every dictator in the Milošević mould, for their Reichs, whether

Keystone or the real thing, cannot endure forever. For all Milošević's power and the brutality of his men in the field, Serbia is decomposing. Although the barrier of sanctions imposed by the West is as watertight as a sieve – supplies rolling in by ship from Russia and Ukraine, and by rail and motorway from Greece – the economy is in ruins, with more and more noughts added to the banknotes. A billion dinar are worth three dollars; law and order crumble, the young torn between degradation and the more titillating adventures of the government's ideology as peddled by the Chetniks on their stalls in the shopping precincts.

'*ČETA*' was the word for an 'armed unit. After the founding of the Serbian kingdom in 1830, the early *Hajduka Četniks* or 'armed brigands' became an irregular but recognised militia within the royal Serbian army. The Chetniks would carry out crude civilian massacres, torture and looting of which the official army could wash its hands if necessary. The first Chetnik divisions were found in the mid-nineteenth century among the Serbs in Bosnia and Croatia, and their role has not changed. In royal Yugoslavia, Chetniks were turned from an extremist but ageing veteran's association under the patronage of the army into a virulent fascistic political force by their leader, Kosta Pečanac. As such, they maintained a steady unofficial violence against Croatian and Muslim civilians, hugely popular among the Serbian peasantry, and in 1940 advocated an alliance with Hitler's advancing Nazi troops. But the movement was taken over by a professional soldier again, Colonel Draža Mihailović, and became committed to nothing but the restoration of the deposed Serbian monarchy and the Greater Serbia. Mihailović sent his Chetnik units an order paper on 20 December 1941 which urged 'the creation of a great Yugoslavia and within it a Great Serbia, racially pure, within the borders of Serbia, Montenegro and Bosnia-Herzegovina' and the 'clearing of the territory of national minorities and non-national elements'.

Mihailović based his units in Bosnia, and at first was

recognised by the British as leader of the Yugoslav resistance, before the Allies switched to Tito. The Chetniks massacred Muslims and fought the Croats, but later rallied to the Italian fascist army (which often disobeyed German orders to attack Chetniks because it was too afraid of them) and the Ustasha. In southern Bosnia the Chetniks even came under Italian command, because Mussolini's men, frightened and militarily incompetent, preferred to fulfil their obligations to the Nazis by giving weapons to the local warlords and leaving them to fight the war against Tito instead.[2]

The Chetniks went undergound with Tito's rule, only to blossom with his death and the advent of Milošević. Out on the front, the real Chetniks kill under the authority of the Serbian army and its Bosnian counterpart, distinguished by their beards and wild demeanour. We stumbled upon a gathering of some eighty opprobrious Chetniks camped down at Prijedor police station in September 1992, on its way back to Belgrade after an ethnic cleansing binge ('fighting', they called it) in the Bosnian Krajina. A neanderthal bunch they were too, gouging canned meat out of tins with their knives and stuffing it into their mouths. They had little enlightening to say, except to register that in the town of Kluj, 'The Turks cannot eat pigs, but they run like pigs and squeal like pigs!' This was Boško Maljević from Niš in southern Serbia, who had taken time off from his factory job to come 'at weekends usually' and 'fight for my country and people'. A local policeman did not like these men talking to visitors, and asked us to wait in his office while they completed their meal.

The Chetniks have a readily interviewable leader in Belgrade (although he charges money for the honour): this is the unimpressive figure of Vojislav Šešelj, a podgy, failed academic who, ironically, has trouble growing the traditional beard. He is supposedly estranged from Milošević, but in reality has the President's enthusiastic support. In August 1992 he appeared briefly at a press conference on concentration camps to bark his comment in his squeaky voice, and for no charge: 'Images fabricated by America, great protectors of the Muslims!' He went on to discuss the 'journey of the Serbian people along their road to Calvary'.

2. The Croats

The newborn republic of Croatia has pulled off one of the public relations triumphs of the decade. It has managed to impress the West with democratic colateral, enjoying the particular loyalty of Germany, while at the same time annexing a sizeable chunk of neighbouring Bosnia, and doing so through the deployment of methods which pale only slightly alongside those of their supposed enemies, the Serbs. At the time of writing, it is the Croatian siege of Muslims trapped in east Mostar and the ethnic cleansing of that area by Croats that presents the most savage abomination of the war. The army of the Bosnian Croats, the HVO, now fights on several fronts in Bosnia, *against* their erstwhile allies, the scantily armed Muslims, and in *alliance* with the Serbs. The sight of Serbs and Croats fighting together embarrasses some intelligent Croatians, but it has its logic. For just as Serbian dogma believes that wherever there is a Serb is Serbia, so vast numbers of Croatians feel the same about their blood brothers of the *narod*.

In the spring of 1991, President Tudjman of Croatia and President Milošević of Serbia held a meeting at Karadjordjevo, in the Vojvodina province of Serbia. It was an unlikely rendezvous, but over one issue these men were the second-hand Castor and Pollux of the Balkans, and that issue was the sole item on the agenda: the division of Bosnia into ethnically pure mini-republics leaving 'just a little bit' (as Tudjman later put it) for the Muslims. The scheme came off the peg; it had a direct precedent and that was the accord struck in 1939 on the eve of the war between the

Serbian diplomat Dragiša Cvetković and the Croat leader Vladko Maček, the 'Banovina', agreement, under which Bosnia was divided between a Medium-to-Greater Croatia, and a Greater Serbia, with a border along the Neretva river which runs through Mostar.

The Banovina map was ripped up by war, but it was revived as the guiding spirit of the Tudjman–Milošević meeting in 1991. The borders correlate almost exactly with those that the Serbs and Croats have fought for in the War of Maps that now ravages Bosnia. History, as ever, could be made to repeat itself. The proposal was put officially on ice as the brandy and cigars of the Karadjordjevo summit made way for Croatia and Serbia to go to war. But that war was only a temporary aberration as far as plans for Bosnia were concerned, for the Serbo–Croat dialogue continued. Radovan Karadžić (representing Milošević) and President Tudjman's viceroy in Bosnia, Mate Boban, met in Graz, Austria, during spring 1991, in order to map out the partition of Bosnia. And there was another consultation: between two members of the Bosnian presidency who did not want Bosnia-Herzegovina to exist: Franjo Boras, a Croatian nationalist, and Nikola Koljevic, who became right-hand man to Karadžić. They said that there was no reason for Serbo–Croat hostility in Bosnia, since there need be no territorial dispute. Some months later, when Bosnian Croats declared their autonomous mini-state of 'Herzeg-Bosne' within Bosnia, their enemy Karadžić heartily welcomed the move.

But for six months, the Croats in Bosnia fought side by side with the Muslims against the Serbian onslaught, although they did so in their own separate HVO, armed and funded by Croatia proper and her allies. Then it became clear that the Croatian and Muslim allies were fighting for different reasons. The Muslims were in combat to defend the frontiers that had been internationally recognised, and, at first, to maintain the multi-ethnic state. But the Croatian project was the opposite: ethnic partition and a racially pure Croatian state which reflected that declared by the Serbs. 'Don't look,' said a young Croatian translator working in Bosnia – apparently trendy, with a pony-tail – 'for a mini Yugoslavia in Bosnia, with people living together. It can't happen.'

Croatian nationalist identity was revived in the nineteenth century with both intellectual and churlish wings. The more intelligent version was that of Josip Strossmeyer, Bishop of Djakovo from 1849. Strossmeyer recognised the need for an accommodation with Orthodox Christianity but believed that Croatia bore a particular responsibility as outpost of true Christendom where Islam, the real enemy, was concerned. Then there were other, rougher, movements, like the Croatian Party of Rights, founded in 1880 (and resurrected in 1991 by Croatian fascists) which judged Strossmeyer to be almost sound on Muslims but soft on Serbs, and advocated a more racially bellicose Croatian cause. Once Croatia became part of the Serbian-dominated Yugoslav kingdom, the hardliners gained ascendancy. Croatia won the 'Banovina' treaty, while from fascist Italy the ultra-rightwing leader Ante Pavelic was building the Ustasha. This is no place to write a history of Pavelic's regime; suffice it to say that Croatia was an enthusiastic and loyal ally to Hitler, more reliable than the absurd Italians, and that at Jasenovac, the Ustasha were trusted to work to the Gestapo's satisfaction without regular supervision. It was a period in which the name of Croatian nationalism was blackened along with that of the Catholic Church, whose priests were implicated in the progroms. Croatians were also murdered in their thousands, by the Chetniks and in the partisan reprisals.

It would be unjust to equate the Croatian nationalist movements which challenged Tito with the murderous excesses of the Ustasha. The nationalist surge of 1971, the 'Croatian Spring', blended an incipient fascistic constituency with a democratic dissident revolt. Part of the push even came from within the Croatian communist party, and one of the unlikely personalities to emerge had been a loyal communist most of his life before a sudden conversion to militant nationalism: Franjo Tudjman. Tudjman's Croatian Democratic Union, or HDZ, is the central column of contemporary Croatian nationalism and was the agent for secession from Yugoslavia. The party is either a very broad church indeed, or downright two-faced. On one hand the pompous but serious Tudjman describes himself as part of the Christian Democrat fraternity of western Europe; on the other hand, the party's representitives in Bosnia are carving out their ethnically pure state, 'Herzeg-Bosna' in the bestial, time-honoured way.

Mate Boban, President of 'Herzeg-Bosna' and of Tudjman's HDZ in Bosnia, is a former supermarket manager and mayor of a dismal little town called Grude, and sits you down to talk about the principles of self-government 'as adhered to by the European community' and which he insists are being applied in 'Herzeg-Bosna', where his troops are engaged in a pale but unmistakable imitation of Serbian ethnic cleansing against the Muslims. Mate Boban did well by stealth and blushed to find it fame. He speaks for the hardline Herzegovinian Croats, and ousted the moderate Croatian member of the Bosnian presidency, Stjepan Kljuić, with Tudjman pulling the strings. Mate Boban from a distance looks like anybody's uncle; a short, white-haired, heavy-smoking man who wears quite smart suits that fail to convince. Close-up, he present a less comforting figure, his hard eyes stare at you with calculating disdain. He is forever surrounded by crews of bravoes with guns, and repatriated Canadian interpreters who refer to him as 'the President'. Outside his headquarters is the flag of the new state: the chequered Croatian emblem with an old heraldic knot on top. On the way into Bosnia to see 'the President' of 'Herzeg-Bosna', the 'border' with Croatia was virtually unmanned. We're in Bosnia, but you wouldn't know it.

Boban is at pains to stress the contrast between his project and that of what he dutifully calls the 'Serbian aggressor'. In contrast to Karadžić's horrific creature, 'Herzeg-Bosna' was 'established purely in the spirit of contemporary thinking within the European Community'. But down the road at one of Mr Boban's camps, Dretelj, 1,400 Muslim men were being held in sheds and underground hangars, drinking their own urine to survive, and Muslim east Mostar, brimful with 'cleansed' women and children, is being cudgelled to death by shelling. But then, like Karadžić, Boban is a mere auxiliary.

Franjo Tudjman ended forty years of communist rule in Croatia by being elected president in April 1990 with the help of $4 million from the Croatian diaspora and the friendship of Bonn. He wants history to recall him as father of the new Croatian statehood. Born in 1922, he was a partisan follower of Tito and organised communist party cadres within the army. Aged thirty-nine, and a fervent Marxist, he became the youngest general in the army's history. But before the Croatian Spring of 1971, Tudjman underwent a metamorphosis. He emerged from a period of seclusion studying Croatian history at the Zagreb Military Institute as a rampant nationalist, ready to write a revisionist history of the Jasenovac camp. He became a leader of the Croatian Spring and was imprisoned after its supression. From then on, Croatians saw Tudjman as the man who hoisted the banned chequered flag of Croatia in the streets of Zagreb and who presided over the war of independence. To meet, he is at first gruff and charmless, but aides describe him as prone to wild harangues and ranting, often close to tears, and harbouring a vainglorious pomposity.

Behind his determination to carry Croatia into the free world, Tudjman swerves illogically between his word and his deed, with a slipperiness that has fooled his European allies. He wants to run with the hare and hunt with the hounds. Tudjman appears more in love with western Europe than almost anyone living there. The twelve circled stars have become almost a second flag in Croatia, even though Croatia isn't one of them. For this, Tudjman is greeted as a liberator, much like Lech Walesa of Poland or Czechoslovakia's Vaclav Havel. But Tudjman is a different animal from these gentlemen; he was elected to office not as a good democrat but as a good Croat.

President Tudjman is not universally admired in Croatia; he has his opponents both on the left and on the extreme right. Among the rebels of the Croatian Spring was an egotistical but likeable man called Ivan Čićak, now a rare voice of centrist opposition to Tudjman. In the melodramatic Zagreb blackout of 1991, as we walked past the old secret police headquarters, Čićak says: 'The same people are working there as when I was inside for a stay as a student nationalist. If they haven't any enemies, they'll produce some.' We are stopped by another policeman, for no reason. 'Just look at all these guys with guns,' says Čićak, 'What are we going to do with them when the war is over? I wouldn't call Tudjman a fascist, but he is opening the way to fascism. We all have to be in one party now, Croatia. But Croatia isn't a political party, it's a country. Milošević is doing the same thing, and look where it has got the Serbs.'

The Croatian nationalist revolt against Yugoslavia was fuelled by a religious miracle: the appearance of the Holy Mother of God in 1981 to a group of children at Medjugorije – not in Croatia, significantly, but in Bosnia-Herzegovina. Since the Madonna's appearance, Medjugorije has aimed to pitch its unspectacular shrines on a par with Assisi or Lourdes. The miracle was a moneyspinner and therefore tolerated by the communists, although local folklore has it that Franciscans protecting the veracity of the vision were persecuted. The Bishop of Mostar has expressed scepticism towards the childrens' ecstasy and appointment with the Madonna, which is still repeated each evening by one of them. But the coachloads still roll in, even with the HVO guns pounding Muslim Mostar not eight miles away. The town has more recently become a focus for other visitors, since it is now a seedy junction for black marketeering and dealing in arms and stolen cars.

The pilgrims come from America or Ireland to pray to God, but for the Croats the appearance of Our Lady has been transformed into a cult charged with political purpose. At the conclusion of peace talks held in the town in May 1993, President Tudjman invoked the miracle in the cause of the Croats of Bosnia-Herzegovina. The Madonna's appearance had, said the former communist, heralded 'the re-awakening of the Croatian nation'. He was not actually in the Croatian nation, he was across the Bosnian border which he had been the first to recognise, but that didn't matter. By 'nation', Tudjman meant the *narod*, wherever it was.

As Croatia went to war with Belgrade, people from the diaspora, mostly refugees from communism, trickled back. Some worked for the government or ran the foreign press centres. Others came to fight, like Tom from the 'Wolves of Vukovar'. Tom arrived from Ohio with 'freelance fighting experience' in Central America and Southern Africa. He dressed in an imposing black uniform (like the Ustasha) and moved in and out of besieged Vukovar to deliver ammunition. He had a pony tail and parked up with his team at the battered Slavija Hotel in Vinkovci, base-camp for the perilous ammunition runs through enemy lines. (This was the hotel where we would sit for a splendid supper in a dining room where the window had been blasted out by shelling, which was so bad one night that the *maître d'* produced his stock of vintage 1962 wine for immediate consumption, on the premise that this could well be the Last Supper.)

Wolfman Tom did not dine with the press. 'The command that started the defence of Vukovar was shit,' he says in the bar. 'But now that has been gotten rid of and the special units are in command.' Tom and his chums worked for the HOS, or Croatian Defence Association. HOS was the military wing of a revived Croatian Party of Rights which adopted the Ustasha's salute '*Za Dom Spremni*', 'Ready for the Homeland', and was founded by a former political prisoner Dobraslav Paraga, a puffy-faced man who speaks in a catatonic whisper. He says he thinks the Ustasha was 'too liberal in the eyes of the Croatian people. If it had achieved what it had set out to do, we would not be in this position now.'

The black-shirted HOS championed the 'Death or Glory' cult imported from American videos and blended it with Ustasha legend. Their recruiting posters showed chisel-jawed young men and girls wearing trendy Ray-ban sun-shades and black leather jackets, and clutching guns with fingers protruding from leather fingerless gloves. They looked like some Balkan mutation of a heavy metal record cover or an advertisement for powerful motorbikes. In Bosnia, HOS was committed not to the frontiers of the Banovina agreement revived by Tudjman, but to King Tomislav's Croatia, revived by the Ustasha, which stretched almost as far as Belgrade. With this aim, HOS was committed to the unity of Bosnia, and opposed to Mate Boban's partition, and there were vicious and bloody intra-Croatian feuds between HOS and Mate Boban's army, the HVO. HOS in Bosnia was run by the man Tom the Wolf had served under in Vukovar, where the defence had indeed been taken over by the militia in the form of the unbalanced but capable military strategist, Milan Dedaković. We caught up with Dedaković not in Vukovar but in Bosnia and asked him how old he was. 'Wine, women and war keep me the man I am,' he replied, modestly.

The most influential expatriate to return to Croatia was Gojko Šušak, who became Defence Minister. Šušak is Tudjman's right-hand man, and had been a restaurateur in Canada. His family origins were not in Croatia proper, however, but Herzegovina. To the despair of more liberal Croatians, the influence of the Herzegovinians has been pivotal to the tone of Croatia's political colours, and sub-sequently to the conduct of the Bosnian war. Herzegovina is the heartland of the nationalist cause.

The loyal Herzegovinian Josip Šišić, who had fought the Serbs in the Croatian war, was now back in his home country of Bosnia and his birthplace of Ljubuški to fight whoever. He is a big man, reticent, coolly cordial, and wears a rosary around his neck, over his fatigues. He worked in Stuttgart for twelve years, in a car factory. 'Why pretend,' he says, 'that this country around here is anything but Croatia? I fought for Croatia against the Serbs and here I am fighting for Croatia against the Muslims. None of them have any claims to Croatian land. There's only one way to secure the future of our people here: no Serbs, no Muslims.' Josip is not a member of HOS, he is a member of the official Bosnian-Croat HVO and a supporter of the ruling party of Croatian President Franjo Tudjman.

Although they fought the Serbs in 1991 and will again fight the Serbs in Croatia, the Croats faced a different set of priorities in Bosnia. The carve-up treaty with Serbia is, ironically, as important to Tudjman as the liberation of those areas of his country still occupied by Serbs. In Croatia, the Croats and Serbs are enemies, but in Bosnia, they have common cause. Mr Tudjman admits that his goal is to 'normalise relations with Serbia on the basis of mutual recognition'. He has begun to exonerate Milošević of his responsibility for the war against Croatia, saying that the war was the 'inevitable result of the disintegration of the communist system and of the multi-ethnic states'. He now insists that the Serbs 'do honour their agreements'.[3] Croatian and Serbian guns may face each other in the Croatian Krajina. But in Bosnia, Tudjman and Milošević need each other, for they suffer from the same inconvenience: two million Muslims.

3. The Muslims

The first thing any visitor will notice about Bosnian Muslims is that they are particularly rotten Muslims; at least they were before the war. Attendance at mosque was about 3 per cent. During the early days of the fighting, charity workers and religious groups arrived from Saudi Arabia, and their representitives would be invited into people's houses or offices in Travnik or Zenica and offered generously filled glasses of strong šljivovic, and maybe a sausage roll. Ahmed Afaudi, a flowing-robed man from the Igassa charity in Jeddah, discussed his findings at Split airport as he prepared to board his flight home. Why, I asked, was the Arab world slow in agreeing to arm the Bosnian Muslims, embargo or no embargo? 'Because,' he replied, 'they have not yet understood the reason for their struggle. They have a great deal to learn. To fight, a Muslim soldier must be ready to die for Allah. These people have not understood this yet, they do not understand their mission.'

'Have you ever met Arab man?' asked Huki in English, over a beer at the Motel Bihać. Huki was a rock guitarist in Amsterdam who had returned to fight for his besieged hometown of Bihać, and the Motel bar was the night haunt for its defenders. 'Arab man is strange man,' Huki continued, 'he no eat pig and he no drink šljivovic.'

The young Muslim fighter up on the Sarajevo front line was pondering the idea of an 'Islamic Republic' with some of his mates. 'I spit on the Islamic republic,' he said, and did so, slightly taken aback by his own bravado. His deputy commander, Jasmin, said more thoughtfully: 'Islamic state? What sort of Islamic state would that be? I am forty, and I have never been in a mosque. If there was an Islamic state here, there would be a lot of Muslims eating sausages in it.' Bosnia's Muslims have adopted some Turkish habits, like grinding coffee in brass coffee mills and serving it from little copper jugs. However, they enthusiastically take Catholic and Orthodox holidays and although their ancestors have built some of the most beautiful mosques in the Islamic world, the call to prayer is hardly greeted by a rush across the square.

But one irony of the war against Bosnia's Muslims is that there are now corners of their country and of its populace in which a more rigorous Islam is taking root in response to persecution, places where both the educated and the hoodlums are starting to act out the comic-strip descriptions of them drawn a year ago by their enemies, but which were then untrue. The young man working in the Commission for War Crimes in Zenica wears an Iranian flag on his lapel. Girls sunbathing down by the river in the same town are asked to cover up their legs and shoulders not by the notorious Arab guest fighters, but by local Bosnian youths. New and nasty fighting units have been set up, the Muslim Armed Forces, which wear the crescent on their shoulder patches, and the words (which translate awkwardly into Serbo–Croat): '*Allahu Ekber*'. The fundamentalists, both local and Arab, are loathed by most Bosnians and by their army, but are the inevitable result of isolation, desperation and desolation.

Far more typical, though, is the view of Emir Tica, a fresh-faced, loyal child of western culture who is in charge of transport for the Bosnian army in Travnik: 'I never thought of myself as a Muslim. I don't know how to pray, I never went to mosque, I'm European, like you. I do not want the Arab world to help us, I want Europe to help us. But now, I do have to think of myself as a Muslim, not in a religious way, but as a member of a people. Now we are faced with obliteration, I have to understand what it is about me and my people they wish to obliterate.' Bosnia's Muslims are over-represented among the intellectual élite of the country. In the towns of the Bosnian Krajina around Banja Luka, now 'cleansed' by the Serbs, most of the doctors, lawyers, schoolteachers and businessmen tended to be Muslim while the political authorities and the peasants would more probably be Serbs.

Bosnia's Muslims had paid heavily for Serbian and Croatian claims and for the revenge against their power during Ottoman times. A Serbian prisoner-of-war called Dragutin Oćko was interrogated by his Ustasha captors on 29 January 1942. He was arrested in Foča, where Muslims were massacred as Chetniks moved in from Goražde and Rogatica, just as they did in 1992. There is nothing remarkable about his documented confession; except that it could have been made, almost word for word, yesterday.

'The Chetniks started picking up civilians, and asked about refugees from Rogatica. They had caught them and killed them all. I did not see them torture the civilians, but they boasted in my presence how many Muslims each had killed and I saw with my own eyes the bridge covered with blood, and in the water under the bridge, corpses. The slaughter lasted ten days, because civilians had hidden in houses, and the Chetniks searched for them, caught and killed them. They had captured and slaughtered the citizens of Foča, and all the refugees that were in Foča. For a month, I did not see a single Muslim anywhere except for a few craftsmen they had left alive to use. I do not know how many people were killed in Foča, but I heard Captain Sergije Mihailović saying "We have got rid of the enemy. We have killed 5,000 Muslims in Goražde and Foča."[4] Fifty years on, nothing has changed.

In the middle of today's ferment, and nominally at its apex, is an unexpectedly shambolic, professorial figure, who greets you with a distracted smile and remarkable blue eyes. Alija Izetbegović is the President of Bosnia-Herzegovina, and has a hunted air about him. Izetbegović is a religious rather than a political animal; he is the only president of a former Yugoslav republic who was never a leading communist.

Izetbegović was a teenager during the Second World War and at the birth of the communist state, having arrived in Sarajevo as a child. A serious youth, he involved himself in religious activism against the communist regime, of a kind similar to that of Christian dissidents in the old Soviet Union. He was denounced by the secret police and jailed in 1948, aged twenty-three, for his writings in a religious journal. He became a lawyer and consultant to the private business sector, but the notion of European Islam remained Izetbegović's passion. In 1970, he published a manifesto which has haunted him ever since. It was called 'The Islamic Declaration' and was a tortured attempt to propose that the Muslim faith was compatible with modern political systems.

Bosnia does not actually feature among the examples of possible Islamic democracies, but that hardly mattered to the Serbian and Croatian nationalists who have since seized gleefully on the document. Izetbegović is now cast and cursed as the white Ayatollah in Christian Europe. The declaration has been adjusted and enthusiastically sold in Belgrade and Zagreb as evidence of the *jihad*, and is sent abroad through the international lobbies which then proceeded to link Izetbegović to 'Muslim centres abroad and above all with specific groups in Iran'.[5]

In 1982, Izetbegović was arrested again, this time for 'counter-revolutionary acts' after the publication of a more considered work about the cultural position of Bosnia's Muslims, stuck between a western view of the world and an eastern view of the universe. Entitled *Islam Between East and West*, along with another book of his called *Problems of the Islamic Renaissance*, it argued for a 'moral revival' in the Islamic world, but stressed that Muslims living in multi-cultural societies should not adopt socially intolerant politics. He was sentenced to fourteen years, but released after only six, when he set about founding the SDA. To forge a party out of his hybrid of beliefs in multi-ethnic patriotism and spiritual Islam, Izetbegović gathered around him a clique of secular and religious Muslim intellectuals based in Sarajevo. If Izetbegović was determined to keep Bosnia-Herzegovina as a unitary, multi-ethnic republic, the sectarian, exclusively Muslim SDA was hardly the way to achieve it.

And Izetbegović put a second blot on his escutcheon soon after becoming President of the Republic. In March 1991, the Portuguese presidency hosted a meeting of EC leaders in Lisbon to discuss dividing Bosnia-Herzegovina into regions in which the three ethnic groups would enjoy 'spheres of influence'. It was partition with a sugar coating, enthusiastically agreed to by Tudjman and Milošević. Izetbegović, with a shortsightedness that has baffled his people ever since, opened the door to the thin end of

the wedge, and backed the idea. Two days later, he was
forced to eat crow; apparently realising his blunder and,
with characteristic naivety, withdrawing his acceptance of
the EC's Greek gift. Despite his Muslim nationalism,
Izetbegović has argued from the outset that Bosnia cannot
be ethnically partitioned because 'it is impossible without
ethnic cleansing. Our ethnic map is intermingled like a
Jackson Pollock painting, There are no ethnically pure
regions.'[6]

The religious leader of Bosnia's Muslims is Mustafa Cerić,
who resides in the offices of the Oriental Library in Sarajevo.
Its courtyard is splattered with shrapnel and shells smite
the gardens outside the elegant room with its sumptuously
decorated ceiling and handsome wooden desk from which
Cerić tries to guide the faith of his people. He smokes
heavily. 'The truth is that the Muslims in this country do
not understand Islam,' he says. 'They do not practise Islam,
they have only their names which are Muslim, and that is a
tradition. Some of them do not even know they are Muslim.
And yet, as Muslims in this country, we live in a paradox all
the time. On the one hand we are European, on the other
we don't know what to do about Europe. We cannot at the
moment love it, we cannot trust it, we cannot hate it, we
cannot deny it, for we are part of it. We are in a similar
position in relation to the Serbs and the Croats, with whom
we share this country, and who disagree between themselves
over everything except one thing: their relationship to the
Muslims, and their common need to destroy us. We simply
do not know what to do, or where to place our faith.

'We are "Muslims" now, because they did not allow us to
be Bosnians. And now that we are Muslims, they all say "that
is a religious category, not a nationality, it doesn't count".
And so we say then can we please be Bosnians after all, and
they, Europe included, say no, because there is no Bosnia
any more. I feel like screaming to the Serbs and Croats:
Why are you so scared of us? Why are you so *obsessed* by

us? Why are you incapable of leaving us alone? Why do you need to exterminate us and our culture? Why does our culture offend you so much that you need to do these things to us?"'

Part Two
Greater Serbia

Chapter Three

Sarajevo, the War Begins

'*If Sarajevo had fur, there would be an international campaign to save it.*'[1]

'It seemed impossible that they would actually shoot,' says Sanja Ruzic, red-haired student of English, recalling the day the war began on the streets of Sarajevo. 'There were so many of us, people from my flats, families, and friends from university. We marched towards their barricades. We believed they were trying to break the country we had voted for and we were going to plead with them not to fight. Suddenly, the police started running down the street; they had seen snipers on the top of the Holiday Inn. I looked up and could see them too, and guns protecting us on other buildings. The Chetniks on the hotel roof fired. People were running everywhere. My mother said afterwards "Why did you go, you fool?" Back in my flats, people stayed on the stairways to sleep for the first time. I remember thinking that night that I knew the war had started.'

Eleven people were killed in Sarajevo that day, 6 April 1992. The government police mounted a grenade attack on the Holiday Inn, which changed hands that afternoon. Throughout the rest of the day, police units and Serbian gunmen fought house-to-house gun battles, and the first mortar shells crashed into the city centre from the hills above, sending a pall of smoke rising into the spring air.

People were still on the streets as dusk fell, crowds of pensioners and miners holding portraits of Tito, shouting 'Down with the murderers! Down with those who would kill Bosnia!' Next day, the European Community and the United States formally recognised the independent, sovereign Republic of Bosnia-Herzegovina. The republic was thirty-six days old, and at war.

Bosnia had voted for its independence from Yugoslavia in a referendum on 29 February. Muslims and Croats had backed the call for secession, and Serbs had staged a boycott. Karadžić had proclaimed the newborn republic 'dead' when it was still an embryo, and now said that whatever the result of the vote, the Serbs would establish their own 'Serbian Republic of Bosnia-Herzegovina'. Meanwhile, the Serbs had been busy. Much of the armour coming back from service in the Croatian war had come through Bosnia, and stopped there. There were 100,000 full-time soldiers of the Yugoslav army working to put the plethora of military bases, air bases and arms factories on another war footing, against another breakaway republic. The Yugoslav army was mobilising men and further weaponry across the border from Serbia, and distributing arms to the Serbian irregular columns being formed in the villages. Along the Drina river, Bosnia's border with Serbia, an Olympian military build-up was grinding into gear: rows of tanks, tents and encampments full of scruffy, beer-swilling soldiers, gathered around bar tables in the warm evenings, waiting. Yards were full of shunting, clunking military vehicles, engaged in the slow, steady business of moving a cumbersome but bountifully equipped army westwards into Bosnia. The word 'Yugoslav' was by now a polite euphemism. All the men wore the striped emblem of Serbia or the crossed Cs of the Chetniks.

Meanwhile, a few isolated units of territorial guards loyal to the government were preparing to defend it. But the government's official policy was, as the deputy president of Bosnia Ejup Ganic explained, 'to try to slowly defuse the mine so as to prevent it exploding. We are just talking, talking, talking. When you are face-to-face with a wolf, the only option is to work with it, until it becomes a pet.' There was nothing domesticated, however, about the wolves stalking the Serbian-held hills above Sarajevo.

The February referendum turnout was 65 per cent of the electorate, with 64.7 per cent (99.5 per cent of votes) opting to establish the new state. The Serbian boycott had held its ground and within hours of the result barricades manned by armed Serbs went up in the capital and elsewhere, provoking the first demonstrations by unarmed civilians. And remarkable demonstrations they were too: crowds of students and families marched under the noses of the automatic weapons and in some cases began dismantling the barricades. The following day, 2 March, President Izetbegović led another crowd through the streets in celebration of what he hailed as 'the defeat of terrorism'. More realistic was the newspaper seller, half-Muslim, half-Serb, who mumbled: 'I wish I could be put in a state of clinical death for two years, because I know how long it is going to take to solve this problem.'2

Two days later, Izetbegović announced: 'The news that groups of armed Serbs are coming from the town of Pale to Sarajevo is confirmed, and we want to prevent them coming in'.3 That night the first Bosnian barricades went up in support of the government, erected by the Patriotic League, an embyronic Bosnian Army founded at the start of 1991 as a paramilitary formation. With the arrival of darkness, the streets into town were guarded by hundreds of nervous civilians and men from the League brandishing ancient weapons and a new flag on their berets: six lilies divided by a diagonal white stripe, the flag of doomed Bosnia.

After the first shells on 6 April, every strand that was to mark the course of Sarajevo's war developed at speed. People trying to leave from the still-operating airport were running a gauntlet of sniper fire along the approach roads. The United Nations refugee agency, UNHCR, was reporting that trucks bringing aid to the swelling number of refugees across the country were being seized by Serbian irregulars, and aid into Sarajevo being stopped by 'Yugoslav' soldiers controlling the access roads. By the end of the month, the siege had begun. Sarajevans recall the first day of serious bombardment, 21 April; Yigal Chazan wrote for the *Guardian*: 'The Serbian assault began shortly after dawn, when up to twenty mortar shells slammed into the Sarajevo television station. Thick plumes of black smoke rose high above the fortress-like building as the Serbs sought to destroy what they were unable to control. The television station has long been a target of the militants, since it has refused to churn out the blood-curdling propaganda that characterises state-controlled television in Belgrade and Zagreb. But despite the pounding, the television staff continued broadcasts to the city's population, who cowered in cellars as the shells rained down.'

There is nothing quite like the Sarajevo feeling – the aura of a sophisticated capital city under seige, faced with the daily onslaught of an unseen army which enjoys an unlimited supply of armour and ammunition. In Sarajevo, you are never out of range. There is the Sarajevo walk: it is relaxed only when protected by the cover of buildings or specially constructed barricades; it becomes brisk and purposeful across a street, and breaks suddenly into a sprint over a patch of open ground, a cobbled forecourt or cross-roads exposed to the snipers' rifles, each with its own bloody history. As for the mortars and shells, they can drop anywhere, at any time, there is no protection. Not even at night: one of the most extraordinary moments of all is when the sky above the city wrapped in darkness is suddenly illuminated by a flare sent up from the Serbian hilltops, which hangs there, diffusing its arrogant light; the wicked messenger. There is a short, ominous interval: the buildings of the city are dragged out of their hiding and displayed in a ghostly, menacing glow before the unseen gunners. Within thirty seconds, the shells hammer in. They may land a good few blocks away, the echo of their thud calling around the valleys, or they may land in the street below, the explosion sending people diving under tables, windows caving in across the room. Or they may land nearby, and thrust flying red-hot metal through the air, which can rip you to shreds.

This is the sight and sound of Sarajevo: when the first shades of dusk have crept across the sky, people may be on the streets, huddled around the entrances to their flats or taking apart the remains of some rusty car that has been blasted off the road and abandoned; the lads are forever hungry for spare parts. Lovers (people do still fall in love in Sarajevo) sit in the porches, holding hands in solemn silence or talking in low voices and the old ladies may hurry home with a prized loaf of bread from the miraculously functioning bakery. Suddenly, two things happen within a split second but, curiously, in slow motion. There is a loud, angry whistling noise overhead, as though the air itself is being cut open and is letting out a cry of pain. It is a deep, not a shrill, whistle. It is a sound everyone knows, and as it proclaims itself we all duck, in perfect unison, torsos horizontal, necks craning to keep our heads raised so we do not bump into anything as we break into a run, and so we know whether we are still there or not. That moment freezes for what feels like a number of minutes, but which is no more than a nanosecond.

You can almost see the sound of the whistle through the air as the missile ploughs into the side of a block of flats: there is the crash of an explosion, a thud more than a bang, and a belch of black smoke. People do not scream like in the movies; apart from the explosion there seems to be very little other sound — for a moment. Then there is bedlam, rubble flung all over the road, breaking glass, a peculiar groan of tumbling bricks and masonry and the odd, blurted human exclamation. Then a scurrying in all directions, either to safety or, in the case of the brave, to find out the damage to the humans caught in the path of this latest pitiless bolt from the blue. On the occasion that the seventh shell in a week hit my friend Hasan's flats, the victim, apart from those caught by flying glass from an adjacent shop window, was a middle-aged woman – typical of Sarajevo's war. There was not as much blood as one might expect, apart from a thick, sticky stream that came from under her torn but still tied headscarf. Her clothes were ripped by the dozen or so pieces of shrapnel that had sprayed her body. The immediate reaction was to look into her eyes, open and only recently functioning, and so it was a while before you noticed that her foot had been almost severed, still in its shoe and tied to her calves by tendons and sinews.

Her name was Amra Hadžisković, and the most compelling thing about her death were the things of which her life had been apparently made on the last morning that she got up in her flat. You didn't have to pry to see what she had packed into the capacious burgundy leather handbag that was lying some six yards from her body: a pocket diary, a handkerchief, a list of some kind (unlikely to be a shopping list, they don't tend to make them in Sarajevo), a powder box, a cleanly sharpened pencil and some small plumbing fitting that maybe she had gone to try and replace in the ramshackle market. She had been a strong, finely built woman and had chosen a pair of sensible walking shoes and a long, brown, thick cotton skirt in which to do whatever business she had planned for that day. Now Amra had been killed by a shell that had come from what felt like nowhere. But that was an illusion. It had been loaded and fired by someone up there, and there would be tens of thousands more who would die like Amra.

There is charisma as well as tragedy in the phenomenon of Sarajevo. The sight of such a city, trying to defend the eroding corners of bygone normal life, is something to behold. The Sarajevans have a certain dignity about them. They are are generally courteous to each other; the girls – many of them very beautiful – take an almost absurd care over their appearance. Cosmetics rank with baby milk and cigarettes as the most prized commodities on the black market.

Sarajevo at the outset of the war was the symbol of a Bosnia that was the exact opposite to that of the War of Maps, and which its army and people were setting out to defend. It was a university city, which boasted one of the two great rock bands to come out of the old Yugoslavia, Bjelo Dugme (White Button). It was a city made up of rogues in dirty suits, students with pony tails and earrings, old men with sticks and women in traditional headscarves, houseproud ladies and hospitality which can almost oppress a visitor. This was a crossroads between Europe and the Orient, where the *narod* dissolved. Sephardic Jews came here in flight from Spain, it was the 'Damascus of the North'; it was Muslim, Serb, Croatian, Austrian, Jewish and more besides. The maze of little lanes around the old Turkish Bascarsija market and the . Ali Pasha mosque was teeming with cafés, flower stalls and the rough traders of trinketry, and the air was heavy with the smell *ćevap* Turkish kebabs. But at each end of the lanes were the Orthodox church and the Catholic cathedral. Selection for the staging of the 1984 Winter Olympics made many Sarajevans feel that *their* Bosnia had been put on the map. My friend Bojan Zec returned just in time for the referendum and the war, after eight months' study at Edinburgh University. Bojan is young and serious, now working for the government in an office whose windows are decked out with sandbags:

'Sarajevo means more than appears to the outsider. The death of Sarajevo would be the death of an idea; if Sarajevo falls or is partitioned, then something dies psychologically as well as physically. We developed a way of life here through who our friends were and the kind of conversations we had. And suddenly we realise what that way of life was: we were going to shut out the historical hatreds. Quite unconsciously, this city was living what Bosnia is all about. But people are now conscious of this. Without it, we would be going mad, or would have opted for an easy life and surrendered. Under siege, the city has suddenly recognised itself.'

Sanja Ruzic was one of 90,000 Serbs who did not join the departure from Sarajevo to embrace their racial comrades in the hills around town, but who stayed to face the siege instead. 'It would have made a great deal of sense for us to go,' says Sanja, 'but I belong here. My friends are here, and they are Muslim, Croat and Serb. We had a letter from relatives saying that if we wanted to go and live in Serbia, we could and should go, for our safety. But I can't. I am nothing to do with those people up there, with their religion and stupidity. I don't care who my neighbours are, I like Sarajevo and I am a Bosnian.' Sanja's neighbours live as she does in a block on 'sniper alley', a tower of charred steel where most of the flats have now been burned out. Her husband and parents avoid using the bedroom overlooking the Tito Boulevard, and instead camp in an inside bedroom and the sitting room. It is a mixed block and Sanja talks about 'our army', meaning the Government Army, in which her husband (also Serbian) is a soldier. She riles against 'Chetniks', although her father-in-law, who was a professional soldier, has languished in a government prison since the start of the war.

Sometimes there would be whole afternoons of relative calm, and then suddenly the black lead mortar bombs would come in like wild rain. The cellars and basements of the city were kitted out with mattresses and camp beds as makeshift living quarters, which became sweaty and smelly during summer, and were to become icy cold in winter. Above them, the ground would shake as the shells came in, plaster dust falling from the ceiling. It would be wrong to say that there was nothing but gloom in the shelters. Some were keenly organised, like that near the old Jugobank, with a separate sleeping area for children, and tables laid out between rows of beds at which men played cards and drank clear, home-brewed šjivovic until late. 'My god!' said a hearty figure called Osman Grebović on the evening the Presidency was hit, opening a can of fish paste he had been saving, 'You've got a Croat here, Serbs, Muslims, a Macedonian, a Hungarian and a Jew, all going mad together. It must be Bosnia!' The women were less stalwart. They said they would only ever go out to take themselves or the children to collect food and to relieve themselves.

Morning, the mists still sitting in the valley, was usually the right time to emerge, take a stretch and a deep breath of air, and wander down to the paltry market to see if peasants from the few outer suburbs still under government control had brought in any cherries or dandelion leaves for sale. As the morgue at the city's Koševo hospital filled up, so the dead were taken to outpost first aid stations instead. And when they could take no more, they were buried in gardens or beneath communal land between the tower blocks. As the evenings grew lighter and longer, Sarajevo was having to use its ingenuity to find cemetery space. The Lion cemetery, once a public park with a few old graves in a corner, had been recalled into use, and by July boasted 2,200 fresh mounds, some already marked by Christian crosses or Islamic wooden headboards. On 25 May, the Red Cross said there were more than 1,000 bodies at the hospital, and advised the Director to start burning them.[4]

In May two massacres stretched the city to its limits. The first turned the war against the infants and the weak: shells aimed at the Sarajevo maternity clinic, setting ablaze the building in which seventy pregnant women and 173 babies were sleeping. The second targeted the guns specifically on the hungry. On 27 May, a shower of mortars killed twenty and injured 160 in a cold-blooded attack on a bread queue which had formed in the narrow Vase Miskina shopping street in the city centre. Television pictures were relayed around the world, showing the dismembered bodies of the dead and not-quite-dead lining the alleyway in pools of blood. They were viewed at the 'peace talks' convened in Lisbon, and the Bosnian delegation walked out. Milan

Gvero, deputy commander of the Serbian troops in Bosnia dismissed the pictures as 'mere anti-Serbian propaganda'.[5] Less than a month later, there was another massacre, this time of a queue to take money out of one of the last remaining banks. This time the dead were victims of one of the many 'ceasefires', people misplacing their faith by daring to come out of hiding. Twenty-one were killed including three children, and 135 injured.

By summer, Sarajevo was traumatised and on the edge of starvation. The UN finally opened the airport and the blue flag was raised above the arrivals lounge. The siege had, in theory, been broken, and not a moment too soon. On the night of the bank massacre, the first relief plane landed. By mid-July the first food since April arrived in the suburb of Dobrinja. Hugh Paine of Reuters travelled with it: 'The guns fell silent, and the people of Dobrinja poured out of their houses into the sunshine to greet the United Nations lorries. They smiled and were grateful but the welcome was subdued because the 45,000 people here know their ordeal is not over.' 'Food OK,' said Samir, a section commander, 'but we need more boom boom. The Chetniks have the big guns.'[6]

The newborn Bosnian army was, like that of Croatia and Serbia, subject to the UN arms embargo. But unlike the other two armies fighting on Bosnian soil, it was landlocked, it did not have a parent state to back it, nor did it have the same weighty international contacts. The Croats were endowed with 1,000 kilometres of coastline, the friendship of Germany and links to the Italian Mafia and arms industry. The Serbs had one of Europe's most formidable armies and arms manufacturing industries at their disposal, and the support of Russia and Greece. The embargo froze the imbalance, leaving the legitimate army of the recognised republic fighting with its hands tied behind its back. The Bosnian army's neutralisation by the embargo suited the other two players well, although the Croats were still Bosnia's ally at this early stage. In what would become a three-sided war, two of those sides, absurdly but logically, supported the ban on arms, because they knew they could get them anyway, and because the Sarajevo government was thus starved of weaponry. The fact that the Bosnian army did eventually get weapons and supplies is one of the more remarkable stories of the war, but at first the Sarajevo army was a rag-bag, dependent on whatever arms its supporters had stashed away, on whatever it could smuggle into its besieged communities and on the wit and determination of its fighters.

In the early days of June, the army – or *armija* as it was now called – launched its first counter-offensive on the noose around Sarajevo. The defending troops broke out with such ferocity from Dobrinja and around the airport that they nearly pierced the Serbian lines. From that moment on, the Serbian plan to push into the city and partition it slipped quietly from the agenda. Sarajevo was now taking 180 mortars for every one it fired out. At the end of June, the Bosnian government said that the war had so far claimed 7,200 lives (more in three months than during the entire Croatian war) with 30,000 people missing. Some 25,000 had been injured.

People were still trying to leave Sarajevo. On 18 May, a ten-mile convoy of eighty buses and 1,000 other vehicles left the city, passed through the Serbian lines and began to make its way, unprotected, to the Croatian border. The convoy was held hostage for two days by Serbian gunmen. An attempt to evacuate children by bus at the beginning of August resulted in the deaths of two of them, one aged three and the other fourteen months, as the bus drove, unescorted, down the airport road. The funeral of the two children was then targeted for a mortar attack. Within weeks, another convoy would leave Sarajevo with greater success: buses taking mothers and their children to Split.

'As much as I am happy, I am very, very sad,' said Borislava Karadglaja, half-Muslim, half-Serb, as she staggered off the coach with her baby Stanko in a pram and her daughter

Anja. As the coaches arrived, the faces of the women were taut with relief and sorrow, those of the little children pressed in disbelief against the glass, noses squashed on the windows as the crowd applauded on the quaysides. Teenage girls chewed gum, and the boys helped to unload the great jumble of bags, pet animals and toys, for re-packing aboard the ferry to Rijeka up the coast. 'It felt terrible to leave,' said Borislava, 'leaving our city and our hopes, our men and our parents. I came just to bring the children out of that hell. For two hours on the bus, I was expecting shells to drop, and only a few minutes ago, I realised that we were here. We will now have to live with people who do not understand, and who have not seen what we have seen. I'm not at all sure that I will be able to enjoy this peace.'

A refugee village at Plošucé on the Croatian frontier was growing into a wretched metropolis. By the end of the month, Croatia had taken 310,000 people in flight from the fighting which was now raging across the Bosnian republic. Attention had been focused almost exclusively on the drama in Sarajevo, but now refugees were arriving in Croatia with stories that suggested Sarajevo to be no more than the tip of the iceberg, and that in the rural reaches of northern and eastern Bosnia, a drama on an even more terrifying scale was unfolding.

Chapter Four

The First Ethnic Cleansing

'Though this be madness, yet there is method in it.'
– Hamlet

'They had been coming to the door for some weeks, with guns, demanding money, jewellery, and anything else. We knew some of them; Miša from the mine, and a boy from the supermarket. Others we didn't know. They started smashing Muslim shops, then blew one up, then another. Soon, there were none left. The police said Muslims would need permits to go into the centre of town, and could only spend German marks. There was a curfew, and they started shooting into the houses, riding down the street in trucks, firing and throwing grenades. They killed three women in a house nearby, just throwing a grenade through the window. One of the ladies was the doctor, Dr Topić; no one dared to move the bodies for two days. Men also came from the political committee and said that if we gave our house away we would be able to leave. People started to go; there was a bus leaving to Banja Luka, and from there we didn't know where. But we thought it would get better. Then they surrounded the town. They came round and said they were looking for weapons, they searched the house and went. Later three rude and rough men came and said they wanted Sahudin, my husband. I said they must be joking, and the man pushed me and swore obscene things. They all had guns and one of them had the bad manners to have taken his shirt off. They took Sahudin, kicked him and hit him in the back with their rifles. I have not seen him since. There was a bus two days later. On the day we left they were burning houses at the end of the street. They locked a family inside, and put men with guns at the door, and then set fire to the house. Only one man, the eldest son Mirsad, made it to the door and he was shot. Other soldiers were sitting on the walls and drinking. I saw them kick the wife of the postman, Mrs Kustura, until she seemed to be unconscious. That's the last thing we saw, the street burning and dead people in the gardens. We took clothes, a coffee grinder, soap and cheese.'

By July Safija Muhanović made it to Karlovac in Croatia. There, she camped down with her daughter Zejna and still looks as though the light in her life has been switched off. She manages to be cordial and kind, and makes coffee in the lovely Turkish grinder, apologising that she cannot be more hospitable than the conditions in the sports centre afford. She came from the mainly Muslim town of Kluj. She was one of the very lucky ones: she survived. Across northern and eastern Bosnia, the Serbs had unleashed a tempest of ethnic violence, bringing to modern Europe the principles and practices of the racial progrom. The 'clearance' of Muslims and some Croats from territory the Serbs wanted for their racially pure republic managed to be both systematic and haphazardly brazen, and used whatever means appealed to the boors who put it into effect: browbeating, destruction, mass deportation and wanton murder. As the world discovered the extent of the progrom, the term 'ethnic cleansing' entered the vocabulary.

Ethnic cleansing was the logical outcome of the mission to 'carve up' Bosnia into ethnic territories, agreed by Presidents Tudjman and Milošević and peculiarly endorsed by the EC in a softer, more tactful edition at the Lisbon EC summit of 1992. The ethnic map of Bosnia was a leopard-skin of blotches – interwoven communities which had been overrun before, but never formally compartmentalised even through centuries of warfare. Why, people said, it cannot be done; the stonger communities would have to physically obliterate or drive out the weaker ones. Sarajevo was full of wise but naive writers and politicians saying that war was unthinkable for that very reason. It was a long time before Bosnia, let alone the rest of the world, comprehended that this was exactly the plan. In 1991 Karadžić first publicly suggested a scheme for 'population transfers' as 'a solution'. 'It could be done over five years with the help of a state agency,' he said.[1] The agency, in reality, was made up of his own soldiers.

The towns most exposed to the Serbian army, as it crossed the Drina and linked up with General Mladić and the hotchpotch of irregulars, were those close to the frontier, like Bjeljina in the north-western corner of Bosnia. The news came through as early as 5 April that 'at least twenty-seven people were reported killed in Bjeljina'.[2] A team of EC monitors were turned back after their attempt to gain entry to the sealed-off town. Some days later photographs appeared which showed what had been happening in Bjeljina: Serbian gunmen had moved in, smashed a paltry resistance and begun the summary execution of unarmed Muslim civilians.

The perpetrators of the Bjeljina violence were a team of killers going by the name of Arkan's Tigers, the most fiendish of the Belgrade-based militias, the Keystone stormtroopers of Serbia. 'Captain Arkan', real name Željko Ražnjatović, was an ice cream salesman who graduated to thug, operating in the Belgrade underworld before being recruited by the communist internal intelligence service. As a government-sponsored Mafioso, he built up a chain of cafés and his latest fixed address was a pastry shop, at which he could still be contacted by anyone capable of breaching the hoodlums around the entrance. Arkan was also leader of the hardcore fans of the Red Star Belgrade soccer team. There is a bar in Belgrade set up around an old London bus which Arkan blesses with an occasional surprise visit, accompanied by a posse of henchmen. The girls, like the journalists, gather round. He cuts an unimpressive figure, and speaks in clipped sentences. 'The important thing,' he pontificates over a beer, 'is for a people to identify its enemies and to banish them. I am a Serbian first, a warrior second.' These were the days before Captain Arkan found his vocation in politics; he is now a deputy in the Serbian parliament, for which he stood in the election of 1992 representing a constituency in Kosovo and advocating deportation of Albanians. Arkan's Tigers, who pose for photographs with a pet tiger cub and balaclavas over their faces, decided that in Bjeljina they had a message to deliver to the Muslims and to the world.

General Mladić's army, with its Serbian patrons and a medley of local cohorts, moved across eastern Bosnia like a grim combine harvester. They linked together the top and bottom right-hand corners of the country, where Serbs were the majority, by displacing, sometimes killing, 200,000 Muslims in between. In Zvornik, on the Bosnian–Serbian border, Muslim fighters hoped to defend their community with hunting rifles by standing on the bridge linking it with Serbia. They disappeared shortly after the arrival of a band calling itself the 'Serbian volunteer force'. The irregulars wreaked the first horror, the army would then move in and remove any remaining civilians and the death squads would 'mop up'. Some Muslims fled, some were taken prisoner, some were killed, others were brought back over the border to await transport by railway boxcar to Hungary.

Meanwhile, the survivors festered in transit camps: harsh, but not specifically established for torture or murder at that early stage. The sports hall of Loznica was converted to take Muslim deportees and Serbs who had fled the fighting, in seperate compounds. Serbs had beds, Muslims did not. Serbs had two meals a day, Muslims had one. Serbs were waiting to be re-housed in the homes the Muslims had been obliged to leave; Muslims were being deported. 'I can almost see my house from here,' said Halil, lounging, disconsolate, in the heat. It was easy to identify his street in the village of Šepak, just over the river and the border.

'We left when they started smashing the windows and firing into the house,' he says. 'Yes, they were armed when they came. We had no choice. We just have to hope that we can get these papers they're promising, and try to start again, somewhere away from here.' The previous night, Halil had asked a Serbian refugee to telephone his home and find out if there was somebody in it (Serbs were allowed to leave the sports hall, Muslims not). The Serb had come back to say yes, there was, and they had asked whether Halil might call sometime and explain how to use the washing machine, which was presenting difficulties.

The houses in Halil's street were slightly, not badly, damaged by automatic fire and Serbian families were busy moving in to find bedding and furniture intact. In what I think was Halil's split-level house, even the larder was full. The Kekić family had arrived from the edges of Sarajevo. 'It feels a little strange,' said Maja Kekić, 'but I don't see it as stealing. We lost our own home because of the fighting in Grbavica. This is certainly a better house, bigger, with new woodwork and I like this two-level thing. No, it's not taking someone else's property, and even if it is, it is preventing the fundamentalists from taking *our* property.' We didn't discuss the washing machine.

The Serbian assault cut east of the Drina to force a corridor which would link Serbia proper with the half-Serbian, half-Muslim Bosnian Krajina in the north and north-west. This passage would in turn connect with the Serbs of the Croatian Krajina. The next stop was Brčko, near the Croatian border, strategically crucial to holding the narrowest point of the corridor. Brčko was cut off; again, impressions had to be gleaned from those who fled, this time to Slavonski Brod in Croatia. Refugees arrived speaking of 'soldiers killing anyone they could find. They were shelling, coming down the streets, torching houses one by one, firing, firing all the time.' This was Ramiza Memić, who later moved to Varaždin in Croatia. 'Some houses they blew up at night; others they locked, set fire to, and watched them burn, the people inside; they were drinking all the while.' Three months later, reporters from the *New York Times* uncovered evidence of a mass grave in Brčko which they estimated to contain the bodies of 3,000 people. On the Drina, the Serbian mobs took over Višegrad, and from there came testimony that a house had been filled with seventy people, including elderly women and children, windows and exits barred, and the building set alight by men who then watched it burn, drinking and singing.[3]

The push towards the heart of Bosnia in April 1992 took the Serb militias to the evenly mixed town of Foča, a community of 10,000 people. They occupied it on the day after Bosnia's referendum, and street fighting trapped 200 women and children in a hospital. Again, the town was sealed off while the business done; UN parties trying to retrieve the patients were turned back. One UN official, Fabrizio Hochschild, was allowed into the town and came out saying: 'I have worked in five wars now, and the situation in there is the worst I have ever seen.' The hospital staff were working without power, anaesthetic, antibiotics or plasma, he said. Foča was 'a ghost town. We didn't see a single sign of life. There are no cats or dogs. Flowers in the window boxes have wilted. The buildings have been gutted by artillery fire and the streets are covered in debris and glass. Many of the shops have been looted. I think over 90 per cent of the people have fled, the elderly and immobile are trapped in their basement.'[4]

A small number of journalists later made it to Foča under Serbian control; one of them was Andrej Gustinčić of Reuters; 'Gangs of gun-toting Serbs rule Foča, turning the once quiet town into a nightmare landscape of burning streets and houses. The motley assortment of fierce-looking bearded men carry Kalashnikovs and bandoliers or have hand guns tucked into their belts. Some are members of paramilitary groups from Serbia, self-proclaimed crusaders against Islam and defenders of the Serbian nation, others are wild-eyed local men, hostile towards strangers and happy to have driven out their Muslim neighbours. No one seems to be in command, and ill-disciplined and bad-tempered gunmen stop and detain people at will'.[5]

By summer, there were only four pockets in eastern Bosnia, where Muslims had been the majority population, holding out against the Serbs: Goražde, Žepa, Cerska and Srebrenica, each of which began the long-drawn-out torment of their respective sieges. But the rest had gone, and at the start of August I took a Serbian helicopter over the terrain, from Belgrade to Pale. The porthole offered a sobering view over the defiled landscape: village after village, tucked into the mountainsides and on the cultivated plains, gutted, charred and lifeless. Houses decapitated as if in some Legoland model which a child had smashed to pieces, the gardens strewn with debris. And nobody there, not even soldiers. I caught the eye of one of the Serbian troopers in the chopper, also looking down. He gave me a smile, as though we were sampling some gastronomic delicacy together.

The most ferocious 'ethnic cleansing' of all had begun in the satellite villages and towns around Banja Luka and Prijedor in the Bosnian Krajina, where in May the Serbs had declared their autonomous 'Serbian Republic of Bosnia-Herzegovina'. Between 150 and 200 homes, shops and mosques were being burned or dynamited every day in the Krajina, sending a tide of refugees towards Croatia which the UNHCR called the 'most serious refugee crisis since the Second World War'. 'Whole communities,' said Peter Kessler, the organisation's spokesman, 'and whole towns have been emptied.' By the end of May, half a million people had been wrenched from their homes, and their number would more than double before the summer.

Not all Muslims left immediately. Driving around this now terrifying area, some houses flew white flags, sheets or pillow-cases from windowsills. Sometimes, entire villages were putting out these signals of surrender, and in one near Prijedor there was a sheet flying from the minaret of the mosque. The Belgrade weekly *Epoka* had run an editoral which explained that 'If the Muslims do not fly white flags from the minarets, we will flatten those villages. Serbian villages will replace them.'

'Those are people who recognise the new order and have made themselves available for organised population exchange,' explained Major Milovan Milutinović from army headquarters in Banja Luka, driving around the subjugated and ravaged villages with a pride in the neatness of the arrangements and a blind eye to the violence on which they were premised. For Muslims waiting to go, codes of practice were being introduced. At Ćelinac, near Prijedor, the new Serbian civic authorities issued a decree that Muslims were forbidden to:

1. Move around from 4 p.m. to 6 a.m.
2. Associate or loiter in the streets, in cafés, restaurants and other public places.
3. Bathe or fish in the river.
4. Drive or travel by car.
5. Gather in groups containing more than three men.
6. Make contact with any relative who was not a resident of Ćelinac.
7. Sell real estate or exchange their homes without permission and only through official channels.
8. Make any telephone call other than from the post office.
9. Leave the town without permission and the necessary documentation.
10. Show contempt for the struggle of the Serbian nation.

Any visit by a Serb to a non-Serb household had to be cleared by or reported to the authorities. There was a further list of thirty-four Muslims who were 'forbidden to contact any person from the neighbourhood or from further away, between 00.00 hours and 24.00 hours, unless they are called to work'. They were local political leaders, schoolteachers and businessmen.

Apart from villages flying the white flags, this was now a desolate, irrecoverable landscape from which life had been blotted out. The drive to Prijedor was through miles and miles where not a soul stirred. Until we reached the town, there was just one bombed, burned, looted, charred house after another. Every mosque had been destroyed. In the town of Kozarac, there was barely a single house left undamaged, and those that stood intact were occupied by apparently nonchalant Serbs. This town of 25,000 had been 90 per cent Muslim, a 500-year-old settlement. Late in May, the Serbs had set about its methodical obliteration. According to relief workers, some 3,000 people were killed. Later in the year, the *Guardian*'s Ian Traynor and Tom Gjelten of US National Public Radio pieced together what had happened: 'The Serbs' operation was clinical, calculated and comprehensive. The local political, business and cultural élites were singled out for extermination . . . Emir Kevljanin, who stood at the crossroads with his wife and teenaged children, part of the exodus from Kozarac . . . said: "they were very systematic, destroying everyone who who could bring about a revival of Kozarac"'.[6]

In Banja Luka itself, the 'Office for Population Resettlement and Property Exchange' had opened in May, with the help of the local SDS party. Here, families who waved the white flag and had 'elected' to leave could register their property as available for a Serbian family, and join the convoys out. Radoslav Vukić, a senior SDS party official, told a group of visitors and the Yugoslav Red Cross that he was hoping to tie up a single population transfer of some 20,000 Muslims that week, despatching them to Zenica and hoping to get some Serbs back in return. And if the authorities in Zenica don't return the Serbs? 'We'll send them all the same,' retorted Vukić, with his spine-chilling laugh. The office lucratively combined the roles of intimidation, ethnic cleansing and extortion. Because Vukić was an SDS leader, much of the 'cleansing' program was organised by him. His thugs were sent to rob, dynamite, kill and torture, which would produce queues of people anxious to flee. The procedure for their transportation would be a contorted one involving a miasma of SDS and independent consultants and agents, and the wheels oiled only by offers in hard currency. The office's business ethos was this: life could be made so awful for the Muslims and Croats in Banja Luka that people would pay their life savings to be ethnically cleansed, which was the political goal in the first place. The more people trying to make departure difficult, the more people would have to be paid. This was perpetual motion between racial ideology and crude larceny.

In the city, a reduced Muslim population hung on, subject to nightly murders and houseburning. By mid-August, Banja Luka was a petrified city. Muslims were scared to be seen talking to any visitor, let alone journalists. One woman came up to us a few minutes before curfew just to say: 'They are killing us, one by one. My husband, my son have gone and are dead, and still they stand around the house, sitting on my wall, the same men, after dark. Can you get me out? Can you?' By the end of the month, Vukić was local leader of the SDS, and he passed an edict that no Muslim or Croatian woman was permitted to have a baby in any Banja Luka hospital. UNHCR officers trying in vain to work from Zagreb estimated that a quarter of a million Muslims were driven from their homes in the Bosnian Krajina alone during one single and brutal wave of 'cleansing' in September. Where they ended up, we did not discover until later.

Some people passing through the office in its early days of operation were, it emerged, being sent to Muslim-held Zenica by railway boxcar. Maggie O'Kane of the *Guardian* heard this testimony from a man called Šehib. This is what he saw at Trnopolje railway station, near Prijedor in June 1992: 'There were ten cattle wagons . . . I only saw a few of the womens' faces and they were sticking their arms out

CROATIA

BOSNIA - HERZEGOVINA

SERBIA

Sarajevo

Largest ethnic groups, pre-war

Serbs

Croats

Muslims

MONTENEGRO

0　　30 miles

CROATIA

Bihac　　　Prijedor

Omarska　　Banja Luka

BOSNIA -HERZEGOVINA　　Tuzla

SERBIA

CROATIA　　　　　　　Maglaj

Jajce

Travnik　　Zenica

Srebrenica

Military control and ethnic groups
August 1992

Kiseljak　　Sarajevo　　Zepa

Jablanica　　　　Gorazde

Foca

Serbs

Croat majority in alliance with Muslims

Muslim majority in alliance with Croats

Mostar

MONTENEGRO

0　　30 miles

of two barred windows high up on the wagon, but I knew the wagons had to be full because of the noise. They were screaming "Water! Just a glass of water". They didn't have a toilet ... At 11.30 at night, the wagons were still in the station. A railway worker telephoned Merhamet, the Muslim charity in Banja Luka, to try and get to the women and children when the wagons reached town.'

'When they finally did,' runs O'Kane's summary of the testimony, 'women and children had been inside for two days under the long hot Yugoslav sun, squashed and wriggling together. They were still screaming, sticking their hands out of the window shouting, "Two children are dead. Let us take out the bodies, let us out, please, water." The wagons reached Zenica on 15 June, it had taken five days.'[7]

This was a different war now. These people were not 'refugees' in the strict sense of the term, in flight from warring armies. Their removal was the *subject matter*, not a side-effect of the war. That these people should die or lose their homes, through whatever means necessary, was the raw material, the aim, of the War of Maps. The assault on the Muslims of the Bosnian Krajina showed the Serbian project at its most systematic. But at the same time, there was a casual, drunken pleasure being derived from the entire procedure.

At this point of the war, the worst had been hidden from eyewitnesses, and could be gleaned only after the event, from victims' testimony. Unlike the siege of Sarajevo, which was there for all to see, the ethnic cleansing programme was not for public consumption. Karadžić's intellectual shadow, a Serbian member of the Bosnian presidency Nikola Koljevic, later admitted to me that Sarajevo was designated a piece of violent theatre which would captivate world attention and draw it away from the principal programme. Professor Koljevic, who has good English and pedantically quotes Shakespeare to illustrate every point, chastised me over tea and cakes in a smart Belgrade hotel: 'It amazes me that you all took so long to get to the point. Poor Sarajevo! That was all you could think about. The crossroads of Europe! None of you had ever been on holiday in Trnopolje, Ha Ha!'

Word was now coming through with refugees into Croatia of an even more astonishing ingredient in the Serbian programme. Roy Gutman of the New York paper *Newsday* began collecting reports of camps which were more than deportation transit centres like that at Loznica. As far back as May, the Bosnian government compiled a report detailing mass executions at a camp in Brčko, and told the United Nations about alleged 'concentration camps' in the Bosnian Krajina. For ten weeks, no serious action was taken. Gutman, however, corroborated specific allegations by meeting survivors of the camps. In a disused warehouse at Brčko, 1,350 people were said to have been slaughtered. Here, according to a witness called Alija Lujinović, prisoners were executed with knives, their bodies thrown in the Sava river or driven by other prisoners to an animal feed production plant. People were also talking about a camp at Omarska near Prijedor, where there were fifteen to twenty executions every day and other men were dying from beatings.[8] Photographs were taken of shaven-headed prisoners at another camp near Prijedor, called Manjača.

The world was bewildered by these reports, not quite knowing what to make of them. The United States government said its intelligence sources confirmed the existence of detention camps. Radovan Karadžić was in London for the latest peace conference when the allegations surfaced, and went on ITN to denounce them as fabrication. Pinned by cameras on a live broadcast, he said that if those making the allegations insisted, they could come and see for themselves. We insisted.

Chapter Five

The Camps, Echoes of the Reich

'I do not want to tell any lies, but I cannot tell the truth,' says the young man, emaciated, sunken-eyed and attacking his watery bean stew like a famished dog, his spindly hands shaking. The guards, swinging their machine guns, are watching and listening carefully. His name is Sabahudin Elezović. 'Let me eat my lunch first,' he says, 'then I'll talk.' The stew in the aluminium bowl is gone within seconds, shoved into his mouth with an old spoon clenched with difficulty by a rangy fist.

This is lunchtime at the Omarska concentration camp or 'investigation centre' run by the Bosnian–Serb police for mainly Muslim internees near Prijedor. The prisoners are horribly thin, raw-boned, some are almost cadaverous, with skin like parchment folded over their bones. Their faces are lantern-jawed, and their eyes are haunted by the inimitable, empty stare of the prisoner, dumb with fear, who has no idea what is going to happen to him next. No one from the Red Cross, the UN or the press had been this far inside the belly of the beast until the day we arrived at Omarska on Wednesday 5 August 1992.[1]

They had kept us waiting in Belgrade for three days, while dignitaries of the Greater Serbian project, like Professor Nikola Koljević, explained the Islamic *jihad* pitched against Serbia by Lybia, Iran, Iraq and their agents in Bosnia. Most important of all, they said, there was no point in our visiting Omarska. There were 'far more interesting places to visit', said the loquacious leader of the Serbian–Jewish Friendship Society, Klara Mandic, peddling a grotesque analogy between Serbia's suffering and the persecution of the Jews.

Finally, we argued our way to Banja Luka and thence to Prijedor by car, with Major Milovan Milutinović, who was anxious to take us to another camp, Manjača, which had been visited by the Red Cross and judged a godforsaken place, although Major Milutinović insisted that 'they have better food and accommodation there than they had in their own homes.' We said we wanted to go to Omarska, were ignored and were treated instead to a monologue of guile about how the Serbs had 'tried to negotiate' with local Muslim leaders, 'in order to save the women and children', but that they had 'wanted to fight to the death'. Then, inevitably, the Second World War and the ravages of the Croatian Ustasha Milutinović pointing out Mount Kozara from the passenger seat.

In Prijedor, a line of women stretching down the pavement was waiting outside the police station. They told variations on the same theme: their menfolk had been taken away, dragged and kicked onto trucks and were now only a few miles away at Omarska or other camps. All these women wanted was some crumb of information from behind the camouflaged wall of silence: what was going on? were their men alive? Serbian guards were patrolling the sidewalk as we tried to make hasty conversation. Rumours were running like quicksilver: executions, beatings, torture. But the police were co-operating only as far as offering the chance to buy exit papers to leave Prijedor. One woman, Edina Poškovič, was at her wits' end; 'What should I do? I am still waiting to know if my husband is alive or dead. Every night, the soldiers shoot into the houses. They have taken everything, and are demanding my house. But I hate to leave while my Zajko is in Omarska. What *is* happening at Omarska? If only they would tell us . . .'

The next hurdle is a roomful of local dignitaries on the first floor of the police station. There is the military commander for the region, Colonel Vladimir Arsić. There is the 'civilian' mayor Milomir Stakic (in military uniform) and his deputy, Milan Kovačević, whose job it is to oversee the 'transit centres', including Omarska, and who was himself born in Jasenovac in 1941. He says that 'what you will find here are not concentration camps, but transit centres. We are a people born out of concentration camps, determined to protect our nation from genocide yet again.' Then we move onto the baloney: 'In the past weeks, we have seen hundreds of Serbian babies nailed to crosses, their eyes gouged out with bottles, floating down the River Una.' He adds: 'I understand your priorities, but I do not have authority to allow you to go to Omarska.' Colonel Arsić and Major Milutonić stress that Omarska is run by the civilian authorities. Manjača is available for a visit, but not Omarska. So it must be time for the video presentation.

The video shows that a copy of the Koran was found in a house in Prijedor! It also shows documents written in Arabic, and a Serbian soldier opening an ammunition case which, says the commentary, itself rather like a machine gun, was found in a Muslim home. The show is followed by the cartography session with Kovačević and then some extraordinary inexactitudes from Mayor Stakić: 'We have tried to get the other side to live in peace with us. Our problems are with the extremists, not the population. We are trying to get Muslims not to leave the area, but to stay and live with us, but they want to go to Croatia and Germany, or back to Bosnia [we are in Bosnia, aren't we?] while the extremists bring weapons into the area, kill the Serbian people and commit appalling atrocities . . . There are no camps, there are only transit centres where people are taken for their own protection. Others are people who want to leave and we are assisting them.' After two hours of insisting on the veracity of Dr Karadžić's 'invitation', we set off for Omarska, under heavy armed guard.

For some unexplained reason, we are not allowed to go down the main road and through the front entrance of the Omarska mining complex. Desperate women are gathering at the turn-off, pestering the soldiers and being turned away. Instead, we take a winding back road through a maze of empty, burned out villages and lanes lined with white flags. There has been no Muslim 'resistance' in this area for months, but as we approach the back entrance to the mine there is a burst of gunfire from a wood, over our heads. Serbs in sunglasses leap from the armoured car ahead – which itself returns fire, high – and take positions in the ditches. 'There are Muslim gunmen all around the camp,' says Major Milutonic. 'It is far too dangerous to carry on.' Common sense told us there were no 'Muslim gunmen' for fifty miles; we ask him to ignore this prank and continue.

Nothing could have prepared us for what we see when we come through the back gates of what was the Omarska iron mine and ore processing works, and are ushered into the canteen area. Across a yard, a group of prisoners who have just emerged from a door in the side of a large rust-coloured metal shed are adjusting their eyes to the sunlight and being ordered into a straight line by the barked commands of a uniformed armed guard. Then, as part of some rigid, well-worn camp drill, they run in single file across the courtyard and into the canteen. Above them in an observation post is the watchful eye, hidden behind reflective sunglasses, of a beefy guard who follows their weary canter with the barrel of his heavy machine gun.

There are thirty of them running; their heads newly shaven, their clothes baggy over their skeletal bodies. Some are barely able to move. In the canteen, there are no more barked orders, the men know the drill all right. They line up in obedient and submissive silence and collect their ration: a meagre, watery portion of beans augmented with bread crumbs, and a stale roll, which they collect as they file along the metal railings. The men are at various stages of human decay and affliction; the bones of their elbows and wrists protrude like pieces of jagged stone from the pencil-thin stalks to which their arms have been reduced. Their skin is putrified, the complexions of their faces have been corroded. These humans are alive but decomposed, debased, degraded, and utterly subservient, and yet they fix their huge, hollow eyes on us with looks like the blades of knives. There is nothing quite like the sight of the prisoner desperate to talk and to convey some terrible truth that is so near yet so far, but who dares not. Their stares burn, they speak only with their terrified silence, and eyes inflamed with the articulation of stark, undiluted, desolate fear-without-hope.

They sit down at sparse metal tables, and wolf down their meal. It is very obviously the only one of the day; if they ate even twice that much, they would not be so gaunt and withered. The meal takes precisely one minute; the guards signal that time is up, and the men make up another queue by the exit. As they form up, some clutch the roll that goes with lunch, to keep for later. Most are too terrified to talk, bowing their heads and excusing themselves by casting a glance at the pacing soldiers, or else they just stare, opaque, spiritless and terrified. Sabahudin says simply: 'I was in the defence force. But not caught in a fight. I tried to get to Trnopolje, the transit camp, but the soldiers caught me on the way and brought me here . . .' and, with the guards advancing towards his table and his minute for lunch up, he rises unsteadily, tries a smile, deposits his metal bowl and takes his place in the line to return to the shed.

As they run back out across the yard, followed once more by the barrel of the beefy guard's machine gun, thirty more men are emerging, ready to take their wretched turn. The guards and a woman called Nada Balban, who translates, produce a variety of people selected for interview, who all appear to be in markedly better condition than the average, but we decline their offers of assistance. We ask to look at the 'sleeping quarters' as we respectfully put it, but were instead bundled upstairs for another lengthy briefing.

In between more waffle about the *jihad* and genocide against Serbs, we learn that Omarska is an 'investigation centre' for men suspected of being members of the Government Army. The men are rounded up, then 'screened' to determine whether they are 'fighters' or 'civilians'. Those found guilty of 'preparing the rebellion' go into 'Category A', explains Mrs Balban. There is no information on their next destination. Those found to have been territorial defence soldiers (but not 'preparing the rebellion') go into 'Category B' and are sent to Manjača, and the rest go to another camp, Trnopolje, down the road. Then there is a fourth category: 'Hostages?' answers Mrs Balban, 'of course we have hostages, people for exchange. We have been offering them since the beginning of the war, but the other side does not want to trade.'

We ask again to see the sleeping accommodation – No. Apparently there is a hospital, can we see that? – No. And the rust-coloured shed: what is it? – No. How many men are there in there? – No. And this white building here? – Definitely not. What is happening in this place? – No. What is happening at the front gate? – No. Despite the inordinate length of the briefing upstairs, there is a sudden hurry to leave, because says Mrs Balban, we are 'behind schedule'. We say we are in no hurry, but Dr Karadžić's kind invitation to see 'whatever you like' now collapses into a disingenuous farce. 'The politicians,' says Mrs Balban, 'are always sitting on two chairs. They make their promises, but we have our procedures, and we cannot do everything.' Whatever Dr Karadžić had promised us, a different message had reached Prijedor: 'You have your motives,' yaps the determined Mrs Balban, 'and we have our orders. He [Karadžić] promised us something different. He said you can see this and this, but not something else.'

'Something Else.' That was the secret of Omarska. We make to approach the big rust-coloured shed door, within which that secret clearly lies, whereupon we are bundled physically out of the camp and back into the vans, just as another line of men emerges from the interior of this corrugated-iron inferno to take their single minute of daily exercise and refreshment. 'Every day is the same,' Sabahudin had told us, 'just waiting for this.' The international Red Cross and the UN have not been admitted, says Mrs Balban, 'because this is a centre, not a camp'. It transpired later in the day, however, that the local Yugoslav (i.e. Serbian) Red Cross had indeed visited Omarska, and given it a clean bill of health. Dr Duško Ivić said later: 'Oh yes, I have certainly visited Omarska and my professional assessment of the health of the people there is very good, apart from some diarrhoea.' The monstrous secret of Omarska would come to light in the days that followed; for the moment, we were moved on to Trnopolje.

More dirt tracks, more burned villages, and finally what was formerly a school in its own grounds, and another startling, calamitous sight: a teeming, multitudinous compound surrounded by barbed wire fencing. And behind the wire, standing in a close-knit crowd under the impenitent sun, thousands of men and women, boys and girls of all ages, as dumbstruck to see us as we were amazed by what was before our eyes.

The men were stripped to the waist, and among them was the young man with the famished torso and xylophone rib-cage who that day became the symbol of the war: Fikret Alic. Fikret had come that morning from another camp, Kereterm, which he said was 'much worse than here. They gave us no food, and would execute people at random. Groups would be ordered to stand up, names read out, and those men would be taken into a room where they would be beaten crazy, tortured and shot. We could hear their screams. Hundreds were killed. Some days, we would be called in to load the bodies onto trucks, or clear blood on the floor – ' the conversation through the wire was interrupted as others joined in; Fikret and his friend Budo Ičić calculated that some 150 had been executed at Kereterm on a single night, 'and many, many more at Omarska'. Fikret had literally been starved into the dismal, malnourished condition in which we found him, after fifty-two days in Kereterm. He tried to talk about a massacre in 'Room Three', but was drowned out by people wanting to speak, and was uneasy as the guards walked past the fence.

Trnoploje is wretched confusion; here there is no pretence at 'A Category' and 'B Category', the camp is just a harvest of Muslim civilians from the area, rounded up on buses and trucks and incarcerated behind the wire. 'Some call it a refugee camp,' says Fikret, through the barbed steel knots in the fencing, 'but it's not; it's a prison camp, although not a PoW camp. No one here is a fighter. They are just people that have been captured.' (Fikret would tell his full, horrendous story, when I met him again, on a later occasion.) 'Let's face it,' says Budo, 'the Serbs don't want us to live here any more. They want us either dead or for us and our families to go. If we can find our families, that is. I have no idea where mine is, I have had no word since the police took me to Kereterm.'

One of the group, Ibrahim Demirović, spirited me away from the guards and took me on a quick tour of the camp. 'It's a nightmare here,' he said, 'I can't tell you everything that goes on, but they do what they want. Beatings, torture, rape. To survive, you just have to keep a low profile.' But some people have come voluntarily to Trnopolje, simply to avoid the rampaging militias plundering their streets and villages. Inar Gornić came of her own accord from Trnopolje village: 'The conditions are terrible, but it is a little safer. There was terrible shooting and bombing in the village, and we had no food. Here, we have no idea what status we have. We are refugees, but there are guards; and barbed wire. But it is safer than at home.'

Igor, a Serbian guard, informs us that his teacher and many former classmates are behind the wire. Igor is looking fit and well on his military diet, which cannot be said for his classmate Azmir, whom he introduces through the fence. Azmir was until three months ago a professional goalkeeper for Rudar Football Club, but is now horribly thin, weak and palid, his dry skin yellow with malnutrition. He was brought here from his village of Rizvanovići after the Serbian militias moved through. The situation is, says Azmir, that he can leave the camp and the area if a relative comes to claim him and guarantees transit papers and transport out of the so-called 'Bosnian Serbian Republic'. 'But how am I supposed to do that?' he asks, with a shrug of his shoulders which look like two tennis balls of bone wrapped in a thin film of dry leather, 'I don't know where my mother or my father are; I don't know where any of my relatives are. Hardly anybody does. It is not easy to stop and think what we are all doing here.'

Not all the guards are quite as genial as Igor pretends to be. 'Every night, the guards and local men with guns come through the new arrivals from the villages in case they still have anything left to steal,' said Stana Ćaošević from Prijedor. 'They beat and kick them and take whatever things they may have. One girl didn't want them to take a locket she had around her neck. The man started spitting on it and said he would melt it and sell the gold, while another older man stuck his hand up her skirts; he would not let go of what he was doing under there for a long time, and this made her cry before they went off laughing. They took another very pretty girl away with them one night, and we never saw her again. We think we know what must have happened.'

There are four lavatories dug into the earth, open to the daylight, full and stinking. Some people cannot face the smell, and find a piece of open ground that might be available on which to relieve themselves, but there are precious few left and they are spreading closer to where people are trying to eat or sleep. There is a small 'health centre' in a classroom where a Muslim doctor, who preferred not to give his name, treated the wounded as they arrived from other camps, and the sick from among the assemblage rounded up from the houses. He gave us a film to take away as we left. The photographs he had taken showed terrible wounds to the bodies of prisoners he had treated: burns, extensive bruising, one skeletal figure after another, open and untreated gashes from beating, stabbing and whipping, and the rot of extreme malnutrition. Back in the world again, we returned late to Belgrade.

The international outrage that greeted the discovery of Omarska and Trnopolje put the Serbs' backs against the wall for the first time since the start of the war. Karadžić said he was surprised by the outcome of his invitation; he promised to bring those responsible to justice (which failed to happen) but insisted that no civilians were being held prisoner and that reports of women and children in captivity were lies. General Ratko Mladić echoed the Chetnik Šešelj's response: 'Detention camps? Those pictures were faked up by the Bush administration to justify the use of American weapons throughout the world.' The token president of the rump Yugoslavia, American-educated millionaire Milan Panić, said that if Karadžić did not open the gates of the camps he would be deposed. The Red Cross drew up a programme which involved visiting 11,000 prisoners a day, and the British Liberal leader Paddy Ashdown arrived in Belgrade and mapped out a speedy itinerary of camp visits over a drink with us in his hotel room. As he did so reports reached the Serbian capital of the hurried shuffling of prisoners to better accommodation in preparation for catching the public glare. Within a matter of days, there was no one left at Omarska; access to the site was still limited but the prisoners had gone, mostly to the less offensive military installation at Manjača. But one witness who telephoned Belgrade to say that buses had been seen coming out of the camp, apparently empty, though people watching from upstairs windows could see men lying down inside. Many reports reached Muslim Travnik during the months to follow of executions before and during the 'transfers' of prisoners from Omarska to Manjača.

We now know what was in that rust-coloured shed at Omarska, and what was happening inside Kereterm, Manjača and in other camps. The Omarska shed was a vast, human hen coop, in which thousands of men were crammed for twenty-four hours a day apart from the excursion to the canteen, living in their own filth and, in many cases, dying from asphyxiation. But that was not all. The taking of careful evidence reveals Omarska to have been a place of savage killing, torture, humiliation and barbarous cruelty. The 'categories' system was a euphemism for a regime under which men would be kept in the shed to await interrogation. After being 'interviewed' with the help of torture, those deemed to have been part of the resistance were then sent to the 'White House' (the building we had seen and enquired about) which meant certain death, usually by beating or stabbing. Only five men seem to have survived it. There was another building, the 'Red House' which, say the prisoners who glanced inside it, was strewn with bloodied bodies. 'Innocent' prisoners were returned to the shed and maybe transferred later, maybe not. Most of the prisoners who helped dispose of the dead were themselves then killed too. One survivor of this work estimates that he was personally forced to help deposit 600 bodies down the mine shaft at Omarska.

People sometimes gild the lily in the self-defeating belief that the more shocking the details, the better chances of the West intervening militarily. There are several unconfirmed accounts – which may be exact or exaggerated – of prisoners being made to bite off the testicles of their comrades, to have sex with each other and with prison animals at gunpoint, of terrible mutilation, castration and worse. There was one case in which two men died from their wounds when they were hanged from a crane, and beaten, having previously been forced to have sexual intercourse with each other and then castrated. Six men have testified independendently to this episode at Omarska.

A concrete and provable truth, capable of convincing a

war crimes tribunal beyond all reasonable doubt, can be constructed by the co-incidence of testimonies, collected independently and in different places, which suffice to illustrate the most barbaric programme of systemised racial atrocity since the Third Reich.

It is remarkable just to sit and listen to Nedžad Jacupović from Kozarac, and to reflect on what he has seen at the young age of twenty-five. Nedžad is one of the five men who survived the 'White House', and his account of ten weeks spent at Omarska can be corroborated many times over. He was moved from the rust-coloured hut to one of the small rooms on the upper floor of the White House, where he watched 150 men whom he had come to know beaten and kicked to death in front of his eyes. 'I think I survived because I had been too badly beaten to be a future soldier,' he says, 'and because all the time I was there, not one prisoner told the authorities that I had had a machine gun.

'They would bring people from the big red hut at eight in the evening, forty of them each night, to the White House. There, they would beat them until they were dead; it could take a day, three days or five days, ripping clothes off with knives, cutting people and then just kicking and beating them to death over a period of days. Then they would arrive with lists of others in the White House who were not yet dead, for execution. They would record the mens' details, take them out, one every fifteen minutes, towards the Red House, where they were butchered. I was counting the numbers; sometimes eighteen, twenty or thirty; the record was forty-two. They were killed just in front of my window. We knew each other by our nicknames. Some people saw bodies piled up inside the Red House.

'In my room, I had dead men at my feet and on my legs. The beating was constant; they were always completely drunk. They used to laugh or sing while they beat people, and sometimes even pray to their God while they were killing. They would to make us sing Chetnik songs and insult Izetbegović's mother or make us stamp and spit

on the Bosnian flag. Sometimes they would bring in the
families of Serbian soldiers who had been killed at Travnik
or somewhere, give them sticks and metal bars and let
them do what they liked. They could kill people if they
wanted to. Every morning, they came and took five men
who could still walk, and shot them outside. In the Red
House, they used knives and axes, and also used to make
video films of the butchery. I could not walk, however, and
for twenty-five days I could not stand. Then I was walking
like an eighty-year-old man.

'Once able to walk, there was only a minute to eat food
in the canteen, and often the men at the back would get
nothing, they would send them away without food. You
reckoned that every other day you probably wouldn't eat.
Sometimes, they would throw their scraps at the men, who
would fight for them. Once they shut 150 of us in for four
days without food or water, and then came with one single
canister. Men were beating each other to get the water, since
only one could drink at a time.'

Another survivor of the White House was returned to
the big rust-coloured hut because he was an old man who
had only come back to Prijedor from Slovenia to arrange
papers for his retirement. Sakib R. calculates that 612 men
disappeared from the hut during twelve days in July. There
was no room to lie down, says Sakib, 'and it was impossible
to organise shifts to sit comfortably. You could only count
the men around you, I reached 700 that I could actually see.
A lot of people went mad, and the mad people were always
killed: when they went insane, shuddering and screaming,
they were taken out and shot'. Sakib's brother was killed,
with his own son as witness: 'They took him outside and
then came back and asked for his relatives. My nephew went
out, I heard a strange gurgling noise, and realised it was my
brother having his throat cut. The boy saw everything.'

'When they took us to the White House, they told us it
was a hospital, but it wasn't, there was blood everywhere,
and bullet holes in the walls. I saw people loading the dead

onto lorries and they were dropping bodies down the mine shaft. On one occasion, twelve Croats were taken out to the toilet. I went in there, and saw bits of their bodies on the floor.'

The testimonies are willing and endless, but the evidence these two men submit is typical, cogent and can be corroborated. Sakib remembers our visit well, and says that only the fittest men were allowed to the canteen during that lunchtime. His mind is old but sharp; Sakib was a counter of men in a place where numbers lost their meaning. One group of 216 men was brought to Omarska shortly before our visit, of whom four, he calculates, survived. During the transfers out of the prison after its closure, one party of 520 which boarded the buses was never seen again he says. The numbers game is impossible to play, but the evidence suggests that some 6,000 men were in Omarska at any one time, and that several thousand were brutally murdered. What we saw that Wednesday afternoon was no more than a hint of the terrifying reality. And yet even Omarska was only the tip of the iceberg.

There is a convergence of evidence on an extermination room at Kereterm, another camp established at a disused tile factory on the edge of Prijedor. It was known as 'Room Three', a large storage space made of concrete with a heavy steel door which opened across half the front wall. Fikret Alic from Trnopolje is among those who testifies to a massacre in Room Three at the end of July, during which some 250 people were herded into the twelve-square metre space. This is how Fikret remembered that night, talking when we met some months later:

'It was the night of 28 June. Men had been brought in the previous day, around 200 to 250. We were in the next hut, and we could hear them beat and kick them. That was normal, it happened to all of us. It went on and on, and all night we could hear the screaming of our neighbours. Then they started singing Serbian songs, the prisoners that is, and the machine guns started. They were machine gunning the men with what sounded like dum-dum bullets, breaking off then starting again. There were more shots next morning, when we woke up.

'Then they opened the doors of our shed and chose five people, to wash down and load the bodies. I was one of them. I stepped into the hall next door. It was nothing but bodies, piles of bodies and blood covering the floor. I cannot remember much more, I felt faint and started to cry. Another older prisoner took my place, but I remember the loading. They had a forklift truck, and prisoners were being made to drive it at the bodies, lift them on the prongs of the truck, and take them to the lorry. We reckoned 150 had died that night.'

Fikret had escaped by way of Travnik. In October 1992, my colleague Ian Traynor found a man who had come out a different route, through Karlovac in Croatia. This was his story:

'"At dusk about ten men entered the room in shorts and T-shirts ... The ten started beating people, cursing them and forcing them to sing Serbian songs. Serbian guards opened fire through the metal doors from the outside, killing those trapped in the warehouse." He said he lost consciousness. "When I woke early next morning, I realised I couldn't walk for dead bodies. I whispered to faces I already knew, 'Are you alive?' Some moved their heads. There were 260 in the room. About 150 to 160 were killed. About eighty survived. Of them, fifty were wounded. Serbian soldiers came in the morning and shot some of the wounded".'2

A university lecturer called Mirsad, who came to London in the clear-out of the camps, spoke about his time incarcerated at the Luka camp outside Brčko. In particular, he described how the guards allowed a pretty young woman called Monika to torture prisoners. She took pleasure in the task and laughed as she performed it: 'Monika was the daughter of a local whore, whom we all knew. She was eighteen years old, and was the most cruel torturer of the

young men. She would break a glass bottle and cut open
their stomachs while the guards watched and laughed. She
had a soft, gentle face. We never expected someone like that
to do such things. But she enjoyed doing it, she must have
done, because she laughed as she did it . . . Other times, they
would take out the young men, one by one, and set Alsatian
dogs on them, dogs who hadn't eaten for days. We had to
watch, they screamed and wept . . . Some of the bodies were
thrown into the river; others were buried at a pig farm, so
we were told by some people from there.'[3]

Four days after our visit to Trnopolje, the fence came down
and the authorities had painted a sign above the entrance
in English, for the benefit of the descending television
circus, reading: 'Trnopolje Open Reception Centre'. But
the armed guards stayed on, and the beatings and the
atrocious conditions continued. The camp remained open
for months after its internationally agreed closure deadline,
because the West refused to take sufficient numbers of
inmates and because the conditions in Banja Luka and
the remaining communities where there were still Muslims
were so terrifying that Trnopolje, where you slept on the
filthy floor, with a straw mattress if you were lucky, was a
perverse haven, a place to which to flee from a home where
life had become intolerable and probably impossible. In
Trnopolje 'Reception Centre', one could be raped, beaten
and robbed, but there was a grim safety in numbers which
the back streets of Banja Luka no longer offered.

When the camps were 'opened', and prisoners 'free to
go', as the Serbs said, a return home would mean certain
death. Of a group of fifteen who tried to return home
from Manjača, thirteen were murdered on their return.[4]
Ivan, a Croatian inmate of Manjača now in London,
said that whole busloads would set out home and vanish
without trace. Intimidation and random ethnic murder were
becoming so ubiquitous by autumn that despite the outcry
over the camps, the Serbs were opening a new detention

centre at Kotor Varoš on the other side of Banja Luka
to accommodate those fleeing the carefully orchestrated
street violence. Every time the Red Cross secured places
for prisoners in Croatia or in third countries, which was
not often, the evacuees would be immediately replaced by
desperate Muslims and Croats in flight from the regime
the Serbs had established. The Red Cross reported that
whenever buses taking camp inmates out of the area passed
through Prijedor, they were stormed by Muslims desperate
to get aboard.

With international organisations now involved in the
inspection of the camps, some idea of the scale of the
atrocities reached the West. The most coherent survey was
an investigation by a US Senate team, which concluded
that Muslims had now been 'cleansed' from 70 per cent
of Bosnia. Reporting on 18 August, the team said that
in territory adjacent to Serbia, 35,000 people, almost all
Muslims, had been demonstrably killed by the end of June,
the majority of them as part of 'ethnic cleansing' rather than
in the artillery bombardments which had initially attracted
more international attention. Far larger, inestimable numbers of people were missing. The report cites cases of extreme
violence – rape, random murder and torture – against Muslims and Croats as they were evicted from home, including
the case of a woman who arrived at her parents home only
to watch a neighbour casually slit their throats on the
doorstep. The Senators conclude: 'There is every reason to
believe these individual accounts are part of a story repeated
throughout Muslim Bosnia-Herzegovina.' The UN and US
State Department came under bitter criticism for their tardy
response. The report says the Bosnian Serbs had made 'a
major effort' to keep reporters and international agencies
away from sites of the worst atrocities and camps. Within
the camps, says the report, there is evidence of 'organised
killing' as well as rape, beating and starvation. The team
adds: 'killing in the camps often appears to be recreational
and sadistic'. They estimate that 170,000 people had been

detained in camps across the country, the overwhelming majority of them Muslims in Serbian detention.

In other places other camps had been established for different reasons. In some of them, the prisoners were not to be tortured or killed, but traded as the currency of war in population exchanges. One such camp was Kula, outside Sarajevo, which we found on 3 August 1992.

'Are you a prisoner?' we asked Fehim Berzić, his eyes filled with tears. 'I don't know. I am not a refugee either, I can't go past those guards. A hostage, that's what I am, a hostage.' Mr Berzić was lying aimlessly on his camp bed in a sparse classroom. All around the camp, artillery fire boomed into Sarajevo, and the crack of small arms fire came back; Mr Berzić's dormitory sits precariously on the edge of this fighting. He was going to fetch some water one morning when he was taken as a pawn in a game of chess played with human pieces. 'I was bringing it back to the house, when the Serbian police said I had to go to fill in some papers. I was never released. We went to the Sports centre in Kut, where we were beaten up and kicked, then brought here. I have been here seventy-four days. I know nothing about why or what they are going to do.'

'We are doing this very professionally,' says camp commander Skipčević. 'It is straightforward population exchange. We take them to the bridge in the agreed numbers and exchange them for our people from the other side. Our problem at the moment is that they are not coming up with the right numbers. Last week we gave them fifty-six Muslims for only nine Serbs. They must be running out of Serbs. This lot'll have to stay here until they come up with some.' There were still 90,000 Serbs in Sarajevo.

More alarming were the stories of those coming into the Bosnian-held town of Travnik, suggesting that every small town, village or hamlet under Serbian control had its own prisons and camps, with men held in small groups in the sheds and barns of Serbian farmers. 'Ethnic cleansing' did not always involve the big trucks to the big centres. The purification of Serbian territory was in force down every country lane, on every hillside, on a scale which it was impossible to measure. Simovic Tajiba arrived in Travnik, thin and weary with bruises on his head, having been held in a barn with ninety other men outside his village of Donij Vakuf.

'There was no daily drill; only when the flour came, and we would unload the trucks. Apart from that, we were three months in the barn, indoors without a toilet. The stink was unbelievable, you just pretended it wasn't real. The torture was usually beating, with sticks and iron bars. They would come about six each evening and call out names. Sometimes it was you, sometimes it was someone else. I watched them beat my friend Ljuban Mirsić to death with rifle butts right in front of me one night, they just kept hitting him until his head was pulp and he lay there dead like a farm beast all night. You couldn't respond or protest, if you did they'd start on you, and worse. Another man was beaten to death a few days later; no reason, they just didn't like his face or his attitude. Other times they would slash and cut men with knives; that made them scream, and if they screamed they would do it again. Then they would rub salt into the wounds. Often, these men fainted.

'Some of the guards came from Banja Luka or Serbia, but most of them I knew from the village. We used to work and drink together, and now they were beating and killing us. The guards told us one day that the big camps had been found in Prijedor, and had been forced to close, but that the journalists would never get here. We buried all hope, any idea that we might get out again. We were in the middle of nowhere. None of us were fighters, all civilians. The younger girls they always kept, and we have no idea what happened to them but it's not hard to guess.

'They fed us on three kilos of bread a day between ninety of us, which we had to share out or fight over. Very rarely there were beans. I weighed 103 kilos when I went in, and went down to forty kilos. I'm back up to sixty now.

They came in one day and said that the Bosnian Army in Travnik had captured a tank crew, and were ready to do an exchange for any prisoners they had. They chose twenty of us, including me. There are still seventy more men left there. When I got here, it was like being born again. It was a like a nightmare, it's hard to believe it really happened. Except at night, when it is all very real again.'

Chapter Six

Meanwhile, the Diplomats: The World Wakes Up

*'Get, thee glass eyes,
and like a scurvy politician,
seem to see the things thou dost not'*
                    King Lear

The revelation of the concentration camps bemused and outraged the world. The response from the US President George Bush was unequivocal: he vowed the West would do 'whatever we have to' to halt the bloodshed and urged the UN to pass a resolution authorising the use of military force to ensure the delivery of aid. He insisted that the issue of the camps be included on the agenda of the UN Security Council. Diplomats from sixteen NATO countries assembled in Brussels on 8 August 1992 and agreed to ask the alliance's military leaders to draw up contingency plans for the deployment of troops. 'To truly end the nightmare,' pledged Mr Bush, 'we must stop ethnic cleansing.' It seemed as though a long and tortuous dance with the idea of military intervention to stop the spiralling violence in Bosnia had reached some decisive step. As the camp revelations filtered out, Serbian guns were busy closing Sarajevo airport, halting the now vital relief airlift.

On the eve of the discovery of the camps, British Prime Minister John Major had told Parliament that military intervention in former Yugoslavia was out of the question. Mr Major was instead placing his faith in a conference in London on 26 August, convened to 'co-ordinate UN and EC efforts to put pressure on the Serbs'.[1] After President Bush's rallying call, Mr Major confirmed that 'all the advice I have tells me that we cannot use force . . . It is the nature of the Yugoslav tragedy that solutions cannot be imposed from outside.'[2] A long season had opened in which initiatives and ideas spawned largely in the US would either be abandoned, or else meet the deadening hand of Europe.

The UN's immediate reaction to the camps was markedly cool. A spokesman said: 'People think it's just the Serbs but that's not the case. Serb civilians who have fled or have been forced to flee Croat and Muslim-held areas also give convincing accounts of mistreatment'. This argument came straight from Belgrade. There were thoroughly unpleasant camps being maintained by the Croats and Muslims, and they were inspected by journalists, but Omarska, Manjača and Brčko presented differents levels of brutality and scale.

It emerged that the UN had been informed about the camps in May, when the Bosnian government reported their existence, and again in July, when it was told about executions in camps and 'a calculated strategy to cleanse the area of Muslims'. A memorandum was filed to the head of the UN's peacekeeping mission General Satish Nambiar of India detailing 'house burnings, deportations and summary executions', following up claims by the Bosnian government about concentration camps with testimony by detainees held in Bosanski Novi that 'in the first fifteen days of May, some 200 persons were taken out of the stadium and shot nearby'. Nothing was done.

Almost as soon as the war came to be discussed at international level, the semantics were indicative: diplomats with the exception of Warren Christopher (now US Secretary of State), talked about the 'Serb', 'Croat' and 'Muslim' armies. This was fair enough after a while, because the overwhelming majority of soldiers in the Bosnian Army were eventually Muslim. But at first, the whole *raison d'être* of the Bosnian army, like the republic, was that it was mixed and care was taken to ensure that Serbs and Croats too held senior positions of command. On the international stage, they were 'Muslims' from the start.

Presidents Tudjman and Milošević had met in March 1991 to discuss their ethnic carve-up of Bosnia, but the idea was not limited to backstage meetings. In spring 1992, within a year of the two presidents' appointment in Karadjordjevo, the Portuguese presidency of the European Community sponsored the Lisbon 'Initiative' for Bosnia, which proposed a similar version of the slice-up, more favourable to the Muslims. It proposed not separate republics as such, but separate 'spheres of influence' for the ethnic groups. The outcome was an EC-sponsored, gift-wrapped version of the carve-up. An unnamed Amercian diplomat described the plan as 'perfect for Zagreb and Belgrade'. A Hungarian diplomat observed: 'Essentially, the EC plan gave Serbia and Croatia *carte blanche* to divide Bosnia'.[3]

In April, President Izetbegović made his first appeal for military intervention 'if the aggression continued'. Later in the month, France suggested the deployment of UN forces on the gound. British diplomats speaking off the record said the idea would 'almost certainly be opposed by virtually all members of the Security Council and the EC states'. But EC Foreign Ministers and the Security Council met back in Lisbon at the end of May to agree a package of sanctions (excluding oil) against Serbia and to devise military action to open Sarajevo airport.

On 8 June, the Security Council authorised 1,100 troops to take control of the airport, with a brief to remove anti-aircraft weaponry and artillery weapons from within a nineteen-mile radius of its runways. On 29 June, the United Nations flag was hoisted as the first French relief plane flew in. The UN was in a bullish mood, and said the airlift 'did not exclude other measures' to ensure the delivery of aid. For the first time, the American State Department said the USA was ready to support the UN effort to relieve Sarajevo, and to provide warplanes 'in a combat role if necessary'.[4] But 'British sources' drew a very different inference from the developments, saying the UN resolution did 'not in itself authorise the use of force' and remained 'adamant that British ground forces will not be deployed in Bosnia in any circumstances'.[5]

On the ground, the French and Canadians at the airport had their own priorities: a ring of armour was being erected around the airport approaches, in anticipation of the arrival of transport planes and attack helicopters for what was gearing up to be a vast international air supply operation, and in which the British RAF was a willing and highly effective partner. Lord Carrington, chairman of the EC's open peace conference, arrived in Sarajevo on the airport's third operative day to confront the fiercest fighting the city had seen for weeks, and to say that he had made no headway with his negotiations.

The next international appointment was in Munich, for the G7 summit of 7 July. Again the atmosphere was gung-ho, with the German hosts demanding that the UN prepare troops to intervene in Bosnia, if necessary by-passing the Carrington peace process. Britain, which held the EC presidency, was the main opponent of this dare-devil approach, saying Lord Carrington needed more time.[6] On the same day, the United States said it was ready to force open a land corridor from the coast to Sarajevo, using air and naval force to stop the interruption by Bosnian Serbs of the deliveries.[7] But divisions within the US government were an open secret. The main east coast newspapers were being told by the Defense Department that the use of ground troops in Bosnia was out of the question, but by the State Department that it was an option.

President Izetbegović made his second appeal for military intervention in Helskinki on 9 July, specifying that if only troops could seal the Bosnian border with Serbia it would prevent another imminent onslaught. He then met with President Bush, who seemed to have turned a few degrees in his direction; 'If our Conference on Security and Co-operation in Europe is to have any real meaning in this new world,' said President Bush, 'then let us be of one mind about our immediate aims. First, relief supplies should get through no matter what it takes. Second, we should see to it that UN sanctions are respected, third, we should do all we can to prevent this conflict from spreading, and fourth let us call with one voice for the guns to fall silent.'[8] Secretary of State James Baker told the rump Yugoslav federal president Milan Panić that 'the world demands deeds not words', and that the Serbs must lay down their arms. But Lord Carrington promptly sent Yugoslavia (now comprising Serbia and Montenegro) a different signal, saying it was 'unrealistic to expect the Serbs to surrender their heavy weapons at the moment'.[9] Bush's idea about being of 'one mind' had been shown to be fantasy within twenty-four hours. The UN Secretary General Boutros Boutros Ghali then made a surreal petition to the Security Council in which he called the Bosnian tragedy 'the war of the rich' and, in a huff, accepted a British 'non-binding' idea that the Security Council might consider UN monitoring of heavy weaponry in Bosnia.

Then, in August, Omarska. Suddenly, the UN, NATO and the Western European Union all began their separate contingency planning and non-planning. 'Safe Havens' – in the manner of the Kurds – were on the agenda, as was the American scheme for a fast land corridor from Spilt to Sarajevo secured by 100,000 ground troops. In the US, a head of steam was building. The *New York Times* shed its shyness to ponder 'massive Western intervention' and to advocate an immediate lifting of the arms embargo on the Bosnian government.[10] The new Democratic presidential candidate, Bill Clinton, said all human rights violations should be internationally investigated and that 'we may have to use force. I would begin with air power against the Serbs to try and restore the basic conditions of humanity.'[11]

Lady Margaret Thatcher had been on a speaking tour of America, and was advocating 'a serious initiative' for 'the restoration of the Bosnian state backed by international guarantees'. Lady Thatcher argued that the West should table a set of demands, including cessation of Serbia's support for the war in Bosnia and the safe return of refugees. 'If those demands (which should be accompanied by a deadline) are not met,' she wrote, 'military retaliation should follow, including the aerial bombardment of bridges on the Drina . . . of military convoys, of gun positions around Sarajevo and Goražde, and of military stores and other installations useful in the war. The Serbian side of the border should not be exempt from the threat,' she added.[12] Even the guru of European unity, Jacques Delors, called for direct military intervention against Serbia; 'in the absence of a credible prospect, and I mean credible, of military intervention, nothing can stop the subtle, deadly strategy of the Serbian leadership,' he told the European Parliament.[13]

In mid-August, the Bosnian government amended its request on intervention. 'We don't want your boys to die in the Balkans,' said its UN ambassador Mohammed Sacirbey, 'All we want is sophisticated air power to get at the gunners bombing our towns and at the other side's air force, and weapons to defend ourselves.'[14] The Council instead agreed on the use of force to achieve 'limited humanitarian goals', with Britain offering to provide military air cover for such operations and now considering the eventual deployment of ground troops. There was also British pressure for a separate resolution on getting aid to detention centres.

In Sarajevo and in the camps they were waiting for the fifth cavalry to arrive. In Pale, the Bosnian Serbs went suddenly coy, asking the Security Council to please kindly spell out what it required 'in order to avoid military intervention and the bloodshed that would accompany it';

UN spokesmen sent out rays of optimism. A diplomat in New York said the West was 'crossing its fingers and hoping that the Serbs won't call its bluff'.[15] The following day, a report arrived at the UNHCR headquarters in Geneva warning of the biggest single wave of ethnic cleansing to date, with 28,000 desperate deportees heading for the Croatian border.

Chapter Seven

Exodus into No Man's Land

By mid-August, some 1.8 million Bosnians had been driven from their homes, killed or gone missing; those alive were on the move, in the camps, sleeping in temporary accomodation or had left the country – the biggest forced movement of people in Europe since the Reich.

More than half were still in Bosnia and some 350,000 were in Croatia. Towards the end of July, the Croatian deputy prime minister Mate Granić said his country could take no more, and appealed to other, wealthier nations to open their borders before Croatia became 'a giant refugee camp'. Croatia would from now on offer transit visas, but no places to stay. At the same time, the UN relief agencies were finding their way through a thorny moral maze, into which they had been cast by Serbian blackmail: by accepting refugees across Croatia's borders and finding third country places, they were merely doing the Serbs' work for them. By refusing to take the refugees, the UN was condemning them to continuing persecution and violence.

The UNHCR's Geneva headquarters took a deep breath and went for the tough option: 'We will not be accomplices to the despicable policy of ethnic cleansing,' said spokeswoman Silvana Foa. The Serbs' front door through which to belch out their unwanted humanity into Croatia was closed. Where, we wondered, might the back door be?

*   *   *

The last eleven miles, on foot, were terrifying and extraordinary even by the standards of the long-drawn-out nightmare of the day.

After being robbed at gun-point of their cars by the last brutish line of Serbian irregulars, the battered exodus of some 1,600 Muslim refugees – the elderly, the infirm and the children among them – was sent trudging and hobbling by dead of night through a mountain battlefield, towards what they had been told was the safety of their army's territory. Wandering like silent ghosts, these dazed and comfortless people carried their babies or a few possessions salvaged from the cars, and hauled invalids in wheelchairs over a barricade of rocks flanked with mines which marked the limit of Serbian-held territory. We were now in no man's land.

It was a lonely mountain road to nobody knew where. Heavy artillery from 300 yards away pounded a little village in the valley below, the shells whistled over our heads, tracer fire lit up the hillsides, and heavy machine guns rattled in the hamlet just ahead. It was here that the soles of our shoes stuck in the blood and we stumbled over the ripped flesh of the last wretches who tried to pass this way.

Looking back up the hill, our procession stretched as far as the eye could see, an epic movement under the moonlight and the gunfire, proceeding with muffled stealth like a silent army of departed spirits. An old man who could barely walk leaned on his daughter's arm, another hobbled on crutches, and a woman with a stoop, walking bent over, held a hand to her face as she shuffled on as though it would shield her from the fire that was pounding onto the road. Some shed tears and muttered as they trudged but most wore faces fixed with disbelief and the haunted stare of the person who flees what is behind and fears what is ahead. As they struggled on, the shells crashed and the guns cracked around them.

It was almost impossible to believe that only this morning these people were forced to bid farewell to their homes, marshalled to order by the Serbian police in the town of Sanski Most, and told they were going to Bosnian

Army-held country where papers were ready for their onward trips to Germany and Austria. Now, eleven hours later, it was clear that nobody on the other side had the slightest idea that we were coming. Every one of us knew that there is one crucial rule in war: never cross the no man's land; never walk towards 'friendly fire'.

Mercifully, the government and Croatian guns kept their peace against the bedraggled human snake that advanced on them out of the night, perhaps because of a T-shirt which was held up, lit by torchlight, as a white flag. There was Serbian fire though, from the woods along the road and the ridges above, its flashes cutting the sky and ploughing into the little village of Cosići below.

Then, an amazed Bosnian militiaman with a young nerv-ous face appeared out of the shadows, and sent word back to his front line; refugees are arriving: hold fire, stop fighting till they are off the road. From then on, the itinerants were ushered off the narrow highway by the militamen, up the hillsides along winding dirt tracks, around the back of the battle. By 3 a.m., passing through empty hamlets and clutches of armed men lurking in the darkness within the burned-out shells of houses, they reached the relative security of the Muslim–Croat village of Turbe, and were then taken by a hastily found bus to Travnik, itself under regular and heavy shellfire, where they joined some 26,000 of their homeless compatriots in the city centre.

As it turned out, we were lucky. We learned that another convoy of people had been cast out along the same route earlier that same night. That time, the Serbian gunmen who had condemned them to this passage had moved around into the bushes that flank the road and ambushed the defenceless procession. Two boys, brothers aged fifteen and seventeen, were killed. It was almost certainly their remains over which we had walked some hours earlier. A fluorescent teenager's knapsack had also been discarded, blood-splattered, on the roadside.

In recent days, the Bosnian Army commander in Travnik

said, twenty refugees had been killed in ambushes by the same irregulars who had ushered them out onto the road. 'They fire at and shell the people as they come through, and to save themselves, people run off the road into the woods, and get lost,' said Commander Haso Ribo, 'Sometimes our soldiers find women wandering in the mountains, half-mad and half-alive, having fled the convoy when they shoot at it.' Five days ago, he added, three people were simply taken off the bus at the last Serbian line and shot. Miraculously, though, none of our human stream was hurt. Maybe the gunmen had met their quota for refugee executions that night.

It transpired that we were with one of scores of such convoys that the Serbian authorities were now channelling into the largely unreported and raging battlefields on Bosnia's central fronts, around Travnik, Jajce and Maglaj, north-west of Sarajevo. Now that the UNHCR had constructed its 'moral deterrent', refusing to participate in the programme of ethnic cleansing, the Serbian response had been simple: to continue the persecution of the Muslim obstacle to their racially pure republic, to harvest those thus obliged to leave, and ship them out the back way into the Muslim- and Croat-controlled zones of this central front, where there was no prying UN and no newspaper coverage. Once penned into Travnik and Zenica, those in flight became targets for the artillery.

That final night march into Travnik was just the conclusion to a long, now seemingly unreal journey for our convoy. All day, the refugees, or deportees as they should more properly be called, had been made to run a gauntlet of fear, hate, arrogance, humiliation and uncertainly on the day that had started with them being bullied out of their homes in Sanski Most. The announcement came over the radio, Radio Sana, that the convoy was leaving, and it had been made clear that this was among the last chances. The previous night had been one of horrific violence, with gangs lobbing grenades through the windows of peoples' homes and firing willy-nilly on the streets of the Muslim quarters. The mosque had been blown up, all Muslim shops burned and looted, Muslims sacked from their jobs and some undamaged houses allocated to new, incoming Serbian families, their names posted above the doorways. Tickets for the journey were purchased from the police, the fare payable in Deutschmarks. People could either use the buses and trucks provided, or take their own vehicles. The convoy left shortly before midday.

We joined it, slipping in as it parked for a rest about an hour later, near Lamovita, east of Prijedor at the turning to Omarska. The Muslims were lined up along the roadside, a ragbag of some eighty cars, buses and lorries heaving with people and baggage. The car in front had a pair of crutches on the roof, one further ahead a child's pram. Behind us was an ageing bus, creaking and brimful, with an armed guard next to the driver, and behind that a battered old truck loaded to bursting with piled-up humanity and its heavy suitcases and plastic bags full of belongings, huddled beneath a tarpaulin cover. Childrens' bicycles were strapped to the sides, dolls' faces stuck out of rucksacks, people sat on each others' laps, luggage and relatives.

These were some of the 20,000 Muslims who once lived in a neat and pretty town, Sanski: most the axis for five villages south of Prijedor. Last night, there were 2,600 left. Now there were 1,000. There was a sudden flurry as a paramilitary guard marshalled his platoon and ordered the convoy to more off. Serbian families and groups of peasants gathered nonchalantly on the roadside and at their windows to cast a passive contemptuous glance at our wretched headway. They had clearly seen all this many times before. Others paid no attention whatsoever.

Skirting the city of Banja Luka, the convoy soon left the main road which leads towards the front line and started to climb the mountain by-roads, past columns of militiamen strolling about, swinging their guns. The old red Volkswagen in front, belonging to a mechanic called Senad, suddenly broke down and we all ground to a halt. Senad emerged from the drivers' seat with his face frozen by panic and fear at the very thought that he might be abandoned without the protection of numbers in the Serbs' mountain militia heartland. As the guards began to open the bus windows to investigate the hitch, Senad rummaged for a tow-rope like a menaced animal looking for cover, ran around to the car in front, hastily attached his own bumper and carried on, lurching up the hillside. Up on high ground, we pulled over for another break.

'Of course we didn't want to leave,' said Senad, examining his engine and trying to calm his elderly father and two friends on board, 'who would want to leave his home? We heard about it on the radio, the Serbian station, last week. They said this was the organised convoy to Travnik, Split and Germany. I figured it was our last chance to get out alive. By this time, they were killing, killing, killing.' Mumir, stretching his legs, was an electrician in town. 'One night two policemen came to my door. They were squabbling over my house, right in front of me, it was incredible. One of them wanted it, and another said, No, he wanted it. It's a nice house, I put a lot of work into it. Then they came to some sort of agreement and told me that I had two days to leave, or else I'd be executed.' A civilian policeman was trying to follow our irregular conversation. He seemed very slightly embarrassed by the procedure; we decided to tell him who we were and in exchange, he admitted of the mass departure: 'They decided to leave. But you could say it was involuntary, given the circumstances.'

Further on up the mountain, the Serbian salutes began, the two fingers of the victory sign and the added thumb. The higher we climbed, the more defiant and mocking the salutes. First, a group of little girls lining the road, three fingers and an uncomely sneer. Then a boy with no shoes and filthy feet, his dirty face corrupted by hatred for those in flight from his heroes. Soon, truckloads of loutish Serbian soldiers came chugging past in the opposite direction, bearded and with ample figures, throwing their salutes high, letting out hoots of triumphant ridicule at those they had subjugated. The dispossessed, for their part, returned the mockery with dumb stares, since anything else would have been suicide.

The last Serbian-held mountain town before the by-road degenerated into a dirt track was called Skender Vakuf, which we reached by mid-afternoon. Gangs of soldiers and irregulars lazed around on the steps of the civic buildings and around the café tables; they would wander out to stop the convoy as they pleased, kicking, punching and spitting at the drivers. A hefty, fair-haired man stepped out of his own group to block the path of our car with a nasty, sweaty grin, while his mates gathered round. 'So who are you with then? Tito? Tudjman? Are you communists or Croats or what?' A foreign language would have been a dangerous and probably disastrous provocation in this town, so I feigned deaf and dumb, a courteous imbecile, while Andrej Gustinčić of Reuters did the talking, as jokily but respectfully as he could. We were just caught up in all this by mistake. 'You're all Ustasha anyway,' barked the man. 'Cigarettes?' It was a demand, not an offer, and after helping himself to the pack he tried unsucessfully to wrench off the windscreen wiper while his chum, heaving with drink, pulled my forearm out of the window to administer a nasty Chinese burn, and then onto the next car. We'd got off lightly. The guards had raised a wooden barrier at the other edge of town, and we lumbered through. Once out on the mountain track, stopping as we lumbered by degrees up the hill, Senad got out of his towed red Volkswagen ahead and graciously put the windscreen wiper back to rights with the first – I think only – smile of the day. It was a delightful, unforgettable moment.

He was quite glad to have got through Skender Vakuf with a punch in the face and not even minor damage to the towed Volkswagen. Soon we lost our bearings completely.

The route became a dry dust path winding through a thick pine forest. In the tunnel of trees, the convoy threw up a dense mist, through which one could see only the sharp rays of sunlight streaming down like columns of light. There were also the silhouettes of armed men moving around in the woods, half-hidden in the dust, or standing guard along the route, made ghostly by the thick haze of soil powder and the sharp contrasts of light and dark. It was an intimidating and almost fantastical purgatory.

Suddenly out on a high open plain, the fields were full of either soldiers or peasants tending to their crops; we thought we must by now be approaching the front lines and the organised handover, which had been promised, to the Bosnian Army. For along a ridge to the south-west were row upon row of heavy artillery guns and rocket launchers, and luxurious supplies of ammunition lined up in neat rows; the upright cones of shells of all sizes. The enemy was at least within range; we must be near the lines. It was now between 4 and 5 p.m. Instead, we pulled off the road again, apparently heading towards some sort of factory farm or set of buildings, huts and barns. A Serbian military helicopter landed in the field beside the complex, and men were getting out and ordering each other about. One thought went through everybody's mind at once: camps. 'This would seem to be the destination,' said Gustinčić, in the passenger seat. We waited about an hour; it wasn't clear what was going on as the helicopter made to take off again. Soldiers were taking some of the convoy's passengers for apparent questioning. Some came back, others did not. Meanwhile, refugee families put rugs out on the grass and unwrapped sandwiches they had prepared for this kind of opportunity.

We moved on. No information, no news, no explanation. 'I do hope we make it through before dark,' said Senad, 'I'm sure we will, I think the worst is over now.' The route became rugged and hard to negotiate by car; tiny ledges along river gorges with sheer drops on one side.

In a cruel war between neighbours, men donned military gear to carve out a patchwork of territories with a maze of roadblocks and checkpoints, often personalised or decked out to intimidate

1

2

3

4

5

6

Dramatis personae:
1. Slobodan Milošević
2. Alija Izetbegović
3. Franjo Tudjman
4. Radovan Karadžić
5. Mate Boban
6. Lord David Owen and Cyrus Vance

Serbian soldiers with mascot

Off to work and back from shopping in Sarajevo

Ethnic cleansing

Muslim soldiers

Travnik voices: *(top)* Emir Tica;
(right) Fahrudin Alihodžić

The buses and lorries lurched their way along with extreme difficulty. On the brief stretches of open land and high, rugged meadow, the fields were spattered with more and more soldiers, alighting from trucks to throw up their now endless Serbian salute and howl their mirthful abuse. Then came the isolated village of Vitovlje, and here was an evil place: they came running down across the fields between the houses, men in fatigues, peasant women and scraggy urchins, to greet those who had abandoned their homes that morning, shrieking '*Zaklaćemo vas! Zaklaćemo vas!*' – Butcher them! Butcher them!, using the Serbian word applied to the slaughter of animals, not the murder of humans. Behind the fence along the roadside, they grimaced at each car, running their fingers across their throats and making sweeping geatures with their arms as if to raze their quarry off the face of the earth.

Out of Vitovlje and back on tarmac, the convoy pulled up to take stock. Three cars at its unstewarded rear had been commandeered in the village, their male occupants billeted in other vehicles. There was an argument going on; we learned later that the young women in those cars had been 'taken prisoner' by the soldiers of Vitovlje. The guards brought the convoy to order, and commanded us to move on. 'I think we must be near the front line now,' said Edhem, driving the car now behind us, 'It's all shit. The whole thing: shit.' The red sun was now sinking below the mountain ridge above the road, abandoning us to nightfall. 'I do hope we are crossing the lines, that this isn't some terrible massacre,' said one man. 'I think the unspeakable has just been spoken,' said a member of our party.

Dusk was falling fast – fighting time. Another stop at a road block further up the road, and soldiers were now moving to and fro along the lines of the woods above the small fields with their weapons poised at their hips. The first shots rang out, fired just over the cars. 'Go to Allah!' one ruffian screamed at us as we descended into the valley and night descended from the sky. We shunted along the valley floor through what was now deep dusk, began to climb again, and then the bus in front of us broke down.

That was the worst moment of the day so far. We were stuck, and the twilight finally faded. Men were moving through the bushes right beside the road, we could hear them talking to each other, and '*click click*', guns were cocking. An hour came and went. Finally we moved onto the next checkpoint. There was a search for petrol and weapons; one aggressive policeman was more than interested to know how we had come by forty spare litres without certificates, but the 'deaf and dumb' driver just waved his arms meaninglessly and the soldiers' attention was then diverted by something more pressing: a woman's personal jewellery, it seemed, had somehow slipped through the net of previous searches and remained in her possession . . . for another few seconds. The official police escort turned back, leaving our progress in the sole and precarious hands of the local outpost irregulars. 'They're taking cars,' whispererd the embarrassed reservist policeman from earlier in the day as he left, 'for heaven's sake tell them you're journalists this time.'

The sight at the next, and as it turned out the last, checkpoint at Smet was a pitiful one. The refugees barely spoke, let alone argued, as the band of armed men stopped each car in methodical succession, yanked out its occupants at gunpoint, made them open the car boots and watched them take out what baggage they thought they might be able to manage on foot. They left behind most of what they had packed, dumping a bag or two on the road, their eyes and faces deadened by obedient, subservient disbelief. One by one, the cars were driven brusquely away, their owners despatched roughly out into the night. The buses unloaded their passengers and turned away, and the trucks were robbed from their owners. It took some time to complete this piece of unapologetic highway robbery. We declared ourselves and after some tricky negotiation and jocular compliments on the quality of the Belgrade soccer team, our car was surprisingly spared.

We were cautiously elected to lead a section of the convoy, with a sidelight shining on a white T-shirt, as a sign to the Bosnian Army lines, presumably ahead, not to open fire. The people walked in a pathetic swarm around our car, as though it offered some kind of protection. The battle before us was getting into gear, with the first flashes lighting the sky and the first gunfire on the road in front, but 1,600 souls knew that anything was better than turning back. There followed almost two miles at a slow walking pace, the bags weighing people down, or piled on the roofs of our car or one of the other six which had for some inexplicable reason, probably their antiquity, been allowed through.

The first blood on the tarmac was just short of the small mountain of rocks that cut and blocked the road – the 'frontier' between what people were calling 'occupied' and 'free' territory. But the rocks were cold comfort, for we were now two miles into no man's land between the front lines, and our route ran parallel to the Serbs' mountaintop positions, from which their shells were punching into the village of Cosići, just a quarter of a mile towards the valley below. Over our heads the return fire answered every few minutes, the elegant trajectory of tracer bullets (one in five is lit, so that the gunner can see his line) gliding above the valley towards the gun emplacements.

The ground to the side of the rocks was a carpet of mines, and so the last cars were bid goodbye and the clamber over the giant barricade began, with some difficulty. Men carried their children and handed them down to their womenfolk on the road. Folded prams and teddy bears, lost shoes and plastic bags were being passed down the other side along with blankets, babies and baggage. The old struggled, getting their feet caught in the gaps between the rocks, helped by the young men, and one invalid had to be hauled over on other people's shoulders, likewise his wheelchair. On the other side, Serb tracer fire was now raining into the valley and onto the route ahead. Some people just sat down in despair by the roadside in huddles to rest, in fear of moving, illuminated by the blasts of firelight and the now fully risen moon, hitherto unnoticed. By its pale, silvery light, they could see the trails of dried blood and torn pieces of human meat on the road. Accidentally, I stepped on a hand.

Then two people emerged from nowhere, one a young man in a vintage combat helmet and the blue fleurs-de-lis flag of Bosnia on his arm, the first we had seen. The other was one of our number, competent, brave, clearly aware of the peril we were in, desperately trying to get the huddled people to move on, and quietly; the guns were now only 300 yards away. The boyish Muslim soldier appeared baffled by the size of the convoy; there was usually one a night, he said, and another had already come through. No, we weren't expected, but at least someone now knew that this was not an enemy approaching, and the terrifying prospect of 'friendly fire' faded just a little. He said he would send a man back to the next village to warn the Croats not to shoot at us, but in the mayhem it was impossible to rely on his assurances. The hamlet ahead was impassable, he said, the fighting too heavy, and we would need instead to cross the mountain using a track which rose up from the road about two miles further on.

They would have been the longest two miles in almost anyone's lifetime. The road cut first through an embankment, against the walls of which a multitude was huddled like barnacles, seeking shelter from the firing and shelling, and also, it seemed, from the day behind them and the uncertainty ahead. A woman hugged her little girl to her breast, stroking her hair and shedding reluctant, silent tears. Tough teenaged lads perched on their kitbags looked as lost as abandoned infants; an old man mumbled to himself. Two young soldiers from the Government Army emerged to operate like sheep dogs, stirring them to their feet, and working from the rear of the slow forward march, walking beside the old stooping woman still shielding her face from the tracer bullets with her right hand.

And thus the hike began. One man with a cap had to use his walking stick to achieve only the tiniest steps, one after the other. He wore carpet slippers and shuffled rather than walked, with nine mountain miles still to go, eventually finding the supporting shoulders of men who told him, in his troubled confusion, that they were his own army. His name was Jasim. I learned later that he died of exhaustion 'and a broken heart', said a soldier, within a week of arriving in Travnik.

We now looked like the phantom parade under this bright, unwelcome moon, making barely a sound. 'There are no words for this,' said Gustinčić. 'It needs David Lean.' The two soldiers and the efficient, brave young man from the convoy kept the rear, ushering people along, and still imploring silence as we aproached the gunners' lines and the fighting in the village drew nearer. The most remarkable thing of all was that the children and the babies obeyed and uttered not a single word, babble or cry; they could read the fear on their parents' faces, despite the reassuring strides forward, and they knew that in that fear was a pleading instruction. After two epic miles, on a corner in the road, there was a soldier, standing and pointing out the mountain track.

The people turned and meandered up the winding dirt road, through the woods, and out onto farmland, the fury of the shooting fading as we left it in the valley beneath us. And at last, a hamlet; news of the flow of people had reached the village of Turbe further along the lane, and here was an outpost farm settlement. The local Croat guards were less than welcoming, louts asking to see our papers and demanding uselessly that people check in with their own separate Croatian militia as soon as they arrive in Travnik.

'I don't know where I'm going,' said one of our procession, 'but it seems to be somewhere.' From now on, the path descended. Every time they reached a water trough from which cattle usually drink, they stopped in groups, took some water, spashed their leathery, dust-covered faces, sat awhile, and then pressed on with the six-hour hike. As we rested, we talked. Besira had elected to leave when her clothes boutique was firebombed. Her brother had been shot dead, and his body run over by an armoured car. The local GP rested his back against a septic tank. He had been the sole survivor when men had lobbed a grenade into his home, killing the two women who had been talking in his front room. He turned out to be one of the men who had secured his baggage to our car, now abandoned behind the rock barricade; he had literally nothing.

Back on our feet, we too pressed on, now chatting with Besira and the doctor about the past they had lost that morning and a future which began tonight but as yet did not exist. Pebbledash buildings lined the way beneath the moonshine, then a small mosque, a church, a main road and finally the forecourt of a sandbagged building, where quite a crowd was waiting, torn somewhere between relief, exhaustion and misery. It was 3 a.m., and this was the first sign that there might be some place which they could call safety.

At the centre of the forecourt was a fresh-faced, handsome young man wearing the first cheery expression of the night. 'My name is Emir,' he announced; and people gathered round him, just to be near his pleasant, efficient manner and to touch the Bosnian army patch he wore on his arm as though it were a talisman. 'And I am with your army. We have buses to take you the rest of the way. Welcome to Travnik.'

Chapter Eight

Travnik, Crossroads of the War

If there is a junction in the Bosnian war, a meeting-point through which its themes of fear, misery, violence, wit and courage have passed, it is Travnik, the ancient town in which we awoke dazed the next morning after two hours' deep sleep in the barracks. The building turned out to be an old restaurant that soldiers knew from weddings and evenings drinking beer or brandy by the stream, Blue Water, that rushed, cool and oddly joyful, under a bridge by the front door. We awoke in a room full of wounded men, and took coffee in the canteen drenched by morning sunshine, with no idea where we were. On the streets, there were soldiers everywhere: Government Army soldiers, Croatian soldiers, black-shirted HOS soldiers; we didn't care who or what they were – this morning, we were on their side. Travnik felt then like some frontier town, a merciful outpost on the edge of territory that had embraced us and taken us in from the madness back out there.

So it was over to Travnik that tens of thousands of deportees were now being herded by the Serbian war machine. With the Croatian border shut, this was the back door. There were 26,000 of them in town already, crammed into gymnasia and schools, all of whom had come along that road. The journey was one thing that every member of this swelling, uprooted community had in common. Simply to have been on that road and to share stories about it was to be understood, if not accepted, in Travnik.

And Travnik would do more before the year was out. Travnik would be the gate that opened to take in prisoners from the camps when they too were cast along that road. Travnik would become the base for the most remarkable brigade in the Bosnian Army, the Brigade of the Krajina, in which every male and female soldier, aged thirteen to seventy-five, had either been 'ethnically cleansed' or a camp inmate. Travnik was itself under bombardment from the hills above, and Travnik would service, with ammunition and ambulances, outpost towns like Jajce and Maglaj under siege at the end of narrow, perilous corridors. And into Travnik the entire population of Jajce would flee when that town finally fell, on one of the most unforgettable days of the war. In Travnik the alliance between the mainly Muslim Bosnian Army and the Croats would hold better than anywhere; but Travnik would also be the centre of the region where the second Bosnian war between the erstwhile allies would ignite and stage its ugliest battles. Travnik would turn out to be the crossroads of the war.

Once in town, at the end of its night through the mountains, our exodus was taken to its new home: the hard floors of the refugee quarters. They queued up to register, recognising each other from some moment or other on the route; some numb, others exchanging greetings. The girls who booked them in were from Prijedor or some part of their lost neighbourhood. There was Senad whose car had broken down way back there, entering his name in the book. 'We did it!' he says, shaking hands, as though at the end of some triumphant march rather than the miserable road away from his life. They were shown through the corridors by Emina from the check-in table, past the wiser, sadder faces of those who had already tried to make this their home, to rows of blankets parked on the floor. There were still a few spaces, and they dumped their bags, and settled. Senad laid out the contents of his plastic bag: a razor, a couple of books, photographs, underpants, socks, shirt and a plate with 'Souvenir of Istanbul' written on it in English.

If Travnik felt safe, it was an illusion. Three weeks later, I returned to take a closer look, by which time another 50,000 refugees had passed through. Mr Ado Brakić must have thought he had reached safety, taking water from the old Turkish drinking fountain in the main street on the afternoon of my return after being bullied out of his home in Prijedor. But his refreshment at the Ottoman freshwater tap was cut short by two pounds of shrapnel ripping into his chest. By evening, his blood was still stuck to the pavement and he was unconscious in a subterranean ward of Travnik's bombarded hospital. When that night's refugees crossed the lines, a pregnant woman and her child had been shot dead at the Serbs' car-stealing checkpoint.

The stories of the road were often more dramatic than ours. Sudbin Musić, a serious young man from Karakovo, near Prijedor, had been here for thirteen days, brought directly from Trnopolje. He concentrates hard as he recalls seeing two brothers hauled off his bus by Serbs looking for men of fighting age: 'They took them to the edge of the bridge, above the riverbank, and kicked one of them over the edge. The other tried to run away, but they grabbed him and then threw him over as well. Later, a Chetnik put a gun into a child's mouth and said that they wanted any jewellery and money we had, and if we did not give it to them, he would blow the baby's head off.' There were other stories, of a man being made to swim across the river, and being shot as he did so. And in the meantime, persistent reports of a gruesome massacre had entered town. Two hundred men were said to have been taken from the buses and from the wheels of their cars between Vitovlje and Smet on 21 August, four days after we took the convoy, and were never seen again, except for two of them, survivors of what appears to have been a summary execution on the edge of a ravine through which a small river ran. I remember the ravine well.

A man called Smajo who moved on from Travnik to Visoko recorded a testimony on the massacre for the War Crimes Commission, in which he says: 'The buses stopped again, just after the regular police had turned round to go back. The new men came aboard or went along the lines of cars telling men of fighting age to get out. We were told they knew a unit of the Green Berets from the resistance at Petrovac had stowed away. There were some fighters among us, as a matter of fact. They marshalled us towards the woods, with their rifle butts. There were so many of us and no one appeared to be in charge, until we came to a valley when they organised us into groups, and some were told to go towards the river, where there was a sheer drop into the valley. Suddenly there was shooting, and I realised what was happening, so I jumped down into the ravine. I broke my ankle with the fall, I think I may have lost consciousness. When I woke up I could see bodies of men in the bushes. I lay quiet for hours, and decided to try and move. I followed the river.' Smajo was found barely alive by the Bosnian army four days later.

It was in Travnik that people had time, too much time, to absorb the changes in their lives, and where the countless stories about ethnic cleansing at its worst, in the outlying villages, could be collected. There were reports of two more massacres like that at Kozarac, in Vropolje and Hrustovo. A boy called Džemo, nicknamed 'the rabbit', from Vropolje told how: 'There were forty-four women and children hiding from shelling in the basement, twelve women and thirty-two kids. When it was quieter, Chetniks arrived and one woman came up out of the basement and asked the men not to shoot, we will do whatever they say. The Chetnik said we do not shoot women and children, and went away. The lady went back down into the basement, where they waited. Then the Chetniks came back and went down into the basement and killed all of them except two, a woman and my teenaged sister. There were children of four and six years old down there.'

Travnik had been Muslim, Croat and Serb, and some of the latter stayed on in defiance of the siege. Indeed, the man co-ordinating the programme for the most stridently

Muslim of the aid charities, Merhamet, was Zeljko Sikanić, a Serb. 'There are still some people, thank God, who don't believe in nationalism, and I am one of them,' he says, 'I am from Travnik, I belong in this city and I also belong to a generation which tried to keep this country unified. There are plenty of places I could go, but I shall stay here. It is a perfectly normal thing to help a friend in need, and all my friends and everything I have, are in this town, which is being shelled by those bastards on the hill, whoever they are.'

In Travnik, the refugees and townsfolk do not mix a great deal socially. But in the hospital, on the exposed edge of town, refugees and citizens find common tribulation in a common war. The hospital is a claustrophobic, subterranean mêlée of beds, blood and hard work, with the wounded lined up along the corridors. Five-year-old Arif has been hit by a snipers' bullet and lost a leg and a testicle is a refugee, hit on his way across no man's land; Selma Mujezinović, next to him, has had family in the town for three generations, and her face is now a cratered mess of dreadful shrapnel wounds. Dr Mirsad Granov, the director, is a pensive, angry and conscientious man; one of the few in Travnik who never lets his manners slip, whatever is happening around him.

His hospital has taken shells almost every day and every night. Its upper windows are all smashed, the top floors gutted. Half of its wounded are civilians, half are soldiers. 'Many of them die, many of them will be invalids for the rest of their lives,' says Dr Granov. 'We have absolutely no experience of all this, obviously. All we have are our old student textbooks, which we follow. But what is motivating us is outrage, a feeling that it is our community and our town that is being injured with every rip into the flesh of its people and those who have fled here. It is the children and the elderly who generally get hurt, Travnik's future and Travnik's memories. Most of the people who come through here recognise that it is quite a special town. Which is why it is all the more sad to watch every facet of this war take its toll here in Travnik.'

Interval

Travnik Voices – 1 – Autumn 1992

Fahrudin Alihodžić

When our convoy of refugees reached the pile of rocks in no man's land, the people scurried over as fast as they could, making for the cover of the bank at the roadside. For some, however, it was harder than that: the old, the crippled and the very young, terrified out of their wits, got stuck between the rough-hewn rocks.

Suddenly, out of nowhere, the unruffled young man appeared, and stamped an unexpected authority on the chaos, helping the weak negotiate the rocks, and waiting until everybody was safely over before scrambling across the 'border' himself. He then told people to space out, the best precaution against a mortar attack, and instructed them: 'Shhh! They are 300 metres away. If they hear you, they'll kill you'. His name, he said, was Fahrudin. Funny, we thought, how moments of desperation throw up twenty-four-hour generals, who save the day and then disappear.

Three weeks later, back in Travnik, I was looking for the commander of the police fighting patrols which penetrate the Serbian front lines. Suddenly, I saw Fahrudin, general of the night, in uniform. We greeted and hugged and I asked him to take me to the commander. 'I am the commander,' he laughed, 'but call me Fahro.' I suppose I should have guessed. Roguish, hyperactive, restless, serious but mischievous too, Fahro was hardly going to join the other 30,000 refugees in town by going mad with inactivity, claustrophobia and fear. 'Oh, they accepted me pretty quickly,' he grins.

In his office, another fortnight later, Fahrudin is shouting. His command comes under the embryonic 'Krajina Brigade'. The barracks is chaos, the odours from the latrine appalling. As evening falls, the courtyard is a remarkable sight: fires burn and refugee children play in their glow; columns of men come marching back from the front, silhouetted in the flames. Fahrudin has introduced two new practices to which the lads are finding it difficult to acclimatise: written, stamped orders, and marching in line upon return from the front. 'I am trying to turn this mess into a fighting unit, not some rag-bag like it is at the moment. I don't care for all this chaos, these Islamic crescents the louts have taken to wearing. People fear me but they respect me. If a guy is arguing or threatening, I give him a gun and tell him to shoot me if he wants to. Sometimes you have to take a soldier into the toilet, put a grenade into his hand and pull out the pin. You have to play games like that with these hotheads.'

Fahro always insists that we sleep in his office. No chance for the moment, however: in one corner a local shepherd is sulking because some of Fahrudin's soldiers have stolen his sheep to eat. In the other is Fahrudin's opposite number from the Croatian police units asking about a Croat prisoner Fahrudin has taken in for looting. 'Do you want him back?' Fahro asks the Croat; 'No,' he replies, 'I want the bastard shot!' Next call is from a couple of bearded men from the local Muslim armed forces, a fundamentalist militia, who want to put their men under Fahrudin's command. Their offer is flatly refused. Then it is late, and time for Fahrudin to go back to his real work, taking his men up to where I first met him, in no man's land out beyond the front, where they have stopped trying to count the bodies.

'It's funny what happens to the boys up there. I say "OK lads, this is your chance to do everything you've been going on about, kill Chetniks." They've watched too many Vietnam movies, and they've no idea. Suddenly there they are, it's for real. And they all crowd round me as though I was some protection. Like this boy' – and he puts his arm around the shoulders of a teenager – 'I love him like my own brother. He's had a pampered sort of upbringing, and suddenly he realises that he's got to kill and could be killed. So I sing some song, and he says: "How can you be like that?" and I say to him: "Just look into my face, and think of it as a mirror. Find yourself in it, and when I'm dead, you'll have it with you to bring you courage. I know where you're coming from, but you don't know where I'm coming from."'

Fahro, one of six brothers, comes from Sanski Most, known as the 'city of flowers'. 'I come from a normal working-class family and worked with stone, ceramics and tiles. There was never enough money, and I used to want to go and work in the West. I grew up with the Serbs, shared good and ill with them. That's the first great disillusion to me, that those friends were the people who arrested me. I remember the first attack. The Serbs had razed Kozarac and we were arguing, people were convinced they wouldn't do it here. Soon the first shell landed and people deserted the streets, except for a woman and two children, for some reason, just staring, terrified. I remember picking up her kids and taking her home, then wondering where my parents were. Mortars were coming in, and I hid in a sewer pit in a friends' backyard. It lasted all night, and in the morning, Radio Sana was broadcasting a demand that we hand in weapons and put white flags on our houses. We managed to keep hold of some guns, but didn't have time to be effective because three days later they told everyone to gather in the square where the driving lessons are given, searched us and took the men away.

'The last time I saw my mother she was crying out to us in that square; the Serbs were taking me one way, holding me so I couldn't even kiss her, and she was being forced another way. I don't know what happened to her. The last time I saw Sanski Most was from the back of the bus to the camp, our town, in flames. Well, not all of it; only one part, the quarter which was solidly Muslim. Something died in me when I watched those streets burning.

'They took us to the local camp and then Manjača. I was there for the same reason as 2,500 other men from Sanski Most, because I am a Muslim. There, unbelievably, my former friends were actually beating us. I have since found out from my brothers (also in the camp) that some of the Serbs we knew were torturing prisoners as well. In fact my best friend, Drago Kovač, whom I had known since I was a child, was a guard at the camp. I was always asking my Serbian friends for help to get me out, but they didn't want to even recognise me. If I want to survive this war for one reason: it is to meet my Serbian friends and see how they justify themselves.'

Fahro was part of a group that tried to mount a pitiful resistance in the Krajina. 'The Muslims were stupid, blind sheep, they couldn't see what was happening in front of their eyes. "Oh no," they all said, "there couldn't be a war in Bosnia, the Serbs are our friends." Yes, there was a resistance, if you can call it that, and I suppose I was its leader in my town. But let me tell you that not a single Serb was killed in Sanski Most. So you have some idea what the resistance was like.

'I was in the camp forty-five days until twelve of us escaped out of the toilet window. We had worked out our route, and we ran. That was May, and my strange life began. I spent two months hiding in burned houses, living off plums from the gardens. We spent three days in one place, without moving, eating or sleeping, five of us. We had buried some weapons but my friend Samir Elic was killed when he tried to retrieve a rifle. If I feel sorry for anyone in this war, it's him; he was a lot like me actually.

'I wanted to fight, and saw a glimmer of hope when I heard they were bussing people to Travnik. We smuggled aboard and every time we went through the Chetnik roadblocks or a policeman came near, I told my friends to sit on the floor so we wouldn't be seen and start any aggravation or killing. At one point, I was lying underneath some bags, with a big woman and her child sitting on top. At Smet, we were told to get off the bus, started walking, and then the firing started. All I can remember is needing to get these people through, angry and shouting at them to abandon their bags and help the elderly so we could move faster, to stick to the middle of the road because of the mines, put their bloody cigarettes out and keep quiet. People were saying to me "This is all we have; if we throw it away we'll have nothing," and I was shouting "Throw it! The important thing is to get out of this alive and help other people get out of it alive." That's when I remember meeting you.

'Once here, I watched things for a while. The Krajina Brigade was just starting up, and the police fighting units. Ten of us from Sanski Most decided they were the best bet, and joined. Within two weeks, they made me police commander. It was in miserable shape, untrained, no weapons, no uniforms. I won their trust by taking no privileges: I eat, sleep and fight at the front with them. We hold positions ahead of the front lines, and kill people in raids. Bringing my boys' bodies back to Travnik is the worst thing I know.

'All I hope is that it is not in vain. I have no respect for any of these people, Karadžić, Boban or Izetbegović. Only Tito. He was a killer but look, if you have three wild criminals at each other's throats, who wouldn't want a policeman around somewhere. I hate this war. These views I hold as a civilian. This uniform was forced on me by those who destroyed Yugoslavia. This fight should only continue as long as the killing of the Muslims, my people, continues. I say "Muslim", but I'm not really religious. I believe in the cycle of nature, but I don't believe that anything is perfect.

I have read the Koran, and it was obviously written by someone very brilliant. But he made one big mistake: he says I must love Allah and fear him. You cannot mix love and fear – that is tainted love.

'I only really love people. I know that sounds daft and a bit kitsch, but it's true, and it is all I am fighting for. I'm not really fighting for Bosnia; look at those children playing out there: I'm fighting for them. I have an idea of justice, and bringing the guilty to justice, but I am fighting the war for children like them and the old people and the weak people who cannot fight for themselves, that's it, that's all.'

Emir Tica

The fresh-faced young man who greeted the refugee convoy as it reached the outskirts of Travnik was Emir Tica, who had organised the buses for the last leg of the journey. 'Tica' in Serbo-Croat means 'little bird'. Emir is twenty-five and lives with his parents in a small flat off the main road into Travnik. He is never home nowadays, spending his life at army headquarters where he does eleven jobs which combine under the title of 'transport adjutant' to the commander.

At school, Emir won a prize for knowing about the history of Travnik: about its role as the governmental seat of Ottoman Bosnia; about the first foreign consulates opened in Travnik by France and Austria in 1807 and 1808 respectively; and about the heroic war by Tito's partisans who, as one of Emir's books says, 'came marching down the narrow valley with firm, unyielding steps, in the name of liberty'. After leaving school, Emir's interests apart from girls were rock music and the internal combustion engine. He was one of 180,000 Yugoslavs who entered for the national heats of the world Camel Trophy for rough-road driving, and got through to the last twenty for the trials in Zagreb. His favourite music is by U2, and Emir has played their tapes as a soundtrack to the war that has turned his life upside down. His preferred track is called 'One' and his 'Bosnia' verse goes: 'Have you come here for forgiveness? / Have you come to raise the dead.? / Have you come here to play Jesus / To the lepers in your head?' 'It says it all,' says Emir. 'It's what I would scream in Europe's face, and at the United Nations.' Emir's own band had split up before the war anyway, due to the lack of female vocalists in town, which were deemed essential.

Meanwhile, Emir had got a job as despatch manager at the bus depot up the road, and that is what the Government Army wanted him for when war came to Travnik. So the Little Bird's job was to be the hub at the centre of an entire logistical wheel, a mixture of the following: managing teams of unarmed drivers prepared to risk their lives on almost every journey they make, despatching and accounting for all military vehicles, running ambulances, overseeing the workshop, procuring spare parts and fuel on the black market or however else, servicing the outpost towns under siege, like Jajce. And every night, he gathers a group of drivers to go towards the lines to greet the incoming refguees. By the end of September 1992, Emir had moved 76,000 people.

'You said when we met that you felt like you had come out of hell into Travnik. But you didn't know that it was hell here too, with the refugees and the shelling. There were 26,000 when you came, there have been another 50,000 since then. It's a nightmare for us, for them, for the city, for me. I don't know what to think when I see them coming; women with no idea where their husbands are, little kids crying, hungry and frightened. One moment they had their homes and normal lives. Then suddenly they become just a number, one of many. I listen to their stories over and over again. Every story is different by name, place and time, but it is all one story: someone came, breaking into the house, beatings and violence, the men to the concentration camps . . .

'My drivers are mostly the men I used to work with at the bus station. They are soldiers without guns, and the best

people in the world. They go out at night, up the line or
to Jajce through a corridor 500 metres wide, unarmed. We
cannot spare the guns to give them. They drive ambulances
to take the wounded from the fronts, collect refugees and
move the troops around. You never know if they will come
back again. They get shot at, wounded and killed.

'Bosnia is a mixed country. There has always been some
kind of tolerance, in this town anyway. In the first days
of this war, I thought there was some terrible misunder-
standing. When they started shelling my city, I understood
only one thing: someone wants to destroy my life, take my
job, kill my parents, wreck my apartment. When I started
fighting, it was just to defend my family, my father and my
mother.

'Bosnia is a complex place. We're European and want to
trust Europe and European democracy. You know me, the
music I like, the movies I like. I'm a Muslim, but I want
to be part of Europe. So when Europe recognised Bosnia,
I was very proud. My Bosnia, united, sovereign, free and
recognised. But now, maybe Europe has changed its mind.
Your leaders are talking about maps, Serbs, Croats and
Muslims, not Bosnia. And if you insist on thinking of it
that way, then I am a Muslim. But I'm not religious, I don't
know how to pray, I never went to mosque. So if Europe
tells me I'm "different", or do not qualify under what I
understand to be European values, then I don't know what I
am fighting for. My country is Bosnia, with all three peoples
in it. I call myself a Bosnian, and I know what that means.

'But the Serbs and the Croats want ethnic cantons, racially
pure. Who the hell wants to live in an ethnic canton? I
don't. It would be like having California for the whites and
Chicago for the blacks, instead of America. It's completely
mad, this is 1992 isn't it? And I think that *my* way of
thinking is the European way. I read about Maastricht,
breaking down frontiers. But Europe is helping those who
want to build more frontiers in Bosnia.

'We do have crazy guys who go around with green

crescents, but no one takes any notice. They want us not to drink, and to pray five times a day, but I'd much rather have five drinks a day. We don't want help from the Arab world, we want help from Europe.

'But it is very important to me to have an identity. If Europe will recognise me as a Bosnian, then I am happy. But if Europe insists that I am a Muslim, then I am a Muslim. If Europe betrays us, there is a danger that these people will become real "Muslims". And then Europe can say, "Oh look, you see it was the *jamahirya* after all, and here comes Islam by the back door, how right we were not to back those Muslims." But that will be said either over the gravestones of our people, or about some Muslim state that we have never wanted.

'Everything has changed for us. But the real difference is that the shelling could start any moment. When your main reason for being alive is *luck*, life becomes very strange. I don't think people who have not been in that situation can understand it. It's not so much a question of whether we will survive, it is a question of staying normal. After all the refugees, the dead bodies and the destruction, all those terrible things, the question is this: tomorrow, when all this is stopped, how will I live without remembering? Will I have a smile as before? Will I be happy as before? That is the question for all of us to answer, but I don't know the answer.'

Nura Čelić

When the waiter brought the tray with glasses of cola on it, Nura Čelić began to cry quietly. Unwelcome but stubborn tears worked their way from her deep, dark eyes, along her cheeks, round the underside of her chin and down her neck. 'I never thought anything so nice would ever happen to me again,' she explained.

We were sitting on the pavement, opposite the old

mosque in Travnik with Nura, aged twenty, from Sanski Most, who had been on our convoy across the mountains. 'The last time I was in a café was three months ago,' she excused herself, and began to smile again with difficulty, for a tune was coming from inside the café which reminded her of her boyfriend. He had been a fireman, and she had not seen him since the day that he had been taken away to the camps.

Nura lived in the gymnasium, where some 4,500 refugees shared the floor space and tried to keep the one women's and one men's toilet as clean as possible. In any such human beehive which itinerants have to call home, there are people who hold the seams together, who remain under control even when they do not feel it, people like Nura Čelić. Nura despatches a posse of rowdy seven-year-olds on lavatory-swilling duty before starting her preparations for 'school'. The only subject on the curriculum at Nura's 'school' (which the refugee children are strongly advised to attend) is 'Bosnian', which involves rounds of story-telling about the lives the children have left behind, or, as Nura puts it, 'making sure that we keep our homes with us, so that we never forget'.

Nura has kept a wad of much-thumbed photographs of her old life: Nura with her brothers in smart Yugoslav Air Force pilots' uniforms, Nura with long hair in a café, Nura with short hair and lots of make-up in another café surrounded by broad smiles and denim around the tabletop. 'These are my friends,' she says, 'lots of them are Serbs.'

'I had just finished school and was waiting to go to college to study English, because I have always wanted to go to England. I enjoyed my life. First, they started shooting into the houses, and then returned with machine guns, and took everything, clothes, fuel, the boys' bicycles. I managed to visit my brother in the camp before we left, just outside Sanski Most. Two girls had been raped there, but they didn't rape me, they just harrassed me and made obscene propositions and gestures. Their last visit to our house was when they wrote a Serbian name on a piece of paper which they put above the door. This was the Serb who was to have the house, who must have been very important because they had said to him that he must have a beautiful house, and the one he picked was ours.

'They had been through town killing for days before that. The Chetniks gave an order to the local gypsies of Sanski Most to put the bodies in pits. They had to go and dig pits on the edge of town, collect all the bodies and put them down there with bulldozers. When the Chetniks came to send us away, they just pointed their guns and said "Walk straight ahead and don't turn back or stop."

'This place is hell, not because of the conditions, we can do what we can about those, but because of what it is doing to people. You can't live like this, there is no *life*, people are slowly going mad. My mother scolds me because my brothers in Travnik joined the army and are fighting, and she says "Why aren't you fighting?" But I am fighting my own war, I'm fighting to stay sane, to look after people, I'm fighting to leave, to go to England.

'It's not a question of hating people. I simply do not trust anybody any more. In the past, I always saw the good in a person, I always have done, I really liked people. But I don't see good in people any more. Before, I could accept the fact that people are not perfect, but still find them good. Now I cannot see good in any man, they just lie, cheat, steal and kill. I can't really describe what kind of a feeling it is to find no good in anything. I can't find the words to describe it to even to my closest friends.'

Chapter Nine

Meanwhile, the Diplomats: Promises, Promises

Ethnic cleansing was creating more than just political indecision along the corridors of power: it was creating a moral dilemma in the form of a tidal wave of human beings that nobody knew what to do with. José Maria Mendiluce, director of the UNHCR in Zagreb, called it 'the worst refugee crisis since the Second World War'.

When Croatia said that from mid-July 1992 she could maintain no more refugees within her frontiers, the rest of the world bowed slowly to pressure. By mid-August the league table went as follows:

Germany registered 135,000 refugees, and admitted that another 65,000 had entered illegally. Hungary accepted 54,000 and then announced its border closed. Austria took 50,000, Sweden 44,000, Switzerland 17,000, Holland accepted 6,300 and plucky Luxembourg 3,200. But apart from these, the doors remained largely shut. Muslim Turkey meanly took only 7,000 of its desperate co-religionists and Italy, a neighbour like Austria and Hungary, took the same. Norway managed 2,300 and Czechoslovakia 1,700. That left France and Britain bottom of the table with 1,100 apiece. Britain further distinguished itself with a strict application of the 'third country' rules and was busy preparing the deportation of some thirty Bosnians, arguing that it was under no obligation to consider applicants unless Britain was the first country to which they had fled (which is physically impossible from Bosnia). The Home Office did later agree to relax its interpretation, and more refugees and camp inmates were accepted.[1]

The discovery of Omarska and other camps further complicated things. The Serbs managed to turn the 'opening up' of the camps into a piece of crude blackmail: they offered to free their prisoners if the international agencies would take responsibility for them and find them somewhere to go. It was a grotesque dilemma, since it forced the UNHCR to either condemn the inmates to further detention, or to facilitate their 'cleansing' from Serbian-held territory. There was the additional problem of third countries being reluctant to take more than a handful of prisoners. At the end of September, the deadline for the closure of camps, the exasperated Red Cross announced that it was obliged to delay the liberation of thousands of inmates because it was too dangerous for them to go home, and because the 'international community' could not agree where to put them.

As a result, thousands of prisoners were unaccounted for, including those transferred from Omarska, and there were reports that many had been executed during the transfers. The Red Cross chief in Belgrade, Thierry Meyrat, said that by mid-September, no European country had agreed to accommodate prisoners on any significant scale. Governments would have to decide, he said, whether to accept them, or have them sent into the teeming areas under Muslim and Croatian control. 'The perversity of all this,' he said, 'is that the conflict is helping a certain type of cleansing, and we are without any guarantee that this cleansing will stop.'

This was the backdrop to the London peace conference late in August, on which high hopes for a settlement were pinned by its chairman John Major. British Foreign Secretary Douglas Hurd was also determined to see tougher enforcement of sanctions against the Serbian frontiers across which plentiful supplies were still rolling. Some of the bountiful gifts from the Orthodox brotherhood of Russia, Ukraine and Greece remained in Serbia, but many of them were passed to the brothers-in-arms defending the faith in Bosnia.

On the eve of the conference, Mr Major pledged 1,800 British troops for Bosnia, under the UN flag and ready to provide protection to UN relief convoys. Under the rules of engagement, the soldiers would be able to return fire in self-defence if a convoy was attacked, but could not 'fight their way through,' said Defence Minister Malcolm Rifkind. The UN had scrapped ambitious plans for a peacekeeping force of 100,000, in favour of a 6,000-strong force compatible with Britain's offer. The EC mediator Lord Carrington said he expected the London conference to secure 'a resounding statement that the partition of Bosnia by force was inconceivable and unacceptable to the international community'[2] – a robust pledge. Mr Major opened the conference by appealing to the people of Sarajevo to take heart and be 'encouraged' by the outcome of the assembly.

Karadžić came to London oozing *amour propre*. The discovery of the camps had brought the West to the brink of action but little had happened so far. He made a magnanimous gesture: 'We now control 70 per cent of Bosnia,' he said, 'yet we claim only 64 per cent'. He was anxious to fend off the apparently serious hostility of the Americans and undertook to gather, withdraw and register all heavy artillery for monitoring above the four main siege towns, Sarajevo, Bihać, Goražde and Jajce. It was humbug, but the 'international community' was delighted.

The warring factions signed a document whereby Bosnia's frontiers would be recognised and respected by all ex-Yugoslav republics, and only changed by universal agreement. 'For the first time,' affirmed John Major, pleased as punch, 'all the parties accept ... the principle that the aquisition of territory by force will not be accepted.' Under his chairmanship, the Balkan warriors themselves had established what he called 'a yardstick by which they would be judged'. Mr Major was 'confident' that Mr Karadžić would keep to his word and 'confident' that the camps would now be closed 'unconditionally'.[3]

Another outcome of the conference was that Lord David Owen, former British foreign secretary and leader of the defunct British Social Democratic Party, would take over from Lord Carrington as the EC's mediator at the rolling Geneva peace conference. Lord Owen would work in partnership with the UN's representitive, Cyrus Vance. The Serbs were upset by what they thought were Owen's hawkish views on the imposition of the London framework. A few days after the conference, the former Polish Prime Minister Tadeusz Maziowiescki published the most damning report to date on Serbian atrocities, after a tour on the UN's behalf. He advocated a tougher mandate for UN troops and an international war crimes tribunal.

As the resolve of the conference dissipated, the troop deployment scheme entered the labyrinth of thick UN red tape. But the British military themselves were taking matters seriously and practically, preparing reconnaissance teams to find out exactly what would be needed on the ground. The UN had come in for a hammering during August and September: an Italian aircraft had been shot down and its four-man crew killed, a Ukrainian soldier was shot and then two French soldiers killed in crossfire.

Within ten days of the revived Geneva conference opening in September, Serbian guns that had come under UN monitoring and supposedly fallen silent had continued to rain down shells on civilians, the monitors empowered to do no more than take a note. Mr Izetbegović said he would not attend the next round of talks while all four cities covered by the agreement were also under air attack. Karadžić threatened a boycott if French proposals for a 'No-Fly Zone' were introduced, which might inconvience his MiG bombers while they destroyed civilian and industrial targets from the air. Britian quickly said it was opposed to a flight ban, but the idea was agreed in principle in October, and then supposedly given teeth by an EC meeting in Birmingham which demanded the cessation of flights from Banja Luka military airport. The Serbs promptly seized the town of Bosanski Brod in a joint artillery-and-jet-bomber push, but conference chairmen Owen and Vance said it was 'understandable' that the Serbs would want to widen their corridor along the Croatian border.

In Washington, the head of the US Armed Forces, General Colin Powell (of Desert Storm fame) published a critique of the interventionist case. On the basis of what he called his 'all or nothing' philosophy, he argued that military force should only be used to achieve a decisive, politically clear result which he understandably said he had yet to hear.[4] And yet the United States did throw its weight unequivocally behind plans for a war crimes tribunal with prosecutions organised along the lines of the 1943 commission which led to the Nuremberg trials. The plan was, however, filibustered into impotence by Britain and France, who involved Chinese help to sink it at the Security Council. The British foreign office wished to make it clear that the Serbs had reacted 'very angrily' to allegations of atrocities published in the Western press.[5]

With winter approaching, the aid crisis was deepening. The UNHCR said it was only receiving one third of the funds it had requested and Western governments were defaulting on vehicles that had been promised. Before long, the world was treated to a microcosm of what was to come when 200 Bosnian fugitives reached a freezing mountaintop on the Slovene–Austrian border and asked to be admitted to Britain. They had been brought out by a Leeds-based charity, with homes arranged, and waited a week in the snow. Home Office Minister Kenneth Clarke was adamant: the regulations would apply, and in any case, they had been recommended for asylum by the Slovenian, and not the international, Red Cross. Austria eventually agreed to open its frontier to them. But: 'We are still trying to get to Britain,' said the spokesman for the 200 in Vienna 'because we think Britain is really great. We still have hope.'[6] By then, the 1st Battalion 22nd Cheshire Regiment of the British Army was encamped at Vitez in Central Bosnia, and doing an infinitely better job for Britain's image than the Home Office.

Chapter Ten

'Top Guns' – a People under Siege

The phrase 'Top Guns' is made up of English words but was crafted in Bosnia and is a favourite among Bosnians who speak a bit of English. 'Top Guns' means the heavy artillery above your town or village, the ones that Karadžić had promised the London conference he would collect for monitoring pending withdrawal. Across the government-held territory of Bosnia-Herzegovina, the fear wrought by the Top Guns had become a way of life by September 1992. In town after town of scrappy pebbledash, breeze-block or plastered houses nestled in wooded valleys below high ridges, their owners trying to live as 'normal' a life as they could under the barrels of the Top Guns. The guns were sometimes quiet for a long while, and would then suddenly break the illusive peace with the crash and echo of another shell or rain of shells wreaking havoc, death or injury on communities quite unable to deal with such tribulation. In some places, the Top Guns were only yards away from these huddles of people, invariably swelled by refugees from surrounding hamlets.

Bosanska Krupa/the Bihać pocket

September 1992
Just to walk around the Muslim half of Bosanska Krupa

is perilous and terrifying for the 5,000 people who remain. They are like ducks in a shooting gallery.

The town sits astride the river Krupa, and on the Serbian side, snipers line its banks and follow you, with bursts of fire as you sprint across the gaps between the houses, until they get bored. Sometimes the bullets are well wide, all you hear is the crack as you run for the cover of the next wall; sometimes, they are closer, and cut the air with a whistle above your head. And sometimes they find their quarry and kill; fifty-nine times, in fact, during the two weeks before our visit, either civilians or the soldiers trying to protect them are hit.

The settlement sits on the edge of what is called the 'Bihać Pocket', an area around the market and industrial centre of Bihać, surrounded by Serbian territory with no open routes in or out. The river Krupa is the Pocket's frontier and front line, and crossing point for refugees in flight from the west of the Bosnian Krajina. Bosanska Krupa is a trap within a trap. The only way in and out of the village is a steep, exposed track up the far side of the valley along which people can be picked off at leisure.

This is now a town of cellars and home-made bunkers, in which young families and old people alike eat fruit growing in their gardens or corn from the allotments. They survive huddled in the gunfire-shadows of what is left of their houses, living behind the back walls that face away from the riverbank. But to leave or to enter the town, or to move around within it, is a nightmarish battle of wits between hunter and prey. The prey must wind through hedges, back gardens, porches, round the backs of trees, along ditches, anything to avoid any possible line of fire from the other side of the river – and then run for dear life across those sightlines that are unavoidable, followed by the crack of the rifles or the rattle of machine guns.

While lying there, in the grass or on the kerbside, or catching your breath behind one house before the dash to the next, there is adequate time to think: 'Who is that at the other end of that gun barrel, looking through the sights and waiting for me to make another run? And how many more houses and gardens have I got to run between before he gives up and starts on somebody else?' And that is how people live, all day and every day. If they want to talk to one another or pick plums they have to run across the gully to the next house – 'Crack Crack' – then wait. Then the next aperture – 'Crack Crack' – and then the next.

Some 30,000 people fled down when the worst fighting started, mostly into the Pocket but others, in desperation, across to the Serbian side, of whom 8,000 are unaccounted for. A horrible silence hangs over the 5,000 that remain, broken only by the gunfire, the booming of the mortar shells and the odd clucking chicken. They are people like the Nokići family, playing cards beside a table wedged tight against their attempt at a bunker, made of piled-up breeze blocks. 'It's home,' says Mr Nokići with baffling resignation, 'so far these bricks have kept us safe.'

We were accompanied by Senada, a soldier visiting her father, and Farud who wished to check that the house he had left when he fled was still there. The drive from the sizeable town of Cazin was through undulating green hills, the soldiers camped in wooded glades and one group busy brewing šljivovic in a wondrous and ancient, solid brass distillery hung over a camp fire. Along the eight-mile road, an occasional procession of refugees from Bosanska Krupa was returning for the afternoon, to collect belongings left behind or, like Senada, visiting. 'We come back just to see our houses,' she says, 'although we could be shot at any time. The people who have left are still nearby, which is strange for them. We are crowded into houses at Cazin, and sad. We come back to see our people, to make sure they are still there and just to put some joy into our hearts, even if it is only for half an hour.'

Then down into the valley on foot, with Bosanska Krupa down below. The two miles of track wind through wood and clearing before reaching hazardous open land and the edge of the village. Is this going to be safe? '*Nema problema,*' replies Farud; 'No problem' is the answer to everything in lackadaisical Bosnia. We had come to learn that 'there's a problem' means 'you are being shot at'. 'No problem' means 'you are going to be shot in a few minutes'. He suddenly pulls us over against a house; 'This is where we have to run'. 'I thought you said *Nema problema*'. 'There isn't a problem, they usually miss': that is meant to be an assurance. This time they held their fire or didn't see us.

Ibro Durakević, his young wife and two daughters peep out of the glassless window of the house which, like so many in the DIY-mad former Yugoslavia, is still being built. They spent two months as refugees in the relative safety of Cazin, but 'came back because we didn't much like the people there, and there were fifty-six of us, crowded into one house. Besides, this is our home and it's important that we stay. If we go, there's no Bosanska Krupa and the Chetniks can just stroll across the river.' Ibro has built an admirable bunker down in the cellar, with table, chairs and a row of camp beds; 'We get thirty or forty people down there when it's bad at night,' he says with satisfaction. Others are less defiant, like Rejzdo, the young man whose lower leg was blown off by a mortar one afternoon, who arrived at hospital in Cazin twenty-eight hours later, and who sits, silent, on a doorstep, holding his crutches, staring at the flagstones and at his stump, and doing nothing.

Munira Durdić has a gash in the side of her house where a rocket came through into what was the lavatory. The cooker is now outside, on the far side of the cottage, where it is safer to sit. Mrs Durdić has thought about leaving for Cazin, but her husband is ill and would never make it up the track. 'So we stay on, me afraid that I will be left alone and forced to choose between running away and staying with my husband. If he stays, he would die in the end, of course. But they would definitely catch him going up the hill, because he is too slow. I've lost my family now; my children left and my brother and sister were both killed. My friends in Krupa and my cousin are also dead. I get used to the shooting, it's the Top Guns that scare me, they could land right on us any time.'

As we run the next gully, towards Dula Kurtović's backyard, there is mighty salvo of machine gun fire. We make it to Dula's yard, and there is another volley, rooting the company to the spot. Then there is a crashing explosion right behind us from one of the Top Guns. Dula, aged sixty-six, is looking after her grandson Nedjad; her skin is tough like animal hide, and so is she. 'You'd best stop here and have some juice. One of those got my cousin, and another got my son-in-law. But I have nowhere else to go. All we can do is to sit tight and smoke our cigarettes – well, not quite cigarettes, we make them by rolling up the leaves from the plum trees, and they keep going out!'

Senada moves on to visit her father, taking a route through the merciful cover of a railway tunnel and in the company of a sturdy bodyguard called Elvir and his Kalshnikov. Father complains a little, insists that he is all right, and Senada advises him to go out as little as possible, to try to avoid picking plums and making visits. Farud finds that his house is much the same as it was last week except for some blast damage. Back to join Dula and a group of soldiers in her yard, serenaded across the alleyway by another crack.

At the time of this visit, Bosanska Krupa had seen no sign of any relief agency. The previous day, a Russian UN Military Observer had approached by road, but was advised to leave town quickly. The single supply of water had been from one stream which had dried up two days ago, and now people collected their bucketfulls from the river. Dula was shot at when she last tried. 'It's too late to try and feed the town in this state,' says a militiaman called Faruk, 'but it's essential that we have civilians here, not to oblige the Chetniks by evacuating. During the good weather, what we need is guns, not food, because we can grow food, and the only hope is to go across the bridge and win a bit of space to protect people. Then it's worth trying to feed them through the winter.'

With that motive in mind, a small band from the Green Berets, an equipped unit from the otherwise hopelessly ill-furnished army, passes by. Ahmed Demirović is their commander. 'We have ten men to every one gun here, and very little ammunition,' he laments. 'We can't get anywhere near the Top Guns, but we can make trouble for them, kill Chetniks and steal their weapons, which is the main thing.' These men laugh at the idea of Karadžić's promise to collect artillery; the armoury is hidden in away forests, woods and houses, and remains intact. The soldiers file off among the wrecked buildings, with their brash but somehow pitiful courage; blind faith that the power of their convictions can overcome the Top Guns, which boom again almost immediately they move.

Senada's mission accomplished, it is time to face the journey back up the track. The first dash is across a piece of open land, one by one: '*Crack Crack*,' down goes my colleague, face into the nettles. Likewise Senada when she tries, and likewise myself. We crawl back to the police station to pick up sturdy Elvir and a posse of lads in search of a better route, and follow them with reluctant trust born of necessity, into the gutted pebbledash maze. We play ninety minutes of cat-and-mouse with the snipers, crawling though back gardens, running in turn between one building and another and then catching breath behind them, ready for the next sprint. Even sturdy Elvir, providing cover with his Kalshnikov but reluctant to spend precious ammunition, failed to conceal his unease. The low ebb came when the lads, armed illogically with crowbars, had an argument amongst themselves over which route to take, each insisting that the others' was much too dangerous. From Senada, fond reassurance: '*Nema problema*'. No problem; next run, please.

All the while, little goups of people would be huddled in their porches, out of the gunners' sightlines, munching on wild apples as we sprint by. They would offer the odd wave, and sometimes even a moderate smile of congratulation as we made it to the next house. We tore across a factory yard, crawled along a long fence and met a soldier coming in the other direction nonchalantly carrying his baby. When we made it to the foot of the still perilous but absurdly welcome track up the back of the valley, it was early evening and the serious Top Guns were just warming up above wretched Bosanska Krupa.

Two weeks later, Senada went to visit her father again, and was told that he had been shot dead trying to move between two houses.

Bihać and its cluster of satellite communities has been caught in a noose of Top Guns and aircraft bombing raids. The Pocket of 300,000 people, 36,000 of them refugees, is cut off to the south and east by the Prijedor hinterland, and to the north and west by the Serbian-occupied area of Croatia. The Croatian Krajina is under UN control and a ceasefire is in force, but everyone in Bihać, including the young British member of the excellent local Military Observer team, knows that the Serbs are pummelling Bihać from the hills on the Croatian 'ceasefire' side too. Bihać is a what a surgeon at the hospital, Irfan Ljubjankić, calls 'a bone in Greater Serbia's throat'; the Pocket blocks a continuous stretch of Serbian-held land from Knin in Croatia all the way through Bosnia to Belgrade.

On a fine Wednesday afternoon in September, the Bosnian Army has the cheek to respond to the usual dosage of shells with an infantry incursion up the hillside. The punishment comes in reliably enough: three mortars ploughing into the side of the town hall, and another two into the hospital grounds, badly injuring a patient hobbling about on a stick. Down by the river, teenagers in bikinis carry on sunbathing, almost beyond care. But in the town centre, the experience of others has become like a wound in itself, into which every raid now rubs the painful salt of fear.

The warren of dank, humid tunnels beneath the school in Bihać has been home for months to those who now scurry back down when the first shell comes in. The Nazis built this subterranean labyrinth as a shelter and operations centre. You leave the scrappy yard above, littered with the debris of explosions, and descend by stone steps into the nether darkness. It takes a while for one's eyes to become accustomed to the murky gloom, but when they have done so they are met by a scene from the depths of Dostoyevsky. An elderly couple is drawn around a low paraffin lamp, eating soup and potatoes with rough, clunking cutlery. The man's leg is wounded and bound, perched on a sack, the woman has a bandage around her head. Slowly, other faces emerge, peering out of the black, those of people lying on bunk beds built against the wall. They stretch back into what is now the half-dark, past arches and into new tunnels, past the shadows of the soup and potato eaters. The shells are landing nearby, up there in the world.

Jusuf and Fatima Hosić finish their meal; a good meal, but the only one they will eat today. They moved down here three months ago; this is home. 'The people who stay out there are those who have not yet had a rocket fired straight into their house. They do not understand,' says Jusuf. 'They think it could never happen to them.' 'We were in our house,' continues Fatima, 'when the shell fell down right onto us. There was an explosion; all I could see was blood. While we were in hospital, our home was hit again. We're lucky to be alive, and have decided never to move around this town again.'

'I am,' said Derviza Smaijlagić, stating the obvious with the dignity that memory brings, 'an old woman.' She is eighty-four years old, her face craggy with deep dimples but her eyes are bright. 'I remember when this tunnel was built. In 1942, German officers used to work in the school. There was always fighting, between Nazis, Utasha and partisans – Muslim and Serb together then – and the Germans extended the school cellar to build a headquarters. I can remember what the Nazis did in this town, it was terrible, and of course that was a bigger war – but in Bihác not as bad as this war now. I was a young mother, and I was left alone. My house was left alone. It was an occupation, and terrible fighting, but they didn't shell the villages at night, we didn't have to go into the cellar. Now, I live down here. I don't like it, I have bad asthma, there is no electricity, we are all living too close to one another. I get out once a day at 6 a.m. and go to look at what is left of my house, where I lived with my husband for fifty-three years. It is bombed, everything torn and wrecked. Ask this girl what she knows' – and old Mrs Smaijlagić points to a figure who has emerged quietly from under an archway leading to another tunnel – 'She won't remember the Nazis, but she has seen worse than I ever did.'

'She' has been listening carefully to Mrs Smaijlagič's conversation. 'She' is what the old woman's generation in Bosnia would call a 'modern girl', in her early twenties, with over-dyed blonde hair which has been layered and, in some now distant life, given a permanent wave. She is pale, plump and very pretty, better suited to Titian's studio than to this infernal chasm. Would she like to say something too? Yes, she says, she would, but asks to be excused for a minute. She goes back into her louring quarters, not quite black as pitch, and returns a while later after some audible shuffling about. In the grime and the soot, she has applied mascara to her eyelashes with great precision, picked out her eyebrows in black, patted a little rouge on her cheeks at each end of her smile; her lipstick is the colour of good wine. The old black T-shirt has given way to a pink, defiantly tight, blouse. Bahra Kadić is now ready to talk, and beckons us through. Next to Bahra's dingy corner, a ninety-year-old woman is asleep on a crude wooden construction which down here is called a bed; the other occupants of the room are all children, most of them orphaned, whom Bahra looks after.

'I sometimes have to think to remember that I reached here alive and that it was two whole months ago. I walked eighty-nine kilometres and was alone when I arrived. I am from Bosanski Novi and I worked as a waitress in a cafe. I liked my job very much, I liked the other girls working there, the owner and the people who came to drink coffee and beer. I liked my life. There was one particular day when it got worse. They had taken the men to the stadium, and now they started firing shells and bullets everywhere. I ran to meet my two friends as we had arranged the night before, and we decided to go. There were people leaving the town, and soldiers were marching them onto the road. I said what about my family, and my friends said let's just go while we can.

'They were marching the people along, soldiers at the side shooting into the people as they tried to run down the road. I saw them killing people, I swear that I saw them killing children, they just fell on the road. After that, we left the road, and came through the woods. We lost one of my friends, but me and my friend Ermina walked for four days in the woods, until we came to Bosanska Krupa. There, two Serbian soldiers let us cross the river, in return for a favour from us which we gave them. Ermina stayed in Cazin because she could not go any further, and I carried on alone to Bihać.'

As Bahra speaks, another shell lands right above us. The walls shake and so does she, or rather she shudders, then composes herself.

'My only plan is that when this war is finished, I will work again. My only dream is to find my family, and go back to work. I miss everything, my mother, father, sister, my café, friends, food, peace and my cassettes of country music. You're going to Zagreb? God I wish I could come with you to Zagreb, away from the shooting. I hate it here, it's dark and miserable. I feel like I could kill myself sometimes. We do nothing; we are simply trying to survive for no reason. I never go out into town, I am too frightened – of shelling, shooting, of everything. I don't go anywhere. All I have to do here is to try to look nice. I am sorry I am not looking very nice today.'

Bahra produces photographs of herself: a snapshot of a giggling Bahra looking voluptuous in a mini-dress, ready for a date. Here, on a shelf is a paraffin lamp that comes with the accommodation, and a small cracked mirror, beside which is the now depleted supply of make-up. Taped onto the wall above her wooden bunk are the other things she carried with her from Bosanski Novi: a magazine centre-spread picture of the cast of 'Dynasty' and a pin-up photo of Tom Cruise.

Jasmin Smajlagić, great nephew of the elderly lady and organiser of the tunnels, has hardly taken his eyes off Bahra for a single moment of her speech and it appears he would be happy to watch her whatever she was doing. Jasmin was a law student before the war, and player for the Bosnian youth soccer team. He was a keen fan of Partizan Belgrade, but 'not now, though, now I support Sarajevo'. Between 1,500 and 2,000 people have passed through, he says, and there are between 100 and 200 eating and sleeping here at any one time. 'A group of us started it for the refugees and the children who arrived alone,' says Jasmin, 'never thinking that we would end up having to house people from Bihać and live here ourselves too. Every other night, I catch the bus up to the front. I think this war will end soon, then we can get on with our real lives.' His glance returns to Bahra. 'It is a war,' says Jasmin, 'and she smells like a flower.'

'Bus up to the front'? That is indeed how the army mobilises in Bihać. Soldiers, young and old, wait in the main street at the close of the afternoon for the coach to take them to the defence lines, as though it were the works bus. What weapons the army has are kept at the front, and the arriving shifts take them over from those returning for a rest. Above Cazin, on a high plain, is the army's main encampment in the Pocket, at a turkey-farming complex whose principal export client before the war was in Scotland. But this year's birds were slaughtered prematurely and the low huts are occupied by billeted boys and men. Some wear uniforms, others wear jeans and sneakers. They drill around the plain, they talk tactics, but they have no weapons. The bullets they do have are singly wrapped. 'We have nothing because of the embargo,' says the senior officer at the camp, Captain Asim Mujić, 'and even if the embargo was lifted, there would still be the problem of getting anything here.'

There are ammunition runs into the Bihać Pocket, but they are precarious ones. Men come from Zagreb, slipping through the forests of the Serbian-controlled Krajina. Male refugees arriving in Croatia from the Banja Luka region are 'conscripted' (sometimes press-ganged) by the Bosnian Army's representatives in Zagreb and sent back along the night routes through enemy territory, into Bihać, carrying ammunition. But Serbian authorities in Krajina have arrested and 'destroyed' (said a Serbian border guard) a number of those making the passage across country. A second supply route had been by light aircraft at night and without lights into the covertly functioning airport at Cazin. But the week before our visit, the Serbian air force dealt out its reply: three MiG bomber attacks on the only airstrip in the Pocket, which ruptured the runway, destroyed a wire factory and killed an old woman for good measure.

By the end of August 1992, 400 people had already been killed in Bihać, and more than 3,000 wounded. The diligent UN monitoring team had been holed up at the Motel Bihać long before any journalists or aid convoys arrived. 'I have seen things here that have made me sick as a soldier and human being,' says Major Helge Ringdal, Norwegian chief of the team. 'Five girls playing in the street down there by the river, mortared at the closest range they can get. On the same day, three refugees were killed when they shelled the hostel. The father of one of them asked me for the official photograph of his son's corpse. It was the only photograh he could get to remember him by.'

In the hospital, Halil Mehić lies on his bed, his eyes burning with anger, frustration and pain. He works his phantom right leg which is not there any more, having been amputated last week after he stepped on a mine. Now, Halil has a second, fresh wound torn out of his side by flying shrapnel when a shell landed through the hospital roof while he slept last night, killing his friend Edin Balić and seriously wounding two other injured patients. This latest attack on Bihać hospital came thirty-six hours after Karadžić's pledge to the London peace conference. Conversation about the irony is cut short by a restrained panic among the exhausted staff: old Rasim Segerić, his head gashed and stomach ripped by shrapnel, has stopped breathing and turned grey, the 109th admitted patient to die here in six weeks.

In the next ward is little Dejana Melkić, who earlier was staring into space, confused by fear and pain, her head covered by a gauze bandage tied beneath her chin. Now she has her eyes closed, and looks deceptively tranquil. Dejana, aged seven, was running with her mother across the garden at the back of her home, heading for shelter at the start of a bombing raid, when a single, carefully aimed sniper's bullet found her skull, narrowly missing her brain. 'We will know sometime soon whether she will survive or not,' said the ward doctor.

Goražde

After 146 days of siege, bombardment and virtual isolation, the people trapped in the eastern Bosnian town of Goražde lined the streets on 17 August 1992 to watch a UN convoy escorted by British, French and Ukrainian troops finally roll in.

It was a logistical and moral triumph for the troops and for the efforts of the white-bearded Larry Hollingsworth, the UNHCR's extraordinary convoy leader rapidly emerging as the man of deliverance in the aid war against time, starvation and winter. And it enabled those who travelled with it to witness one of the most wretched scenes of the war. Kurt Schork of Reuters was among them: ' "This is the first time we have stood outside without fear for four months," said Hajruhdin Causevic as the first UN vehicle pulled onto a bombed-out plaza in the town centre . . . Local residents and UN soldiers mingled briefly in a festival-like atmosphere amid the bullet-riddled cars, broken glass and blasted masonry which litter Goražde.'

The celebrations ceased abruptly, however, when the UN team visited the Isak Samokovlja hospital: 'The young man looked like death,' reported Schork, 'in the gloom of his hospital room, a pale wraith with a short stump wrapped in blood-soaked bandages where his left leg should have been. "This man had an amputation without general anaesthetic," said Dr Alija Begovic, "we don't have the painkillers or facilities for major surgery here" . . . Nurses held down a three-year-old girl as she screamed with pain and a man writhed while a doctor probed deep into his shoulder for shrapnel . . . "Those were like battlefield operations during Napoleon's era," said Lt-Col Erik de Stabenrath, whose French Marines had provided the convoy's military escort.'[1]

Some reporters stayed behind after the UN convoy left; one of them, Alec Russell of the *Daily Telegraph*, sent this report: 'An hour after the UN convoy pulled away, Goražde was suffering one of its heaviest bombardments of the last month . . . "*Bon Appetit*, bye bye", said Mrs Dada Tatarevic scampering across the street with her dog, "at least we'll die with full stomachs."

'The defenders are relying on home-made hand grenades against the unstinted ordinance of Europe's third largest army. The intensity of the assault and the efficiency of the blockade make the siege of Sarajevo seem almost humane.

'The suffering is probably most acute in the refugee quarters. Three weeks ago, the Serbs shelled the Iva Lola

Riba sports stadium, a temporary home for 3,000. It burned for two days. It is now a charred skeleton still exuding the fumes of melted rubber. The survivors are housed in a school cellar. Last Saturday, cowering from a sudden attack, they stood in 90 degree heat and darkness, coated in the smell of their own urine . . . "My wife is missing, my child is dead" – the stories took on an almost ritual quality, becoming a litany of human degradation.'[2]

Although the rope around Goražde tightened, the overnight ammunition runs from Sarajevo, and those from Tuzla to Srebenica, continued, usually carried on the backs of mules whose trails would weave through the enemy's wooded territory by night, or else carried by shepherds in backpacks. At the same time, Radovan Karadžić said that he was withdrawing some of the guns around Goražde, in accordance with the London agreement, and there is evidence that some positions were in fact dismounted. The Bosnians chose to take unwise and vicious advantage of the withdrawal.

The following month saw the most unexpected series of victories and atrocities of the war to date. Small units of the entrapped Bosnian Army suddenly broke out of both Goražde and Srebrenica, moving through the Serbian-occupied hillsides, mounted startling guerilla attacks on Serbian military positions and convoys and attacked civilians and villages. One village in particular, Bratunac, was temporarily taken, and its remaining civilian population massacred in cold blood – Serbian television showed pictures of rows of slaughtered victims, some of whom had had their throats cut. Other villages in areas comfortably under Serbian control fell to the Government fighters, and burned: Drinjaca, Novo Selo and Podravanje.

The bewildered Serbs reeled from the ferocity of the counter-offensive. Their own partisan legends were being turned against them by Muslim units fighting across classic partisan terrain. Soldiers in ambushed Serbian military trucks saw the slightest trace of their attackers. Wounded

Serbian fighters in a hospital at Uzice said their lorries were driving down what had been considered a safe road when they were suddenly sprayed with machine-gun bullets by unseen gunmen.[3]

Roger Cohen from the *New York Times* travelled with Serbian troops to the scene of the massacre of a civilian convoy at Kukavice, near Goražde: 'Even by the standards of a dirty war, the scene here is one of horror. Four bodies, charred and putrid, lie sprawled beside overturned cars, scraps of clothing and broken glass. The blackened skull of another burned corpse has fallen from a vehicle onto the road . . . Western analysts say they believe that such attacks by Muslims on Serbs are likely to become a feature of the war.'[4] But 'Western analysts' were wrong. It took little time for the Serbs to regain their military composure, if that is the right word, dig out the guerillas, kill them, take back the lost villages and re-lay the sieges of Goražde and Srebenica with even greater intensity. Overlooking the barbarism which they had wrought on the Muslims for five months, the Serbs began talking about 'revenge'. Within ten days of Cohen's report, word was reaching Serbian-held Foča that 200 Muslims had been summarily murdered in vendetta killings north of the town. Michael Montgomery wrote for the *Daily Telegraph*:

'Colonel Marko Kovac ordered a squad to clear away stinking heaps of Muslim corpses from nearby hills, and said "Neither side is taking prisoners any more." About 150 bodies lying on a track were making operations "difficult", his men are complaining . . . A similar pattern of violence is emerging in northern Bosnia. About 200 Muslim men and youths were allegedly executed by Serbian policemen in retaliation for an attack on a Serbian patrol.'[5]

By the end of November, Goražde, Srebrenica and Žepa were digging in for the winter, under heavier fire than ever. There were 70,000 trapped in Srebrenica, most of whom were refugees and for all of whom the nightmare was only just beginning. For the moment, though, Goražde and Srebrenica held on. Over in central Bosnia, another siege had tragically ended.

Jajce

It was the largest and most wretched single exodus of this now unrelenting war against the common people: a river of bedraggled humanity fleeing on foot and by tractor, trailer, armoured car and wooden horse-drawn cart – almost the entire population of the fallen town of Jajce and the army that had defended it but now surrendered, trudging through an October Saturday down the perilous, rugged road, past blazing Serbian guns, into Travnik. 'Vietnam Road' it was called.

It was the exodus, too, of the carthorse: hundreds of them, heaving their burdens of people caked in dirt and piled onto the farm carts on top of the plastic bags, childrens' toys and machine guns. Their heavy hooves clip-clopped all through the night of Friday 30 October, and throughout the weekend, down the tracks and through the streets of town. Occasionally the fine beasts, as resigned and weary as their peasant masters, were rested to munch at straw. Farmers from Travnik brought up lorry-loads of hay and along the route into town, and mothers, old men and children lay down with the horses to try to sleep for the first time after two nights in the wild, under fire.

Then up again, to move on, talking of looting, shooting, betrayal, killing, loss and bloody feet. Lame mongrels, unaccompanied, limped as best they could to keep up, and to take the odd offering of stale bread. Shepherds with their trusted dogs had herded entire flocks of sheep along the thirty-mile road and through the shelling that accompanied these people as they walked on. 'They are my life,' said one old man, barely able to carry on but for his sturdy stick with which he stabbed the dust. 'Without my beasts I cannot live, and now they are all I have got. How could I think of leaving them. Chetniks kill our animals too, you know.' Eleven people had been killed that morning out on the road, and more than sixty badly wounded. They were carried piggy-back or with their bloody arms around those who could still move.

By the middle of the Saturday afternoon, more than 30,000 escapees from the bloody mayhem left behind in Jajce – and the pitiful ramshackle remnants of an army, some 7,000 soldiers – had crossed the new, retreated Bosnian front at Karaula and now jammed every square of Travnik. The smoke of their campfires and broilers filled the air as they pitched camp on any spare stretch of grass, concrete or flagstones they could find; the very young, the very old, the peasants and the doctors or businessmen, reduced to a vast, itinerant encampment on the already war-weary streets of someone else's town. The soldiers wandered aimlessly among them and their beasts and wagons, as lost and destitute as the civilians. It was like some woeful landscape from Tolstoy, or a war from another time: the life of a country town and its surrounding villages uprooted and driven out by war, with all its flotsam and jetsam. And another 15,000 were still out there, trapped by gunfire on the front at Karaula.

The defence of Jajce had been serviced from Travnik up an umbilical twenty-five mile corridor through Serbian territory of rough track, wooded undergrowth and mountainside, and sometimes only 500 yards wide. Only the fiercest of fighting had kept it open during the five months of siege. Attempts to get to Jajce by night were turned back by successive outbreaks of heavy fire along the corridor, the track littered by a debris of vehicles blown off course by mortars, or their drivers caught by snipers' bullets. 'Why do you want to go to Jajce anyway?' asked police commander Fahrudin Alihodžić after a request to go with one of his fighting units. 'Jajce is a toilet full of fungus, and you probably wouldn't get back.'

Emir Tica's ('Little Bird's') vehicles kept Jajce alive and fighting until its final surrender. Night after night, his

unarmed drivers would finish their Turkish coffee in the
refectory at the 'Blue Water' command and set off with
their ambulances, which took medicines in and brought
back the wounded, lorries and trucks. At dawn they would
usually return, exhausted, invariably with another couple of
holes in the sides of their vehicles. Every truck that went to
Jajce tells its own story; like the blue bus that was bringing
some civilians out one night, hit by machine gun fire. Three
people were killed, and the side of the bus, with its rash of
holes, tells you how.

Now the toilet of fungus had been flushed out by a Serbian
offensive which had deployed fresh troops from Belgrade
and which now afforded them an easily imagined boozy
night of celebration among the ruins and a swift advance
to the gates of Travnik. Meanwhile, the accursed human
tide of their victims came ahead of them.

They began coming in on the Friday evening in trickles,
with terrible tales to tell. They were at the head of a ten-mile
column of people on whom the Serbs had opened fire as they
fled Jajce on foot, entering through the outpost checkpoint
on the edge of Turbe and boarding Emir Tica's buses. He
personally greeted all of them. On the road behind, the
sky flashed with shells and mortars, with shots ringing
out across the valley as dusk fell. The Civa family was
finally re-united at the checkpoint after hours of troubled
searching. Jasmina, aged twenty-six, greeted her sick and
exhausted father and elderly mother from who she had been
separated when the refugees broke ranks under fire.

The end had been terrifying, said Jasmina. The edges of
town were ablaze and the shelling had become relentless;
'all the time, all day and all night, we couldn't even go out
in the early mornings. For weeks, people had been living
in cellars. Even when the food arrived from Travnik, it was
often impossible to get to it. So many were killed trying.
We simply lived underground, unable to leave the basement,
and when food arrived we would run for the trucks and back

again. For the last few days, it was quite terrible, and now my life is in this suitcase.'

Word had gone round that the Serbs were about to come into town. The Croatian army, the HVO, was rumoured to have pulled its men off the defensive lines, and the Bosnians had been unable to hold them alone; for the moment the reasons for the fall of Jajce were a mystery charged with acrimony and accusations of betrayal by the Croats. 'We left because the civil authorities said there was going to be a massacre,' said Mr Mustafa Civać, 'and that we should leave while we could, the whole town at once. We were climbing muddy slopes, among the first, climbing up five paces and sliding down three. We left everything and fled because we were afraid we would be butchered. The last time I saw Jajce it was in flames, and I will never see my town again, which I love beyond words. I built my own shop, and now I look like a beggar, I *am* a beggar, and all that I have worked for is vanished in an instant, and I do not understand why.' His son was killed by shrapnel during the siege.

More crossed the checkpoint, and then more still. 'They were firing at us as soon as we started to leave,' said Tramisa Mulanović, walking through with a child on each arm. 'We have been up to our ankles in mud and water, it was the most terrible part of it all. The shots came close to my feet and someone in the group ahead of me was killed; just fell in the road. We tried to revive her, but she died almost immediately, it seems . . . I've left my husband at the front, I don't know where he is . . . The last two days were the worst, a bomb every second, I swear it.'

The sight that greeted Travnik when the town rose the following morning was among the most dramatic of the war; Jajce had arrived and pitched camp. 'We have been totally overwhelmed,' said Anders Levinson, the tireless co-ordinator for the UNHCR in the area. 'We have never seen such large numbers coming in at one time, anywhere.'

An army in retreat is a thing to behold. In the village of Karaula a new front line had been established, spread out across the meadows the soldiers now, and ushering thousands of people trapped in the village overnight back onto the road. But all along that road, the downcast soldiers trudged or packed the lorries, or else cadged lifts on the peasants' carts, their faces comatose with humiliation. Their heavy vehicles chugged pointlessly past us and past the old men and women leading their packhorses. The sound of gunfire carried on the wind from the new front, now close by as defeated soldiers came pouring through Turbe just outside Travnik, disconsolate and past recall. A sniper's shot cracked nearby and a ramshackle armoured car came by us as we walked, with one boy lying, bloodied from a fresh wound, in the arms of a comrade, hit just that instant. At the checkpoints, the local Croat and Bosnian armies had come out from Travnik to meet and disarm those in retreat, aiming to recruit them in defence of the town. There were fist fights; men objected to surrendering their weapons; bad blood, bad feeling. Many insisted that they hold onto them, and were allowed to, in the interests of calm.

The defeated soldiers went to gather outside the headquarters of their respective armies, Croat and Bosnian. And from all of them came the angry, abstract charge of betrayal, some deal over Jajce, between Radovan Karadžić and his opposite number Mate Boban. Pejo Jurić, a Croat from Skender Vakuf, fighting way up towards the Serbian heartland, was fairly explicit: 'They can both go and fuck their mothers. There were rumours for weeks that we were going to be sold. We didn't need to surrender. This is Boban and Karadžić dividing up Bosnia. Well I'm not going to fight for Bosnia any more, and I won't fight for Mate Boban and his 'Herzeg-Bosna' either. We feel pathetic. We've walked thirty kilometres on foot, behind the civilians, and we feel like cowards.'

No soldier can tolerate the stigma of defeat, and some regained their manhood with drink, filling the bars, lurching around the girls and singing in some hollow pretence at defiance, parading their machine guns around town and firing into the air. One unit remained disciplined and marched down the pavement in formation: the new 'Muslim Armed Forces' with a green Islamic crescent on their arm. 'Idiots,' said Nadja Ridjić, from the Bosnian Army radio station, 'they lost Jajce and now they think they're heroes in Travnik.' But they were all silent by about 10 p.m., when the Serbs sent in their first message to those who had fled them in Jajce: three heavy shells, exploding right in the centre of town.

By then, heavy rain was lashing the streets, where several thousand still remained in the open, trying to shelter under the eves of the buildings or guarding their drenched possessions in the yard outside the high school. 'This umbrella is now my home,' said Asan, trying to comfort his wife Velega and little daughter Armela, as icy water splashed into their ripped shoes. 'They say a bus may come tomorrow sometime; we have no money, no dry clothes and no idea where we're going.' This family too had walked through the mud, seen the man in front of them shot in the head by a sniper's bullet and lost their friends and relatives along the way.

The lucky ones, like Naim and Hamida Karaga, found a space to crouch on the floor of a corridor in the school already packed with refugees from northern Bosnia. 'Everything we had was destroyed,' said Naim. 'We walked, drenched, there was shooting all around us . . . We'll have to stay here for a while, but not for long I think . . . Where to? God knows. Europe won't have us; that's clear, perhaps the Arab countries will look more kindly, but I'm not an Arab! Only one thing for sure, there won't be any Muslims left in Bosnia.'

Some people, unable to bear the confusion and the driving rain, elected to go on, to wherever was further down the road. All night and throughout the following two days little convoys of carts, horses, lorries, tractors, sheep, cattle and men and women on foot, set off again aimlessly, out onto the road, the Muslims heading east to Zenica, the Croats south towards Herzegovina.

But most who went back out onto the road were without destinations, like Safet, who said that he would take his father and his fine riding horse on, walking, but would have to leave behind his cart and the old carthorse Miki where he was grazing beside a rubbish tip. 'He's done well, but he's just too tired to go any further,' said Safet, 'we'll just have to say goodbye here.'

Chapter Eleven

Sarajevo, from Siege to Torture

*'We are very satisfied with your military interven-
tion,' said Jasmin Hamzar, a petrol pump attendant,
'tell Mr Bush thank you very much.'*
— card player's message to the *New York Times*
from a Sarajevo bomb shelter[1]

The city had changed since spring. By October 1992
Sarajevo was not just under siege — the Serbs could have
taken it if they had really wanted to — it was on the rack.
The capital had become a torture chamber and the daily
dealing out of death, injury and mourning had become
an endurance test beyond physical loss and suffering. The
shelling was cynical and calculated to terrify as well as to
kill. One evening, coming back with driver Hasan, a mortar
sliced the air over our heads and hewed into a block of flats
just ahead, sending up the usual puff of grey smoke. The
people scattered, as they now knew how, and began to
run past us on the road, away from the explosion. Hasan
did an estimable U-turn and was making to drive back,
along with the flow of people, when a sudden second shell
came in, a hundred yards ahead, right in the path of those
running instinctively away from the first; clever, nasty and
deliberate. Hasan hastily found a third route out, so it was
only later we learned that two lives had been taken by that
little game of cat-and-mouse.

It was always hard to understand those who talked about 'getting used' to shelling. Of course, one's capacity for self-control and common sense expands with each experience of shellfire. But the looks on the faces that peered round the hollowed-out doorways of the flats in between those two shells that evening showed nothing that could be described as 'getting used' to the sound of those grey metal cases landing, exploding and splintering into flying shrapnel. People looked out as though the air itself was menacing them and could tear their bodies to shreds, their faces vitrified in the frozen effort of concentration and fear.

Now the bus depot on the Tito boulevard was a litter of rusting mechanical skeletons. Every wall of every building was, if it remained at all, pock-marked and splattered with shellfire. Whole blocks of flats had been reduced to blackened concrete or steel with a few isolated floors maybe still habitable, and the fine twin towers opposite the Holiday Inn had been incinerated by raging fires, left like towering twin monuments to the city's destruction.

By now people knew the ropes. They knew exactly where to start sprinting with their shopping bags, and when to slow down again into what was becoming the more forlorn trudge. They had learned to start running for cover when their own side sent mortars out from its dugouts. They would still stand captivated when the boys' valuable ordnance climbed the hillside and plunged into the greenery behind the enemy's lines, but very quickly they would then scatter into the doorways and alleyways, even though it was quiet, because they knew that what goes out must come back, multiplied many times over.

At the end of summer, the UN 'information' machine started playing strange games. The city's pulse had quickened with the Americans' talk of intervention, and the UN political staff were wary of the climate. A UN report was ostentatiously leaked which blamed the Bosnian Army for some of the most notable atrocities of recent months in

Sarajevo. 'Muslims', for instance, were accused of shelling the cemetery during the funeral of the two children trying to leave on the Children's Embassy convoy. Off-the-record briefings featured the possibility that 'Muslims' had also shot up the buses in the first place. 'Muslims' were even blamed for the bread-queue massacre in May. The idea was that 'Muslims' would mount these spectacles in order to win over world opinion and increase the pressure for military intervention. The suggestions were all made *sotto voce*. A senior civilian affairs officer in Sarajevo, an agreeable Icelander called Mik Magnusson, was forever dropping hints, not for attribution, about dark 'Muslim' motives for attacking their own people. The director of civilian affairs in Zagreb, Cedric Thornberry, would organise briefings through his German secretary at which he would advise, unattributably, on not only the dangers of military intervention but also the 'Muslims' interests in firing out from near UN installations in order to invite return fire back at the UN troops. When the ABC camerman Dave Kaplan was shot dead by a sniper on the airport road (under constant Serbian fire), UN officials said the killing was 'unlikely' to have been the work of Serbian snipers. The UN's curious behaviour persisted despite the fact that its own soldiers were coming under fire from Serbian guns.

This turbid war of words caused consternation among the Bosnian soldiers, one of whom banged his head against a brick wall in frustrated disbelief when he heard his own army was blamed for the bread-queue massacre; 'If I believed for a moment we were killing our own people, do you think I'd be here?'[2]

The opening of the London conference had been marked by a mortar attack on a refugee hostel, the Europa. Two were killed immediately, and others shot as refugees tried to flee the blazing building. Within a week, the Bosnian Army attempted to break the lines around the western outskirts and pressed the Serbs back a few houses, in territory where the rival trenches sometimes faced each other across a back garden. The immediate reprisal for such audacity was a heavy 105mm shell aimed right in the middle of the marketplace while it was bustling with people looking for something affordable to eat. Television cameras showed the butchery that followed: elderly victims torn limb from limb, lying in pools of blood between the stalls, then loaded onto lorries to be taken away.

But the long-term response was even more significant: the Serbs mobilised ten tanks, hidden from the UN armoury monitors, for a push which only came to final fruition several months later to cut the road which linked the airport to the city. On 8 December, the first Serbian tanks moved onto the road, slicing the city's lifeline to the outside world. UN troops trying to get down 'Sniper Alley' to the airfield were fired upon and neighbouring homes pounded by tank shells. The local UN commander, General Hussein Abdul al Razek, said the UN mission in the city had 'failed completely' and that the UN should consider intervention with force to stop the amputation of the airport link.[3] Just as Serbian tanks severed the airport road, Pale, the Bosnian–Serb 'capital', went on a simultaneous propaganda offensive, with an offer to civilians: they should prepare to leave if they wished, for safe passage out was guaranteed. The flip-side was a perverse appeal to the outside world: life in Sarajevo was becoming impossible, bleated the Serbs, because of 'famine and cold weather'. The UN command replied that it would play no part in 'ethnic cleansing' the city.

Sarajevo's own mass media somehow managed to keep going, as did its attempts at a cultural life. A run of the musical 'Hair' was somehow put on and local radio was thriving, not least because of a new service: 'War Recipes', with hints on window-box vegetable growing, stretching the contents of a UN food parcel and the health risks of eating the pigeons that flew around Sarajevo. There is a show on Bosnian TV now called 'The Little Survival

School', which specialises in making UN food packs taste spicier. The only trouble is that no one has the power needed to watch television.

Extraordinarily, the daily paper *Oslobodjenje* – Liberation – was still published from a bombed-out building, once one of Sarajevo's modern architectural showpieces, on the exposed western edges of the city. The paper lost two journalists in the fighting, and came to be showered with international awards for its remarkable gallantry in linking Sarajevans to the rest of the war and the world outside. The paper had been founded along with the federal republic in 1943, and now its driving forces were the figurehead and editor, Kemal Kurspahić, a tactful man wounded in the leg when he crashed his car in a sniper attack, and his sharp-witted deputy Gordana Knežević, who describes herself as an 'anti-fascist Serb'. The paper's political line was supportive of the government in the last resort, but tended tortuously towards the more youthful radical stance of its tireless staff.

There was one particular group of young people setting out to resist the Sarajevo siege with a freshness of attitude that astonishes in retrospect even more than it did on first meeting. The peculiarity and magnetism of war is that amidst the violence and despair things like Radio Zid emerge; at the start of 1993 it was preparing to hit the airwaves. 'Zid' means 'Wall', and 'Radio Sarajevo Wall' was founded by a leader of 'alternative' Sarajevo called Zdravko Grebo.

Sarajevo's street life and the 'urban' lifestyle were now held hostage in the back rooms of incinerated blocks of flats. Under such conditions, Radio Zid set out to put the café conversations, the bar-room debates and the art-room banter on air as a rock-and-roll station. Zid's logo shows a comic strip figure with one bare foot, a rough smock and scruffy hair trying to heave away a brick wall with the strength of his shoulder. The studio is a room at the foot of a shabby block of low-rise flats opposite the home of the army commander and down the road from a multi-storey car park full of mortared cars pillaged for spare parts.

In between doses of Bob Dylan and what was called 'Yugo-rock', Radio Zid featured discussions seeking to define a 'Rationalism and urban mentality' which might emerge from the war. They were often serious, sometimes funny and usually irreverent towards the government. There were tirades against ethnic intolerance; attempts to make sense of why the 'liberation' of Eastern Europe had gone wrong. Grebo's 'International Manifesto' of Radio Zid, written in English, is one of the more original documents to emerge from any war. To the Western eye it recalls the outmoded vocabulary of 1968, but this was not written from a pampered student commonroom at the Sorbonne.

> Dear Friend,
> You must have seen more than once the images of dev-
> astated and massacred Bosnia-Herzegovina, and among
> these the singularly horrifying images of Sarajevo. But
> what could not be recognised in those images was
> the slaughtering of the civic spirit and culture of
> the country's urban parts. The demolished buildings,
> collapsed bridges and other edifices will be restored
> more easily than *the urban and civilisational spirit* that
> had been created over the centuries.
> Deeply aware of such grave reality, Zid in Sarajevo
> has started a media project that is primarily a *mission
> of cultural and spiritual renewal*. That project is a local
> (FM) radio station ('*Urban Radio*') whose *spiritus
> movens* is striving for democratic principles, spirit of
> tolerance, civic norms of behaviour. This Sarajevo
> identity is in crisis today, as is everything else to
> that matter.
> Why the name 'Radio Sarajevo Zid'? Not long
> ago, there was a town divided by a wall. The wall
> was toppled down and millions around the globe
> thought that the world had made a step closer to
> Utopia. Then the war in Bosnia-Herzegovina started.
> Sarajevo is not divided by a wall, Sarajevo is divided
> by hatred. Nationalistic fanatysm and madness emanated
> by people that have never been Sarajevans, who have

never been citizens. This whole city, together with
other Bosnian-Herzegovinian towns, has become a
wall. *The wall* in front of which the consience and
morale of the world's mighty ones is stopped, unable
to go over it.

As an independent radio station, *Radio Sarajevo Zid*
shall have a defined *autonomous political attitude*. It will
not come from any ideology, dogma, party codex. It
will not be a mere instrument of a holy scripture to
the disobedient reality. The political attitude will be the
attitude of common sense, of social sagacity based on basic
European idea of *rationalism and urban mentality* ...
And last but not least, that spirit is trying to preserve
sense of humour.

Sarajevo was by now fighting its own war. It was the
capital of a state that had been hewn to pieces and continued
to resist as a symbol of that state's doomed will to survive,
but estranged from the war that was raging in the rural
outback. Winter drew in, and every tree that lined the
boulevards and the patches of green was cut down for
fuel. In November, the first cases of typhus arrived at the
hospital. The snow fell two days after Christmas, but it was
a mercifully mild winter. The Bosnians now played their
own progaganda card, and the face on the card was that
of Borislav Herak. Herak was a Serbian prisoner-of-war
whose confessions were tape-recorded by his captors; he
was also extensively interviewed by John F. Burns of the
New York Times, and this is what he said, for instance, about
the occasion when he and two other soldiers gunned down
ten members of a Muslim family at Ahatovići, five miles
from his prison cell:

'We told them not to be afraid, we wouldn't do anything
to them, they should just stand in front of the wall. But
it was taken for granted among us that they should be
killed, so when somebody said "Shoot!", I swung round
and pulled the trigger three times on automatic fire. I
remember the little girl with the red dress hiding behind
her granny ... We were told that Ahatovići must be a

cleansed Serbian territory.' The family had been found cowering in their basement before Herak and his friends found them.

Herak recounts all this, on tape and to Burns, in a matter-of-fact way which contrasts with the way he recalls slitting the throats of three soldiers taken prisoner by his 'Serbian Volunteers'. One of the three was called Osman: 'I have pictures in my mind of many things I did, and they return every night. I sleep, I wake up in a sweat, I sleep again, I wake up and smoke, and Osman is always there. I have dreamed at least ten times of Osman saying "Please don't kill me, I have a wife and two small children."'

The Bosnians accused Herak of killing twenty-one other Muslims by his own hand and playing a part in, or bearing witness to, 220 other murders. He told his captors about a massacre of 120 men, women and children in a field near Vogošća in which the victims' corpses were taken to a pit, doused with petrol and burned. Burns heard that Herak also witnessed the incineration of thirty men from a Muslim village called Donja Bioča; some had been shot before being slung into the oven, but others were bundled in alive. Herak also details the use of Muslims as 'human shields' in battle, and saw the bodies of 60 men killed after being used as body protection for Serbian troops on the Zuč mountain outside Sarajevo.

But how to transform a man from an unremarkable background into a cogwheel of a deranged killing machine? There is a clue: drill sessions on a farm near Vogošća, at which Herak and two other young men were trained by an older soldier to wrestle pigs, pin them to the ground with their heads held back by their ears and then cut their throats.[4]

There were eight further charges against Borislav Herak. He had confessed to raping and murdering eight women. He said that men were encouraged by their superior officers to rape women and to kill them afterwards. But

Herak's eight victims were not isolated cases; they were part of one of the most abominable facets of the Serbian progrom which was only now beginning to come painfully to light.

Chapter Twelve

Rape – 'Reward against the Innocent'

In March 1993, Maggie O'Kane of the *Guardian* found Sabrija Gerović and her daughter Samira at a hospital in Tuzla:

'Her hair was in a pony tail, and she had big brown eyes that gave no hint. The doctor's report noted that Samira was born in 1989, that she had difficulty urinating and defecating and that she had been sexually violated. Samira told her mother that "a man touched me". She never spoke of it again . . . Purple puncture marks on Sabrija Gerović's breast where she says she was bitten when she was raped, and a gynaecologist's report of her child's broken hymen are the only evidence of her testimony.'

Mrs Gerović tells the story of what happened one night at a chicken farm near Cerska, where she and ten other women were held. Two men came into the room and took her daughter:

'She was gone for twenty-four hours. At midnight the next night a man came in and told me to come and take my child. I went into a room. It was empty and there was only a table. They told me to take off my clothes and I was completely naked and there were seven of them. Then they all raped me. They had been drinking, but only two of them were really drunk. One of them was biting at my breasts . . .

'There was a curtain across the room, and when they had

finished, they said: "Go and get your baby," I went behind the curtain, her head was blue and she had foam on her mouth. She had no pants and there was lots of blood streaming down her legs, and I knew they had raped her.'[1]

The first victims of multiple rape by Serbian soldiers began to arrive in Zagreb as early as August 1992, sent from Trnopolje camp to Travnik, and then out through Split. Their pleas that such violations were 'typical' were largely overlooked in the cyclone of violence and in the assumption that rape was part of the conduct of any war. In Trnopolje, to our shame, we had not even asked about mass rape, although prisoners did refer to girls being 'taken away'. But as refugees kept arriving in Travnik, Zenica and Sarajevo, evidence emerged of a debauched and monstrous progrom: the systematic violation of women and their detention for that purpose, as well as wanton rape when Serbian soldiers stormed and took Muslim and Croatian villages.

A centre was established in Zenica to take testimonies on what it called 'rape and other abuses against women, girls and female children of non-Serbian nationality', and what emerged was a programme integral to the genocidal violation of one people by another. The exact figures are incalculable and were even tastelessly haggled over by journalists and various propaganda interests. For what do they matter; it is beyond doubt that several thousand women, girls and even children were, as the Zenica commission puts it, 'served to the Chetniks for the satisfaction of their low instincts'. Months later, an EC investigation into the accounts of mass rape, led by the retired diplomat Dame Anne Warburton, concluded that some 20,000 women had suffered sexual violation. Testimonies of rape of Serbian women at the hands of Bosnian Government soldiers were subsequently made in Belgrade.

The Zenica centre also sought to offer what psychological, gynaecological and theraputic support was possible, and to organise the transfer of some of the victims to hospitals in

Zagreb. From there, some remained together in Croatian refugee camps, others dispersed. Many became pregnant, and either aborted or gave their babies away for adoption. This is the story of one of them:

Nezira (not her real name) now lives in Slovenia, at Maribor close to the Austrian border. She shares a flat with her cousin, married to an electrician from Ljubliana.

Maybe Nezira did once have the terrified, injured face of the women photographed upon their arrival in Zenica to break news of the horrors of the rape camps; after all, Nezira was one of them, although not photographed. She is a composed woman, aged twenty-six, but appears older; serious and sorrowful but not morose. She speaks with a quiet, fixed concentration, almost completely lacking in overt emotion. This is how she recalls her last weeks in her home town of Rogatica:

'When the Chetniks were taking people from their houses, inhabitants were separated into three loose groups. Men, the elderly, and then most younger women, who were told to stay. I would be lying if I said I didn't suspect what was going to happen because of course I did, we were not stupid. We were not treated roughly at first, more with a mixture of roughness and politeness which made me sick and scared.

'I have made a long and detailed statement to the Genocide Centre in Zenica, and I am not going to go through the exact details again. But I will tell you that we were taken to the local school. We were first made to sit in the lobby before being assigned classrooms with blankets on the floor, and there were already some women there. We didn't have to ask what was going on. In fact we barely spoke. The women were between fourteen and thirty-five years old, most of the younger girls I presumed had been virgins. Some were mothers and daughters. There were about twenty to twenty-five of us in three classrooms.

'On the first night, nothing happened. They even gave us some food. On the second night, it began. They came in after 11 o'clock, after fighting or drinking, or both. They would come to the classroom, and nod, point or shine torches at the girls or women they wanted. The first violence was when one mother tried to stop a man with red hair taking her daughter away. They kicked her against the wall. Although I knew what was going to happen, I was still surprised. The kind ones would say there was nothing to worry about if I did what they told me to. Others were violent, verbally and sexually, and foul-mouthed. They used to turn the tapes and radios up so other people would not hear the noise that was going on, especially when young girls were involved. They would insult us, insults which I cannot repeat to myself let alone to you.

'The first time I talked about what they did to me was in the kindergarten at Zenica to a woman from the genocide office. These things have been repeated by some women on television, but I don't think it is necessary for the exact details to be gone over because although these things may be printed with good intentions, they can be stimulating to some people who read them who have the same mentality as Chetniks.

'I will tell you that I was violated at least once every other night on average, for a number of weeks. This was in various places, buildings, houses and the command centre. Some of the men I knew by appearance. Women and girls used to come back to those classrooms beaten and exhausted, sometimes after an hour, sometimes not until morning. I myself just closed down as a human being.

'I became pregnant quite soon which was lucky in a way, because it meant that I was exchanged, with thirteen others. I was also lucky to be early enough to have an abortion, which others were not. I hated the thing inside me. In Zenica, they were very understanding, and a gynaecologist looked after us, and also the womens' group in Zagreb where they took us to another hospital and organised our papers. I have not had a single regret about having an abortion.'

*   *   *

Among the responses from the outside world was an appeal
by the Pope for the women to bear their babies, 'turning
an act of violence into one of love'. Lord Owen said at one
point that it was 'difficult to talk to the Serbs about this
kind of thing'.

The violation of women and girls took place either during
the ethnic cleansing purges, in homes, barracks or public
places, or else at the special 'camps'. Some victims reported
that they were told to 'go and deliver fighting Serbs'. The
centre at Zenica has accumulated evidence of seventeen
'rape camps', mainly in motels, schools, saw mills or private
houses. Other women were taken from their homes to the
fighting lines and subjected to 'the most bestial of abuses'.
In Foča, women tell of rape in public, in front of husbands
and children, neighbours and other soldiers.

The most infamous rape camp was the Kod Sonje, a
motel at Vogošća outside Sarajevo. Testimony gathered by
the commission includes that of a thirteen-year-old who was
raped in front of her mother and who later died. Other cafés
and motels were used, in Doboj and at Brčko, and schools
were used at Foča and Kalinovik as well as at Rogatica.
At a spa near Višegrad, the Hotel Vilina Vlas was used
to keep women as well as being a military headquarters.
Women were reported killed after being raped there, and
their bodies thrown into the Drina. In northern Bosnia,
women were taken from the Trnoplolje camp to be raped,
and kept for that purpose at a saw mill near Kozarac.

Among the hundreds of testimonies kept in Zenica is this
one of E.N., aged fourteen, from Foča, who testifies in the
presence of her mother:

'The commander was large, fat, dirty and grey haired,
with a white tuft on his forehead. He wore camouflage
uniform, and he smelled of brandy, he was stinking. He
nodded towards me and ordered me to stand up. He took
me to a room, my legs were shaking, and I could not walk
properly. He pushed me and everything inside me was
shaking. I thought he was going to cut my throat. Then

he asked me – she looks at her mother and asks if she can carry on with the narrative; her mother nods – "Have you ever fucked?" I said, Sir, please don't do that, I was begging him. He pushed me, and hit me and said "Get on the couch". Then he tore my dress and hit me again. Then he closed my mouth with his fist.'

The girl's mother now takes up the story. 'I heard my daughter screaming. She was calling me to rescue her from this maniac. I heard him grunting. My own womb was tearing apart. He was shouting "Have you had enough, bitch?" Then he left the room, and said angrily, "Don't anyone touch the girl!" In another room, the daughter of my sister was abused in the same way. One Chetnik watched me and my sister all the time, telling us not to shout. Then they said we could go in, and we found M. almost unconscious, and naked, and E. crying with torn clothes and injuries.'

To go on repeating the testimonies would be gratuitous; they cover every conceivable dark cranny of sexual sadism and male violence, and often overtly associate racial and sexual obscenity and subjugation in the most bestial manner. Children were often witnesses to the violation of their mothers, or else were close by. One account reads: 'He threw me into the pantry. My son was screaming at the door, he wanted to come in. I had my *dimije* on [traditional Muslim baggy trousers] and the Chetnik pushed me and said "Take off your *dimije*". I said I wouldn't. He said "Yes you will, or I'll kill you!" . . .'

Public humiliation of women is as prominent as brutish private gratification. One girl of fourteen was tied naked to a tank and driven around her village near Prijedor. After being raped, she was, as the collector of the testimony says, 'thrown in front of her parents so that they could see her half dead'.

The woman who received the women when they arrived in Zenica, who took their testimonies and co-ordinated the various projects to re-settle them into what passes for 'normal' life, is Selma Hećimović. A schoolteacher, she herself needs to control tearful anger when discussing the evidence. Each one, she says, 'is a scar across my soul'. There is little point in adding much more to this most pernicious chapter in Bosnia's war, beyond Selma's own reflections:

'We will never know the real truth, and we will never know what all these women have been through. This has gone further than a "war crime", this is not a war crime any more but an attempt to destroy a whole people. This isn't the kind of rape that is the consequence of any war, this is organised rape, a stage in a programme. Maybe people out there think rape camps have to be camps of the kind we used to see in films about the Second World War, organised by the Nazis. There aren't such camps. We regard a "camp" as a house or school or café or hospital in which they violated people.

'At the end, I get a bit tired of constantly having to *prove*. We had to prove genocide, we had to prove that our women are being raped, that our children have been killed. Every time I take a statement from these women, and you journalists want to interview them, I imagine those people, disinterested, sitting in a nice house with a hamburger and beer, switching channels on TV. I really don't know what else has to happen here, what further suffering the Muslims have to undergo – only because they want to live like the rest of the so-called civilised world – to make the so-called civilised world react.

'This is only my personal opinion, but it is the end of civilisation if somebody can do all these things and then be rewarded at the end.'

Chapter Thirteen

Fikret Alić Revisited

With his rib cage behind the barbed wire of Trnopolje, Fikret Alić had become the symbolic figure of the war, on every magazine cover and television screen in the world. We had met briefly at the camp, held a hurried and charged conversation, and it was strange to meet him again seven months later. He had fattened out a bit, but was immediately recognisable in the lobby of a hotel at Ljubliana, with the clean diagonal break to his front tooth and a look in his eyes somewhere between sadness and mischief.

After the greetings, the long conversation began at a bar in the centre of Ljubliana. Fikret is the son of a lumberjack, born in 1970 at the village of Alići in the Kozarac national park. He left school at fourteen, and trained as a weaver before national service and a job as a security guard at a mine. Fikret recalls his Serbian boss warning him of what was about to happen; 'He said "Alić, get out of here, you're not safe any more."' Fikret was picked up in the neighbouring village of Svici during a bloody assault by Serbian militiamen in which they systematically executed all prominent figures in the village, dynamited houses and took every male left alive to Kereterm camp.

There is a verb in Serbo-Croat: *'iživljavtise'*, which translates roughly as 'to inflict pain and to derive pleasure from doing so', and this is how Fikret introduces his description of Kereterm concentration camp. Quite apart from the massacre in Room Three, he says: 'We didn't have anything to think about, we only thought about when we were going to see the sun rise and the new shift arrive, because when they did it was always hell. On the second day, this man Zoran Žigić came, called out five of us with the family name of Alić and started beating us. We could endure that, but not when they started to cut us with knives. Then the killing started . . . In the mornings, there were bodies all over the parade ground. They used to switch on the headlights, and fire on people from a distance with anti-aircraft guns. Then they washed them down with cold water, loaded them onto a truck like cement, dead and wounded, and took them away. Or else they would just shoot at us inside the dormitory; we had to spend the whole night lying face down with our hands on our heads and if someone tried to get up, they would kill him. One man was killed sitting on the toilet just fifteen minutes after I had been in there.

'At one point, a UN van stopped right in front of the camp, and did a U-turn. We were all there, in the yard, but they didn't look at anybody. We were all stunned, and sad that they hadn't seen us.'

Fikret was transferred to Trnopolje, where our paths crossed. News of what happened after we had left came as a shock:

'It was the happiest day of my life when you came. We thought that after you had gone, they would stop beating us. However, next day a man called Hasan Karabašić was beaten and died. And then some of the people who had spoken to the journalists were killed. From Trnopolje, people were allowed to go to the village to get water, and they let this one group out and killed nine people. Most of them were the ones who had talked to the journalists. Two were shot by snipers, through the throats, I don't know how the others died.' Fikret thinks these deaths were 'nothing in comparison to how many you saved by coming that day' – but that is not for us to judge. The discovery that our visit cost the lives of nine men was a cruel reminder of how none of us could really be bystanders in this war.

Fikret himself went into hiding in the depths of the school compound:

'The Red Cross came with food, then more journalists, with all the papers and pictures of me. But I didn't see them, I was hiding, wondering whether I would survive or not, and planning to flee. People were to go to Croatia, but they only sent seven buses, for women, children and the elderly. Other buses came, and some of us dived onto the floor and hid among the women and children. I sat in the middle on the floor, and kept quiet. This was the bus to Travnik.'

Fikret took the same road as us, out over the mountains, off the bus at Smet and on foot to Turbe. 'I don't remember it all,' he says, 'I was so ill and exhausted, but I do remember crossing some awful rocky ground, and then when we were too tired to walk, some people came in cars to bring us to Travnik.'

We moved on from the bar to eat, which Fikret still did like a hungry dog, with the appetite of three. Not only had we taken the same road to Travnik, but there was another coincidence:

'At the barracks, a man smiled and said: "Hey, are you that guy who is on TV non-stop?" But I didn't know anything about this, and I couldn't believe it when he showed me the pictures. I knew who he was, a man who deserves a lot of gratitude, because he tried to organise resistance in the Prijedor area, Fahrudin Alihodžić.

'I had come to the barracks with my comrades, and we had put uniforms on. But this Fahrudin said I'd be no good for fighting in this state. He said there'd be no problems now, and told me to go to the Krajina unit, get food and accommodation, and recover. Then he fixed for me to go on a convoy with some other camp people to Zagreb. At first I hated seeing the picture of myself. I couldn't believe I had been through that and survived and was now free. I can't believe that I can greet people, have a chat and a coffee and there is no beating or kicking. I am disappointed to see that picture and be able to say that I am a free man. It is strange to be alive after that . . .

'Why? I was a normal guy with a modest kind of life, I lost my father as a child and was the breadwinner in the family. I worked to get money for my mother. And now I have nothing, and I hate those people. I never did anything to harm them. I hate Vjeko Žigić, who killed my grandfather and uncle, who had never harmed him. I never saw any difference between Serb or Muslim or anyone. But now I could never look at them or greet them or live with them again. We liked each other for forty-five years, and in the forty-sixth year, we hate each other.'

Part Three
Greater Croatia

Chapter Fourteen

Blackshirts and the Rule of Madness

Grude, in the baleful mountains of western Herzegovina, looks less like an imperial capital than almost any other place on earth. It consists essentially of a main street lined by ramshackle concrete and pebbledash cafés and shops, from which a dishevelment of other buildings crawl up and down the hillside. Along its sidewalks, gangs of boors strut or stagger, depending on the time of day or night, swinging their guns and clomping their heavy boots. There is no enemy for miles around, but the silence of night is invariably blessed with the rasping rattle of automatic weapons fire. It is an obdurate little town, and a stranger to good manners: people talk with a curl of the mouth, if at all. The windows of some of the cafés and shops are adorned with photocopied portraits of Ustasha dictator Ante Pavelíc. In winter the air feels especially sodden with damp and thick fog.

And yet this is the administrative centre and acting capital of a grand project called 'The Croatian Union of Herzeg-Bosna', an elaborate way of entitling the mini-state carved into Bosnia by the Croatians as a mirror-image of the Bosnia–Serb state declared at Banja Luka. The hotel in Grude has been converted: down the dimly-lit stairs and past the lout with his boots resting on the 'Reception Desk' is a large, sweaty basement adjoined by a meeting room which can be sealed off by drawing a sticky curtain. This is the imperial palace of 'Herzeg-Bosna', epicentre of the fiefdom over which Mate Boban – supermarket manager and mayor of Grude – set out to rule in July 1992.

Croatia was the first and most enthusiastic country to recognise the frontiers and government of Bosnia-Herzegovina in its secession from Yugoslavia. And yet from the beginning of the war, the flag that flew beside the ubiquitous checkpoints across Herzegovina was not that of its government, but one of two variations on the red-and-white chequerboard emblem of Croatia, known as the *Grb*. It featured either the insignia of the new country governed from Zagreb, or else the earlier version tainted by the Independent State of Croatia of 1941 to 1945.

When the Serbs began their offensive across Bosnia, the Herzegovinian Croats fought not under the auspices of the Bosnian Government Army, but in their own military formation the Croatian Defence Council, or HVO. The HVO was established with the suspicious approval of the Sarajevo government, and under its theoretical command, and for a while the cautious alliance held. In central Bosnia, while the two armies came under seperate commands their respective insignia would hang next to each other on buildings they shared. In some places the soldiers even crossed over the ethnic divide. The HVO in and around Mostar mustered hundreds of Muslims, not least because of its superior weaponry; the HVO was always better-equipped with armour if not with men since it shared suppliers with Croatia proper and enjoyed Croatia's access to 1,000 kilometres of coastline.

The alliance was formalised in July 1992 by an accord signed in Zagreb between Presidents Tudjman and Izetbegovíc, forging a joint military and political front. In yet another blunder, Izetbegovíc naively agreed to allow the army of Croatia proper to mobilise in support of the alliance within the frontiers of his country, and confirmed the HVO as an 'integral part' of its defence forces. The agreement was a confirmation of the existing arrangements, for several thousand 'volunteers' from Croatia proper were already fighting inside Bosnia with weapons brought in after the end of the war in Croatia. The weapons were Greek Gifts for Bosnia, but the alliance was was re-affirmed as late as September 1992 by a 'Defence Pact' against the Serbs agreed during peace talks in New York. Croatia, however, was cardsharping. Her ambitions within Bosnia were deliberately unclear in both agreements.

The alliance between the Bosnian Army and the HVO celebrated its zenith with the liberation of Mostar from two months of bombardment and part-occupation by the Serbs. A joint push across the Neretva river at the end of June drove the Yugoslav/Serbian army out of its strongholds in the old town on the east bank, and up into the hills. Although the Croatian government denied sending heavy guns as well as volunteers into Bosnia, there were now regular units and some hundred artillery pieces in Mostar belonging to the Zagreb army. 'The arms embargo,' said one Croatian officer to the *Daily Telegraph*'s Robert Fox, 'does not really affect us.'[1]

The cost of the Serbian retreat from east Mostar came to light weeks later, when mass graves were found with the remains of 200 putrid corpses in them. The dead were mainly Muslims, with some Croatians. The pathologist who inspected the bodies said they had been shot with automatic weapons at close range; that is to say a massacre, which included women and elderly men. The victims were caught in villages through which the Serbs had retreated.[2]

The fighting left Mostar shattered and under siege from the new Serbian lines. It had been one of Bosnia's most beautiful cities, an ancient settlement nestled deep in the valley and astride the Neretva, with its renowned Turkish marketplace and the Ottoman bridge, a symbol of the republic's oriental heritage. The bridge's architect, Hajrudin, was threatened by his employer, Sultan Sulejman the Magnificent, with execution if it fell down. It had survived thirty earthquakes, graced a million tourist postcards and was now covered by a corrugated iron roof, constructed by citizens anxious to protect it from the shelling, which began reliably and ferociously each evening.

'If you had come here four months ago, you would have seen children playing, women walking with prams, and people with their dogs in the morning,' said Sead Vidimilíc, a militiaman with the Government Army surveying 200 makeshift graves in what was the little park on the newer west side. The graves were earth mounds capped with either crosses or crescents, bearing dedications like that 'To the Unknown Man from Žitomoslíci'. Some empty holes had been dug, awaiting their occupants.

The liberation of Mostar concealed the imminent break-up of the alliance. At their meeting in Graz in May, Mate Boban and Radovan Karadžíc agreed to a rolling series of bilateral negotiations on the future borders between their territories, and how much might be left to the Muslims. Karadžíc was keener than Boban to discuss the progress, saying they had agreed to trade territory in order to 'delineate' their respective borders.

At the beginning of July, the Croats founded their 'Union of Herzeg-Bosna'. The new (unelected) authority would be based at Grude although the plan was for Mostar to assume its role as capital as soon as the city could be 'secured'. Sarajevo was outraged: Defence Minister Jovan Divjak called the move 'a knife in our back which will seriously undermine our defences'. An editorial in *Oslobodjenje* said the declaration was 'a direct result of talks between Milošević and Tudjman'. The Bosnian Serbs, however, heartily welcomed the development. Karadžić praised what he called an 'expression of their right to self-determination' by his Croatian counterparts.

'Herzeg-Bosna' was an initiative from Herzegovina, with the backing of Zagreb, but did not speak for all of Bosnia's Croats. Further up country, in the capital especially, Croats did not necessarily share the brusque bully-boy culture of Herzegovina, notably one of the three Croatian members of the rotating Bosnian presidency, Stjepan Kljuić: 'This,'

he said, 'is outright treason.' Kljuić now works out of a
dingy basement wearing a bow tie and slightly foppish suit.
Soon after the declaration of 'Herzeg-Bosna', his position
as Croatian representitive on the presidency was taken from
him and given to a Boban nominee, on Tudjman's express
orders. Kljuić tells his story with a ponderous sorrow. He
set up the Sarajevo branch of Tudjman's HDZ party, elected
at an assembly in Mostar in 1991 to be its representitive in
the new republic. Mate Boban had been among the losers
to Kljuić in the vote; he conceded defeat and kissed the
victor. 'It was Judas's kiss,' says Kljuić now. Kljuić was
close to Tudjman, and had his trust. 'But Tudjman,' he
says now, 'began to arrange the partition of Bosnia by
negotiation with the Serbs. I could not agree with this.'
The Bosnian and Croatian wings of the HDZ met in secret
on the border: 'They were all against any alliance with
the Muslims,' recalls Kljuić; he resigned and Mate Boban
moved into the vacuum. By now the HDZ had become the
viper in Bosnia's bosom; and the president of the Bosnian
Croats in all but name was now the supermarket manager
from Grude.

Boban loves to say that 'Herzeg-Bosna' was established in
the spirit of the European Community, and, surrounded by
his uncouth, grunting cohorts, makes a sortie into political
philosophy to explain why it was necessary to subvert the
Sarajevo government in the interests of democracy: 'The
Muslims,' he says, 'want a citizens' state, without specific
rights for Nations [*narods*]. They guarantee Rights of the
Individual, but not of the *narod*. For this reason, it was
necessary to create a community spiritually, culturally and
economically tied to Croatia, because we are historically
part of that *narod*, but unfortunately separated by historical
circumstances. There is no bond with Sarajevo while it is
working against the Croatian people.' So, the Sarajevo
government was now 'the Muslims' and the principle of
individual liberty was 'working against the Croatian people'.
'Bosnia-Herzegovina,' he concluded, in resonant language,

'is historically a living space for the Croatian *narod*. But the contemporary world does not recognise these facts. Never in history has a multi-ethnic state been organised on unitary lines. We are taking steps to ensure our right to decide our own future. This time we are equipped and armed to secure the freedom of the Croatian people.'

It took a long time for Mate Boban's HVO to stamp its authority on 'Herzeg-Bosna', and to collect up the farrago of thugs into the ranks of a single army. In the meantime, the region was a lawless embroilment of militias, fighting their own wars against each other amid what would become a bedlam of violence. There was the HVO, the Bosnian Army (each with its own military police); the fascist HOS, and any number of free range groups like the Croat 'Falcons', 'Yellow Ants', 'Black Legion' and whatever. The roads on the way into Mostar told their own story: some were manned by the HVO or its military police; others by HOS, very few by the official Government Army and most were minded by men in camouflage but with no markings of any kind, and some by gunmen with no uniforms at all – just the local gang, armed to the teeth. The atmosphere was menacing in the extreme, the quiet broken only by the odd crack of inexplicable local gunfire, the thudding of the Serbian shells into Mostar and the clomping of boots.

The various factions had no argument over driving out the Serbs, but there were plenty of other things to divide them among themselves, often to do with the plethora of Mafia, blackmarket and arms deals for which Herzegovina was becoming the Balkan crossroads. For the moment, the worst internecine violence was between two wings of the Croatian side, Boban's HVO and the fascists HOS. The conflict was between those who wanted partition (backed by Tudjman and Boban) and those who didn't. While Boban was negotiating with the Serbs, HOS was loyal to the unity of the country in the hope that all of it may become a component in Greater Croatia. Things became so serious that in mid-August nine members of HOS, including its commander General Blaž Krajlević, were gunned down at an HVO roadblock. For a week after the roadblock killings, there was a sabre-rattling mood at HOS headquarters in Ljubuški. Black-clad sentries with sunglasses and berets, their machine guns to attention, hung their heads each side of a shrine on which candles burned in honour of the dead. Inside, no one wore anything that was not black, with Catholic rosaries around the fighters' necks and fascist girls (also in black) manning a radio station playing sullen patriotic music. Milan Dedaković, hero of the defence of Vukovar, had been drafted in to be the organisation's military strategist. He was a raucous, vainglorious bantamcock who confessed humbly: 'I have a character of steel. We are absolutely not interested in politics or political dealing. The Muslim parties and the HVO are interested in power and in doing deals. We are only interested in fighting Serbs. Whenever our units enter a village, the enemy civilians flee from us. The only people who stay on are a few Chetnik irregulars, which makes our task easier. This area of Herzegovina is now clean. There is no open resistance left.'

Dedaković believed that the heroic defence of Vukovar, of which he was commander, had been sold out by Zagreb in a deal with the Serbs. Now fighting in Bosnia, he believed that a similar deal was being done to divide and 'sell out' that country, which happened to be perfectly correct. The difference between Mr Boban's HVO and the HOS was that for HOS, Greater Croatia was even bigger than that organised at the various Serbo-Croat carve-up meetings. 'The carve-up,' Dedaković protested, 'would leave 55 per cent of Croats outside Croatian rule' – also true. The united Bosnia, he said, was a 'first step' towards the aim of the greater Greater Croatia. Because of HOS's ferocious anti-Serbian stance, the organisation was, extraordinarily, one third Muslim. Young Muslims were impressed by the bravado and by the commitment to national unity.

But back in the park-come-graveyard in Mostar, Bosnian soldier Sead Vidlimlić said as he surveyed the wreckage of his town, and the posses of various militiamen stomping up and down: 'Poor Mostar is paying a high price for these divisions'. Indeed it was. Mostar had come under a rule of madness, the real Beirut of the Balkans. At the locked entrance to the block of flats where Sead's family live, a civilian sentry is stationed. People rarely go out, and instead socialise on the stairwell where tables and chairs are set. There was the Panetić family, Serbs who had remained. Sead's family were their Muslim neighbours, and both families downstairs were Croats. 'It was the extremists on our side who started this war,' admitted the Serbian Mrs Panetić, at coffee with her Croatian and Muslim friends on the landing as her compatriots in the hills sent in the first shells of the evening. 'And as a result, the innocent on our side are suffering the consequences. Everyone suffers in the end. Everyone is terrified to talk or to tell other people who their neighbours are. The only thing to do is to stay in the shadows. They are taking people to the tribunals, Serbs and anyone else they might suspect. The various police forces take them away. Some come back, others don't.'

'These people are Serbs and they are our friends,' said Sead's Muslim mother and the Croatians in the company nod their agreement. 'We know there are Chetniks and fifth columnists in town, but we also know that they are not Mr and Mrs Panetić. We are all afraid of the tribunals.' The Serbian fifth column was looking for 'collaborators'; the Bosnian Army was looking for the Serbian fifth column, the HVO was looking for Serbs, 'fundamentalist' Muslims, HOS or even Croats who had shunned them and fought with the Muslims. HOS was looking for the 'partitionists'. Under the law of the freelance gun, protection rackets were rife in town, and everybody was looking for money.

Most of all, the hunt was on for Serbian civilians that could be captured and used as hostages in the 'prisoner exchange' business booming in the Herzegovinian outback. Human beings could be exchanged with the Serbs for other human beings, cadavers or money. And another of HOS's functions was the running of the 'prisons' in which this currency was stored.

'Let that remain a secret,' said Major Miro Hrstić, in his black uniform with the Ustasha symbol on his cap. 'You cannot know everything. A journalist is like a soldier. The less you know, the longer you live.' It was a straightforward enough warning.

The secret was this: a warehouse in the middle of a prison compound staffed by HOS. The concrete building with metal doors would be an oven in the heat, and appeared to be a shed for munitions or stores in the now disused Yugoslav army barracks at Dretelj near Čapljina, south of Mostar. The steel door was half open. A guard said the shed was full of provisions. It was not. Through the door, scores of women were visible, crouched on the floor around the wall of the dark shed, on or beside matresses, confined in a narrow space. Some gazed wearily up into the brilliant sunlight of the doorway as we walked past. They looked desolate and subjugated. It was a quick but conclusive glance, but nothing more. One of the six black-shirted guards who accompanied us with machine guns slammed the metal door, echoing the major's view that 'you do not have to see everything'. The atmosphere was not conducive to argument; the authorities' hospitality came to a decisive end.

Both HOS and the HVO said they only detained prisoners of war captured with weapons. Access to the HOS camp had been granted by Dedaković, 'not just with my blessing, but on my orders', in an attempt to rival Dr Karadžić's unfulfilled offer to make free inspections of the infinately worse Serbian camps. 'We are holding only fighters,' said Dedaković. We arrived at the camp escorted by a HOS 'staff car' sporting a portrait of Ante Pavelić and treated by Major Hrstić to a history of massacres and 'war crimes' committed against Croats by the British during the Second World War. Major Hrstić explained that 'you cannot interview the prisoners unsupervised'. A conversation with women internees working in the kitchen was cut short when one woman started to say: 'It's all a terrible mistake, my husband is a Muslim, and . . .'

As we entered a male 'PoW' shed at the end of the compound, about 120 prisoners ranged around the inside wall on mattresses stood obediently to slouched attention. They were a pitiful sight, though in better condition than their counterparts in Omarska. They showed no signs of beating, but were thin, horribly browbeaten and constrained. Hand-picked interviewees were brought forward to speak. One was a teacher, Momčilo Micić. While anxious not to offend the major, he clarified that some or many were civilians; he had been taken out of his flat by gunmen eight weeks beforehand. Another Serb was even more eager to please, and said that he 'understood the fight of the *narod* to be in their own land'. As we went away, the order was barked: 'Sit!', to which the men replied in grim unison, 'Thank You' before lowering themselves to the floor.

Although HOS was in control of daily drill at the camp, there was an oddity: the prison doctor arrived in a car marked 'HV', identifying it as belonging to the army of Croatia proper. The doctor, who declined to give his name, said: 'I am not HOS', as though to distance himself from the rabble, 'I am a member of the army of Croatia'.

The filthy, cramped prison beneath the official HVO police station in Ljubuški contained, said police commander Rudolf Jarkec, 'only prisoners of war'. His charge included some unlikely 'prisoners of war', however, and his own jailer, 'Charlie' Ereš, said that only twenty-one out of the ninety-six current prisoners were soldiers. 'There are no women here,' said Commander Jarkec. 'They all had weapons when they were taken, and were fighting on the other side.' In one tiny cell were a mother, Mrs Kojnević, and her daughter Dariuka aged sixteen. They had been fleeing the fighting at Tusovići during the liberation of Mostar when the neighbour driving them was shot and killed. The two of them had been held at Čapljina police station for two months, and thence to Ljubuški. 'It is like a bad dream,' cried the schoolgirl, 'I do not believe it is happening. I wish I knew why I was being kept here. Why is this happening?' She spent her time, she said, writing poems 'about love'. Unsupervised interviews were allowed with seven men in a basement room measuring twenty-five by eight feet. They were unlikely soldiers, variously aged in their fifties and late sixties. They received a thirty gramme sachet of fish paste plus a plate of beans a day. A man called Djuro from Mostar said: 'We were taken from our homes and from the streets. I was watching television. They said "We want you for exchange, nothing else." I've been waiting four months.'

Although 'Herzeg-Bosna' was for the moment an incoherent mêlée of militias, there was a clear driving motive behind its creation: to expand its boundaries and secure steady annexation to Croatia proper that would not offend the 'international community'. And although the HOS was an important military organisation, the real powers in the territory were Boban and his HVO. The border with Croatia was one of Europe's flimsiest; only aid convoys, foreign cars or cars from Muslim towns were seriously checked. The flag was the Croatian flag, goods were bought in Croatian currency (or else Deutschmarks) and new 'Herzeg-Bosna' number plates were being manufactured for issue in the new year, showing the Croatian flag.

A subtle pattern of fighting was emerging, which signalled the impending carve-up; the Muslims were being militarily squeezed out. The HVO was moving into Muslim-controlled areas in which there were more Croats than Serbs; this was Croatian territory. The Serbs were taking Muslim-controlled areas in which there were more Serbs than Croats; this was Serbian territory. In October, Karadžić and the new Serbo-Yugoslav president Dobrica Ćosić said they were ready for a ceasefire with the Croats, and without a document being signed, fighting between the two all but stopped across most of Bosnia. It was one of the very few truces to work.

'To achieve their partition of Bosnia,' reflected the moderate Croat Stepjan Kljuić in Sarajevo, 'Tudjman and Boban need to talk with Milošević and Karadžić. Dealing with the people who still occupy one third of Croatia! They strike compromises over maps. The Serbs have now all but completed their war against the Muslims, and have "cleansed" most of the land they want. But not Tudjman and Boban; they have not yet started the war they need to fight to "cleanse" their part of this country. The agreements by my former colleagues with the Serbs makes war between the Croats and the Muslims inevitable.'

What was less predictable was the suddenness and the ferocity with which the Bosnian Croats would strike against their allies, and the perverse encouragement they were to receive from the international community.

Chapter Fifteen

A Knife in the Back

The word '*prozor*' means 'window', and the little town of Prozor was thus baptised because it sits deep in a valley beside an azure lake at the gateway to central Bosnia, down the valleys from Travnik and at the northern tip of Herzegovina. When we drove through Prozon on the afternoon of Friday 23 october 1992, the Croatians were coming out of late Mass, women in their traditional black-and-white peasant dresses and headscarves, and the Muslim and Croatian couples were walking their children home in the last of the autumn sunshine. The Muslim cafés were open for business, and people took coffee at the sidewalk tables. The church bell was ringing and at the far end of town, the minaret of the mosque rose against the steep, lush mountainside towards a clear, deep sunset sky.

Prozor was a safe distance from the Serbian front line and undamaged, although both Croats and Muslims had for six months been fighting together against the common enemy. It was a town of 15,000, one third of them Muslim, sitting on what had become known as the 'Road of Salvation' along which winter aid was to be shipped up to the desperate, predominantly Muslim towns of central Bosnia. Fighting in Mostar had closed the main road towards Sarajevo and made this route a crucial supply line to the capital as well. Whoever controlled this road controlled access to food and ammunition.

When we returned four days later, Prozor was suddenly

and horribly transformed. Almost every Muslim house was
either torched into a charred wreck, or else smashed by tank
and shell fire from the hills above. The Muslim cafés along
the main street were sprayed with machine gun bullets and
ransacked. Every single window in the Muslim quarter was
smashed or sprayed with gunfire, and the brickwork of their
houses was blackened, the sickly smell of fresh fires hanging
in the damp air. The shops were empty apart from beefy
HVO soldiers helping themselves to drinks, packet foods
and fruit. While children played and young girls chatted
on the walls of the Croatian side of town as though
nothing had happened, the only people to be seen in
the centre were teams of strolling Croatian militiamen.
One long-haired bruiser was trying out the remains of a
child's bicycle, but disguarded it as beyond use by kicking
it roughly against a wall. Some wore Nazi regalia, most
wore the official chequerboard of the HVO. Each trooper
wore a red ribbon tied to his epaulette to distinguish him as
the gangs moved into town to complete their operation. A
spokesman for the HVO at its base in Tomislavgrad issued
a statement saying simply: 'Prozor is now cleansed and
under control'. Under the leaden dusk, a dead horse lay
in the road leading out of town. Human bodies reported
lying in the street earlier in the day had apparently been
moved.

Conversation with the hard-faced gunmen was not easy.
'The Mujahadeen [the new word for the Government Army
in "Herzeg-Bosna"] tried to fight us,' said one cocksure
trooper. 'We won.' But a rough chronology could be
pieced together: There had been an argument with the
local Government Army over supply trucks passing up to
central Bosnia. HVO units had arrived from Tomislavgrad
at the edge of Prozor on Friday evening and subjected the
town centre and Muslim quarter to an all-night artillery
barrage. Then, as dawn broke and people started to flee,
mobs had moved into town, firing willy-nilly, and then
begun to torch, loot and 'cleanse' the town. A huge,

fresh graffiti, in English, had been painted up on a wall: 'CRO TERRITORY', it proclaimed. One awful question remained, impossible to answer that night: Where were the 5,000 Muslims of Prozor?

We made it up to Travnik, to try to glean some clue from the Government Army headquarters. 'We have no idea where they have gone,' said Commander Haso Ribo, who in one month had turned from a teddy bear-ish Tank Corps officer into the troubled ganger of a desperate army. 'All we know is that all Muslims have left the town. Some have presumably fled, but others were seen being removed in groups under guard, and we are trying to locate them. It is my assumption that ethnic cleansing has now started in this area, but we are so mixed in heareabouts that I don't know how it could come into anybody's head to try. We do not want this conflict. All I can do is to appeal to whoever is giving these orders to please stop it.' The road to Travnik itself had completely changed. One month previously, it had been crammed with heaving aid lorries, and it was being widened and laid with tarmac in preparation for the winter. Tonight, it was almost empty, and the building equipment idle. Instead of the bustle of road works, a new maze of front lines was being staked out: hundreds of Croatians had taken over a hilltop beyond Prozor, and had brought up heavy guns looking northwards towards the predominantly Muslim villages. In the valleys, new roadblocks had been mounted by nervous soldiers of the Government Army, manifestly unprepared for what was about to be thrown at them.

Next day, we set out in search of the missing 5,000, and turning down a road from Prozor towards Muslim Jablanica came upon a pathetic procession of women with their children wandering through the rain, lost, soaked and lachrymose. 'How many are you? What happened?' A minicab driver from Prozor pulled up and advised us all to get off the road quickly. Croatian patrols were moving up and down, taking or killing anyone they could find.

The cabbie told us to follow him up a rough and winding mountain track, if we wanted our questions answered.

'We are looking for caves in which to hide,' said Farida, one of the bedraggled procession making its way up the track in what was now no man's land, her clothes and bedroom slippers drenched. 'I have lost my three children; someone came and put them in a car when we were running away from the machine guns. I don't know where they went. We have been walking these hills for three nights now, living in the forest, looking for caves to keep us dry where the soldiers cannot find us – ' and she was cut short by her own tears. They were roaming the mountainsides in their pitiful hundreds, if not thousands, looking for their families and without food or shelter, the escapees of bombardment, killing, looting and expulsion by the gunmen of Tomislavgrad and Prozor.

There were reports of a massacre, with people saying they had seen columns of men, women and children being

The Croat push
Oct 92 – June 93

- Serbs
- HVO push against Muslims
- Muslim-Croat alliance holds or Muslims keep control

CROATIA

Bihać
Prijedor
Banja Luka
BOSNIA -HERZEGOVINA
Tuzla
Maglaj
Jajce
Zenica
Travnik
Vitez
Srebrenica
Gornji Vakuf
Kiseljak
Žepa
Prozor
Sarajevo
Jablanica
Gorazde
Tomislavgrad
Foca
Grude
Mostar
Capljina
SERBIA
MONTENEGRO

0   30 miles

marched out of town at gunpoint by HVO guards. One man said he had seen captured Muslims forced to load the bodies of their dead onto a trailer being drawn out of town by tractor. Escapees said they had seen bodies lining the streets as they fled. Looking out across the bleak landscape, there was an extraordinary sight to behold: groups of figures meandering around the distant slopes, visible only for the brightly coloured cloth of their dresses, wandering and wondering whether to try to find a way back to their savaged town, or to stay up in the cold, wet wild.

'I was at home when it began,' said Nadja Avdić, a woman in her fifties, barely able to speak for bewilderment. 'The shell hit our house, and we went down the basement. Next morning, they came into town, shooting everywhere. My son grabbed me and we came out through a sewer ditch while they were firing all around. Other people were running out of town on the road above us; some of them made it, others fell.'

Nadja, her hair flat and dripping and her sodden shirt clinging to her shoulders, was hiding in a tiny mountain hamlet protected by boyish government soldiers, who had themselves been pushed back towards the hillsides. 'My husband works in the hospital, and I have no idea where he is,' continued Nadja, 'They have taken him away. I also have three other children and my grandmother, and I simply don't know where they are. The soldiers came in so quickly people just ran as fast as they could. I came here barefoot and in my nightdress. The clothes were given to me by people in this village. All I have left is the key to my basement,' and she brandished it, the last pathetic token from a home of three generations now burned to the ground.

A soldier called Sadan said he had seen the bodies loaded onto trailers during the late morning, and towed away. Another elderly man called Arif Ćimić said captives had been forced to help with the loading, 'No one knows how many were killed,' he said, his eyes haunted with confused grief, 'We were just running as fast as we could to get out.

All we know is that there are no Muslims left in town and hardly any of us know where our families are.'

'All our Croat neighbours,' said Sadan, 'left their houses on the Friday afternoon. When they did so, we thought the Chetniks were preparing something. Some of them even said that, but they didn't tell us to go too! Then we thought something was wrong when leading Muslims had their houses burned on that same first evening.'

'Mine was burned that first night,' said Nusret, who had owned the hardware store on the main street. 'We were their first target, anybody in town who owned property, had some standing or taught in the school. The headmaster, I have heard, is dead. I do not know what the Croats want. We agreed to everything. We accepted their state and their flag in our town. We fought alongside them for months. And now this. When they came into town, there were people shouting down megaphones: "Come lads, get them, it's the filthy gypsies."' An old man with a beret mumbled under his breath, 'There is no going back to Prozor now.'

Perhaps he had some idea what the town looked and felt like as we drove back through it: burned out, a heavy silence, and one group of rowdy churls making a souvenir video of their handiwork. Some of them posed outside a small bombed supermarket, displaying their swag to the camera operated by one of their colleagues. On the road back from the mountains into town, from which the cabbie had hustled us away, was a car which had not been there before, which had obviously wheeled out of control, crashed and been abandoned. The driver was nowhere to be found; the windscreen had been shattered by two bullets.

The mountain road back to Tomislavgrad that night was lined with trucks carrying their loads of HVO troops, packed tight and returning home after a job well done. They held their bottles of beer and slivovic aloft, swung them in unison and swigged a toast to their achievement. Even above the chugging of their wagons, the valleys rung with the swaying choruses of their victory songs. In town that night, there was a festive atmosphere.

One was never allowed to forget for a minute that Tomislavgrad was the Coronation site of the ruler of the great Croatia from 925 to 928. And the town had by now decided to fulfil its destiny by becoming Operations Headquarters for the push north into Muslim territory that was being prepared by the authorities of 'Herzeg-Bosna'. To the Herzegovinians, King Tomislav's abode is the nearest place to the Elysian fields save Medjugorje; to the outsider, it is an insalubrious slum at the heart of the Heart of Darkness. The streets and bars had become meeting places for freebooters and crooks of every shape and size. The bar of the King Tomislav Hotel was the intersection between the Herzegovinians and foreign mercenaries rallying to Mate Boban's squalid cause. They wore cowboy hats with their black uniforms, or else fatigues or a combination of camouflage and jeans. They parked their guns against the walls before settling down to beer-drinking sessions and perhaps the odd song. Conversation with journalists was usually reluctant and straightforward, like that with Damir from Imotski just over the Croatian border: 'You British have your nation. The Serbs have their nation. We have a nation, which is here. The Muslims do not have a nation. How can you call a religion a nation? . . . Oh you saw Prozor that day? It was the Chetniks who did that.' (The same line on Prozor had been spun by the respected Split newspaper, *Slobodna Dalmacija* – 'Free Dalmatia'. It was a lie.)

Not everyone in the King Tomislav bar and its adjacent restaurant was Croatian. Underneath a tawdry painting of the coronation of King Tomislav, three unmannerly young men were devouring meat and chips, speaking another language; they had shaven heads and spiders' webs tatooed onto their necks, and other heraldic tatoos on their arms. Gunter, Manfred and Eberhardt were quite happy to chat. They had come from Hannover to 'fight for Croatia' against

'Turkish Muslims and communists'. They had arrived the previous day and had had their meeting with the HVO's Canadian–Croat deputy commander that morning. It had gone well; they were all set to join up. After a few banalities about the Libian threat in Bosnia, we moved onto the lads' domestic problems back home, notably 'big problems with immigration', which vexed the boys and seemed to require a reference to Germany's generous asylum laws, then in place. 'That law is a Jewish law,' Gunter kindly enlightened us, 'passed by Jews.' We moved quickly on to a discussion about soccer over a further glass of beer.

Tomislavgrad was temporarily blessed with another, unforgettable and more sociable visitor, and that was the representative of the European Community Monitoring Mission, to whom we decided the Prozor atrocity should be promptly reported. The EC monitors, dressed in crisp, laundered white, were a varied bunch, sometimes genial, more often arrogant, sometimes efficacious and sometimes ineffective. But Geoff Beaumont in Tomislavgrad was something special. 'Five thousand Muslims, mainly women and children, in the hills looking for caves,' we told him, dutifully. Beaumont, a tall, inscrutable man with blond hair, a stoical smile and big ears, started up from his chair: 'Were they armed?' he enquired, hurrying over to his map to locate the moutainside in question, felt-tip marker in hand. To Geoff Beaumont, '5,000 Muslims' constituted a guerilla army.

Beaumont described himself proudly, in a confident colonial accent which had gone through the best of the British educational system, as a 'White Wog'. Born in Kenya, he had served as a 'senior officer' in the British army, but would not say where, to which rank or in which regiment (which usually means the SAS), and was enjoying his new job enormously. He had made good local contacts, and it was he who later introduced us to the HVO's commander in Tomislavgrad, Joko Šiljeg, the colonel with the twelve maps of Croatia down the centuries. Beaumont's room was a little different from that furnished for the usual EC Monitor, who

Tearing Bosnia apart

Above: Fikret Alić, Trnopolje camp, August 1992
Below: Manjača camp, August 1992

Trnopolje

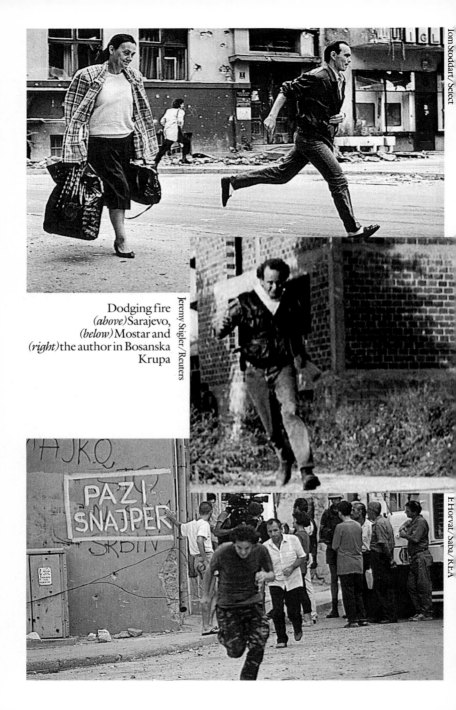

Dodging fire
(above) Sarajevo,
(below) Mostar and
(right) the author in Bosanska
Krupa

Tom Stoddart/Select

Jeremy Stigter/Reuters

E Horvat/Saba/RExA

Above: Hundreds of women reached Zenica, Sarajevo and Zagreb with
accounts of mass rape by soldiers, sometimes over periods of months
Below: Another family mourns in Sarajevo

Above: Men of the 1st Battalion 22 Cheshire Regiment arrive in Vitez,
October 1992
Below: In the war of ethnic cleansing, millions of Bosnians were turned out
of their homes and wandered the mountains in search of safety

Above: Get out: a Bosnian Croat soldier in Prozor warns off reporters after the expulsion of Muslims from the town in October 1992 began Bosnia's second war – between Croats and Muslims
Below: Muslim bodies: the war comes to Vitez

Above: Surrender: Srebrenica, April 1993
Below: Defending the remains of Muslim Mostar, September 1993

has at his disposal all the facilities (indeed, luxuries) he needs or wants. Beaumont's room contained the following: one low-scale laminated map of Bosnia-Herzegovina, covered with felt pen markings showing detailed troop movements, daily updated; one pair of black British army boots polished to shining perfection (which combined interestingly with the Monitors' all-white uniform); a dependable supply of black boot polish; a bottle of Scotch, a cassette player and tapes of Isaac Asimov reading his own science fiction novels, and of early baroque music of the mathematically pleasing variety; and finally a zip folder, which he now picked up off the floor with the simple but puzzling announcement: 'I am ready to move across this country without a vehicle'.

The zip folder contained Monitor Beaumont's survival kit: the usual supply of sterile medical equpiment, blades, compass and tools. Beaumont described the function of each article with a blend of pleasure and quiet pride, fixing his impervious smile, until he got to a piece of wire with two handles at either end and a marble-sized ball welded into the middle. This was EC Monitor Beaumont's garotte, should he ever need one. 'And look!' he said getting up off the floor and heading for the door, 'It can be used as a saw', and he held both handles tight, flipped the wire over the top of the hotel bedroom door and began, with a see-saw motion of each hand, splicing the wood. We returned many times to enjoy an evening with Geoff Beaumont, always pleased to find him but half expecting to look up a mountain slope from the road one day to behold a figure dressed in white, a slaughtered sheep across his shoulders, moving across country without a vehicle. Instead, we returned one day to learn that instead the European Community had very sadly transferred him to Hungary.

The sacking of Prozor was the beginning of the second war of civilian ethnic cleansing, but the war between the HVO and the Government Army had already started. A few days before the fusillade against Prozor, the first serious battle between the soldiers began, centred, of course, on the crossroads of the war, in Travnik, or rather in the satellite town of Novi or 'New' Travnik. It was strange, crouching behind a wall for a good hour while the Croats strafed the government positions with anti-aircraft rockets, to think that for the first time in months of war in former Yugoslavia, the Serbs were not involved. Indeed, the Croats and the government had turned against each other right under the barrels of the silent and waiting Serbian guns arraigned on the mountain tops above them. The Serbs were simply watching and listening.

The fighting broke out the day after Mate Boban had declared Travnik, with its Muslim majority, part of 'Herzeg-Bosna', and simultaneously moved a huge number of Croatian troops up from Tomislavgrad into the Travnik area. For a time now, Boban had been edging the ill-defined northern frontiers of 'Herzeg-Bosna' beyond Herzegovina and deeper into central Bosnia, engulfing mixed communities and the city of Jablanica, which was 70 per cent Muslim. The fighting in Novi Travnik was the first armed consolidation of Croatian territorial ambitions beyond its Herzegovinian heartland. 'It is,' said Emir Tica, 'the beginning of the end of the war against the Serbs. It is completely mad.'

The fighting began after a row at a petrol station. Under the etiquette of the Croatian–Bosnian government alliance, fuel supplies were shared. This particular Wednesday, a Croatian officer had refused to give the Bosnians their share. There had been an argument and the Bosnian soldier was shot dead. Within hours, the two sides were fighting. That night, smoke was billowing up from the town centre, and the madness spread; first to Vitez, next town along the valley, and then followed the Lašva River towards Sarajevo. Within three days, fifty people were dead, and at Travnik hospital it was clear who the inevitable victims of this latest war would be. Among the wounded filling the corridor of the underground wards were two young boys: Salko Halep, a twelve-year-old Muslim, was crying with pain after shrapnel had ripped his stomach open; next to Salko was Ante, a Croatian boy also aged twelve, with a gaping sniper's wound in his right leg.

The day after Boban ignited the fighting in Novi Travnik, the HVO headquarters in Mostar issued a statement saying it would not tolerate 'Muslim extremists' in any area where there were Croatian citizens. The HVO command simultaneously declared that it no longer recognised the legitimacy of the Sarajevo government or its defence forces. Three days later, the HVO suddenly clenched Mostar in an armed vice-grip, giving the Government Army an ultimatum to either come under direct Croatian command or to hand over its weapons, and HVO units were despatched to seize key civil and military installations.

The Mostar ultimatum came on the very day that Boban now wrested official control of the HDZ party in Bosnia from the moderate Stjepan Kljuić. The following evening, with Kljuić neutralised, Mr Boban told us in the basement of his headquarters, with a newly decisive tone: 'We have our political platform, and anyone who disagrees with it will either have to step down or leave in some other manner. Not a single Croat will participate in the Geneva talks other than those you see in my company and or authorised by my signature.' He concluded by pronouncing for the first time that: 'I do not recognise the army of the republic of Bosnia–Herzegovina. It is a purely Muslim militia. We, the HVO, are the only effective army in the freed territory. If they want to call themselves the Bosnian Army, that's their business.' In Mostar, he declared bullishly, 'They must come under our authority.'

On the ground in Mostar that weekend, the putsch had impregnated the most important city in the region, in which Muslims were still the biggest population group, with the embryo of the vicious urban civil war which would explode months later. There was no more than a little fighting, and no casualties thanks to the naivety and restraint of the Government Army, but there was an ugly tension which could only spiral in one direction; downwards. The HVO commander Miljenko Lasić had sent teams fanning out across the city, erected a cordon sanitaire of thugs around his headquarters, and produced Scotch whisky over which to tell us that his troops would be 'much stronger and better organised if we removed the Bosnian Army altogether from Mostar. I told them yesterday, they are free to remove themselves from the front lines.' Squads of his soldiers were moving around in trucks and buses taking over the courthouse, police station and main post office and telephone buildings. The Muslim SDA party headquarters was raided and the guard outside it disarmed. The Bosnian Army was asked to move its headquarters from the west bank of the river across to the exposed east bank, beneath the barrels of the Serbian guns.

The speed of the HVO's coup was such as to persuade President Izetbegović, forever weakening, to say that he would consider an ethnic division of Bosnia in order to maintain some agreement with the Croats. But on the ground, his lieutenants in Mostar accepted the challenge. There was an atmosphere of enraged bewilderment at army headquarters, of hurried coming and going, and acute anxiety. HVO soldiers had marched in and smashed and confiscated the broadcasting equipment used to transmit the army's radio service. 'We just had to watch them,' said the commander's bodyguard, Emil. 'What kind of humiliation is that? They just walked in, pointed their guns at us, tore it apart and walked out again. We had orders not to resist them, but there's little chance they'll hold because people are too charged up; I didn't know whether to shoot them or not.'

The situation was complicated by the fact that a number of Muslims in Mostar had joined the HVO because it was better armed. In Mostar, the HVO was 15 per cent Muslim, in Stolac to the south, it was 90 per cent Muslim.

The Government Army also contained several Croats and some Serbs who remained within its ranks as a matter of political choice. Emil the bodyguard was a Croat come to study and live in Mostar: 'The Muslims are being offered the chance to be "Croats of Muslim faith". That is the exact flip-side of what the Serbs were offering them,' he said. 'I just want to defend this country. What am I supposed to do if the Croats are marching around telling me I can't have a weapon even though I am a soldier? Yes Sir, No Sir, Three Bags Full Sir? If I refuse to surrender, that makes me a Muslim fundamentalist, even though I'm from Zagreb!'

Emil's commander Arif Pašaljić is one of the central figures in the war. The day he lost his radio transmitter, General Pašaljić laid down for us the response to the Croats which was to remain the army's line and ultimately lead it into facing one of the most brutal offensives of the entire war, the Croatian siege of eastern Mostar. 'We will not lay down our arms,' he said. 'How can you do that in the middle of a war? This is not local squabbling. It is a systematic coup by one of the two forces defending this city. We cannot give up our weapons, and this can only lead to war within the city.'

The non-military columns of Muslim society in Mostar were equally concerned, as civic buildings filled up with refugees newly cast out of their accommodation within the city itself. The headquarters of the Muslim council were now teeming with hapless families who had fled the Serbs into the city and were now expelled from their temporary accommodation because they did not have HVO-issued permits to stay there. The council's president, Faruk Ćupina, a former lawyer decked out in the odd combination of military fatigues and a smart brief case, tried to be as judicious as his quiet rage allowed him to be: 'Of course it is too early to talk about "ethnic cleansing" or anything comparable to what the Serbs have done to us. "Herzeg-Bosna" is so far a tragi-comic farce. But there is a tumour spreading through the body of our Croatian neighbours, and we hope that together we can cut it out before it kills off the body of the people with whom we have lived and wish to continue living.'

General Pašaljic's deputy, a secular old military sage called Captain Tetak, was at work in a bunker beneath the barracks. That day, in prophecy of the war as yet unborn, he said this: 'Now our allies are turning against us, and just look at their maps, and those of the Serbs: there is nothing for us to do except fight for our own survival. If we Muslims do become the Palestinians of the next decade, a people without land, then there is little else we can do but fight as Muslims. I have to think that it will not be like that. There must be a world out there – the West, the democratic world, the Arab world, the UN – somebody who will say: "enough!" Meanwhile, we still stand for an indivisible society in Bosnia, in which all three peoples live equally, and we shall fight for it against whoever, but I don't know how long that will be realistic. If the HVO wants our guns, it will have to come and get them. If the Croats insist on this course, all that will happen is that everything so far, the killing and rape, will get worse. And it will certainly mean war within Mostar.' This was October 1992.

The Croatians did insist, and the second war spread like a dry savannah fire across southern and central Bosnia. And into the early stages of this inferno marched the soldiers of another army, the British army.

Chapter Sixteen

Meanwhile the Diplomats: A Foreign Field that is Forever England

For a while, the diplomats had to yield the international limelight to the men they had despatched into the field, the soldiers of the United Nations Protection Force, or UNPROFOR.

'We shall be smart, we shall clean our boots and we shall salute the ladies,' promised Martin Forgrave, a debonnair Captain with the First Battalion, 22 Cheshire Regiment of the British army which hoisted its colours and the Union flag outside a schoolhouse in Vitez late in October 1992. 'And although soldiers here do not normally salute each other,' observed Captain Forgrave, 'we shall salute them, and already they are starting to salute back. It is very important that we have the right image. Politeness and professionalism will be our watchwords.' Goodness knows what bewilderment the wizened old peasant women and the gun-toting backwoodsmen felt when confronted by the display of resolute courtesy that was unfolding before them.

It was a damp autumn night, with a pluvial fog in the air, when about a dozen officers and men from the Cheshires first camped down on the floor of the school gymnasium to inaugurate 'Operation Grapple'. After months of war in the inhospitable Balkan hills, it was extraordinary to be asked politely if I would like a cup of tea, and in a reedy accent from the Lancashire dales about the Liverpool versus Manchester United result. Meanwhile, the French were bunkering down in Sarajevo and the Spanish in Mostar, with Belgian, Dutch and Norwegian soldiers at other bases. The Serbs refused to allow Canadians into Banja Luka, and they eventually set up at Visoko in central Bosnia.

During the careful preparations, Vitez had been chosen by the British as a good forward base because of its advanced position up the aid supply line it was mandated to secure, and also for its relative security behind the Travnik front line, in safe Croat–Muslim alliance territory. The calculations could not have foreseen the sudden outbreak of the fighting between the Croats and the Government Army, which erupted the very week the Cheshires arrived. 'We had quite a show last night,' said a corporal dutifully fixing a local child's bicycle while his comrades watched the exchanges of fire from the schoolhouse doorway.

The army's brief was to secure routes along which winter aid was to be shipped north to the packed towns of Tuzla, Zenica, Travnik and the villages in between, and to ensure its delivery. The problem was that the route came through Prozor, Gornij Vakuf, Novi Travnik and Vitez, the corridor of conflict. And so from day one, the Cheshires' task was to stretch the mandate with a series of delicate tasks: meeting the warring leaders, crossing their battle lines, clearing their road blocks, all of which had to come under the title of 'Liaison Work'. The liaison officers could not have been a more level-headed and affable bunch, ready to put their best foot forward. On their second night in town, we sat over steaming PG Tips at a table in the school gym to go over the implications of a steady machine gun dialogue in progress outside.

'Well, it's certainly an eye-opener,' said Captain Bob Ryan, a stalwart type. 'We have not been shot at, but we've been shot near to, over and in between. We have to keep calm and be seen to be taking it, and do our job getting to know people and making sure they know who we are.' The British had run into what was cooly described as 'fire across the bows' by Captain Simon Ellis, an officer of sanguine conviviality. 'We were deliberately crossing the lines in order to meet and deal with both sides. We are here to help the United Nations deliver aid and I think people understand this. However, these incidents could hamper their effort. If the aid does not get through, both sides must understand that it is their people who will suffer.'

'Route Diamond' was the name given to the sixty miles of dirt track that was the aid route running up from Tomislavgrad to Vitez, quickly baptised as 'The Ho Chi Minh Trail'. This was the route the HVO was determined to control so that while advancing its frontiers northwards, it would also have its hands on the tap that switched the aid on and off, and could divert supplies to its own communities. By late November, sappers from the Royal Engineers were working with local contractors to turn the rocky paths into roads capable of handling the convoys of relief trucks which were to serve all of landlocked central Bosnia, and if need be Sarajevo.

By their own admission, the soldiers were going to be eyed with suspicion by both sides. 'There is an assumption that you are assisting the other side,' said Captain Forgrave, 'the idea that if you are not with us you are against us.' Reactions to the troops' arrival among the citizens of Vitez, Tomislavgrad and Travnik were varied. Down in Tomislavgrad, where the Royal Engineers and others were establishing a logistical base, we checked in at the HVO's military police station one night and asked how our army was settling in. 'British army is communist army,' grunted the Croatian soldier in English. 'Winston Churchill war criminal.' We reported the observation to a stoical captain from the Engineers over dinner: 'So we're communists now are we,' he sighed. 'British man is fuck-man,' said a Croatian bravo on an HVO checkpoint in Vitez. 'They have Bolshevik Protestant army in Ireland.' The boys from Manchester were underwhelmed.

Meanwhile, however, the children enjoyed running down the garden paths to wave at the impressive authority of the white Land Rovers with their radio masts and UN flags, even if some did prefer to offer a Nazi salute. There was some good soccer in the school playground between the British soldiers and the local lads, and a tournament was planned between a British army team and sides compiled by each of the warring communities. The superior British players were advised that drawn games would make for the desired results in the matches they played.

Among the Muslims and the Government Army, the reception was a little more approving, if only because it was hoped that the Protection Force might be a thin end of the wedge of military intervention. And yet it was a Bosnian Army roadblock in Vitez which was the first to feel the gale-force, boisterous authority of the Cheshires' Commanding Officer, Lieutenant Colonel Robert 'Bob' Stewart. His party of Land Rovers was greeted by an *Armija* roadblock as it chugged down the main street on day three of the Cheshires' tour of duty, a bus parked across the thoroughfare. '*What's this?*' thundered Colonel Stewart, six inches from the face of the bemused local soldier, who mumbled something about manning his checkpoint. '*Well move it!*' shouted Stewart, and the soldier did, immediately.

Colonel Bob, as he asked to be called, climbed the stairway of the school to inspect his and the officers' new quarters on the first floor. 'Right, we'll have a proper officers' mess in this room for a start,' he ordered as he breezed along the corridor between the classrooms. 'I want some brandy sent with the next supplies, and I mean good brandy. Also beer; there will be an allowance of two beers per soldier per evening', and he smiled at the idea as though to say that this rationing might not be too strict, and need not apply to the officers' mess and its guests.

Colonel Bob became one of the flamboyant figures of

the war in central Bosnia, universally known, and held in either famous or infamous awe by the locals. He had a bombastic, confident manner, was very much his own man and to those who liked him epitomised the mix of lofty decency, precision, efficiency and a stubborn sense of almost imperial, upright morality that characterises what is best about the British army. The popular British press of course took more interest in a love affair between Colonel Bob and a Red Cross charity worker called Claire, from Switzerland, than the fact that he liked, as soldiers say, to 'lead from the front'. He had to be involved, and he manifestly enjoyed being involved.

Stewart was a pleasantly immodest man who had no fear of talking on or off the record about what he felt about his task and the conditions for its execution – which was only partly appreciated by the first army press officers who arrived to funnel the system of information and briefings which had already been informally established at Colonel Bob's late-night, fairly boozy 'Sit. Reps' (as we would call them in cheerful mockery of the military jargon for 'Situation Report') in the converted classroom. Colonel Bob liked to tell a good yarn, spicing his tales with the inimitable humour nurtured at public school, Sandhurst and through the ranks of military authority.

'The key thing is to stop people fighting each other,' said Bob, laying out his manifesto one evening, 'and to return them to some kind of civilised lifestyle instead of the anarchy that we have at the moment.' People are afraid because other people want to kill them for the simple reason that they live in or are trying to move across this area. Our task is to enforce the rule of law. I hope that by our very presence a British battalion can act as a deterrent to this killing. I met an old lady on the road today, clearly distressed, and I said to her: "We are here to look after you. You are a European, and the British people want us to look after you." We are here to assure people like her and to familiarise them with the standards of the British army. So don't be surprised when you see my regimental band marching along the high street down there!'

There was also the matter of escorting the UNHCR aid convoys, to which end Colonel Bob was already prepared to interpret the mandate beyond the cautious mumblings along the corridors of the Ministry of Defence in London, consistent only in their capacity to vacillate. 'I will not,' affirmed Colonel Bob, 'be forced off any road. There are all sorts of implied tasks, because I cannot be here in the middle of a battle and fulfil my mission. My mission is to get aid through, and nothing is going to stop it getting through. When the British army gives its word, it keeps it. If necessary I'll load up the aid in armoured vehicles and take it myself. There will be hitches, because this is not a perfect world, it is Bosnia.'

The armoured vehicles were Warriors, due to arrive in a matter of days and about which Stewart spoke with the enthusiasm and affection he no doubt bestowed on model aircraft when he was a boy. 'I love Warrior,' he admitted with a coy smile, 'for its fire power, protection and mobility. I don't want to have to use its fire power, but I will if I have to. I want the guns to be there and to act as a deterrent against anyone being silly. The protection is that which the British public expects for British soldiers, and it moves at forty miles an hour.

'It is a three-pronged plan. One: talk to the local people using the liason officers, and if necessary using armour to "talk" as well. Two: position Warrior and other means at my disposal along the route like a close picket. Three: run the convoy through, hopefully without having to fire. I want to use military power, not military force. But, I repeat, I won't be forced off any road by anyone.'

That was Colonel Stewart's bold plan, but even this language, when published, caused back room discomfort among the grey suits in London. 'Quite honestly I don't give a damn what they think,' retorted Stewart next morning, already enjoying his status as purveyor of tough but civilised standards, in contrast to the harum-scarum of Vitez and the flummery along Whitehall. 'Don't apologise! We have told these poor people we are professionals, and that is what we are.'

British officers would bring the warring commanders together, broker and negotiate their ceasefires and even try to enforce them. On one occasion, the truce was written down, passed around a table and counter-signed by one British officer and the tireless Anders Levinson of the UNHCR. A witness to the scene said: 'They were rather aghast at having to put their names to the document, but if they hadn't signed, no ceasefire.'

The unforgettable day that the refugees from fallen Jajce invaded every square foot of Travnik came during the British army's second full weekend in Bosnia. By then the liaison officers had become well known at Travnik command of both the *Armija* and HVO, and throughout the Saturday evening, British medical officers were working to treat the worst cases of exhuastion and sickness. It was a performance that would have caused bureaucratic eyebrows to be raised in alarm back at the Ministry, but which was saving lives on the ground. In a remarkable reversal of the normal role, a small circle of journalists willingly agreed not to report the Cheshires' more imaginative endeavours.

The soldiers' rules of engagement were: 'If we are fired upon, we do not fire back unless we are actually hit, and cannot extricate ourselves without casualties.' The first serious fire came during the terrifying afternoon of 7 November, near the outpost village of Ribnica, on the road to Tuzla, bombarded from Serbian front lines which skirted the route. The party of soldiers, unmistakable in bright sunshine, was ambushed by Serbian guns and mortar fire as it left the bombed-out village, and took some five minutes of sustained fire. Mercifully and against the odds, the attack claimed no casualties, but it did invoke the first return of fire by British troops, a decision endorsed and defended by Colonel Bob on the men's return to base.

The convoy of three clearly marked Land Rovers and two cars with reporters from the *Guardian*, Reuters and ITN, set out to examine the viability of routes and bridges along the mountain tracks being used by almost all traffic to Tuzla. After some hours of climbing up hill and down dale, the convoy passed through the Bosnian Army roadblock on the way out of Ribnica. A soldier called Hasan was waving and shouting at our car, which was bringing up the rear: 'Don't go that way! They'll shoot!' The usual route to Tuzla turned to the right, but the convoy was intent on examining the road ahead also. Thus warned, Andrej Gustinčić of Reuters and I accelerated alongside the army Land Rovers to try to alert the leading vehicle, but as we did so the first burst of fire came in.

Our convoy sped behind the cover of an embankment lining the road, where the Cheshires' senior officers, Bob Ryan and Mark Cooper, spread their maps over the bonnets and decided against carrying on into what was clearly the lion's mouth. The only thing to do was to use the shadow of the embankment to U-turn, and to run the gauntlet back. And run it we did: for about a mile we pressed accelerators through the floors while the rattle of machine guns followed us, peppering the bank at the side of the road. But that was only the beginning.

Rather than go back through the Bosnian roadblock to Ribnica, Captain Ryan instead turned left up the usual road to Tuzla, presuming that the move to which the Serbs had objected was the fact that we hadn't taken it in the first place – and we followed. But now came the main strafe of fire, with neither the Land Rover nor our battered, trusty Citroën able to make a clean about-turn in the narrow road. Captain Ryan manoeuvred his vehicle around first. Through the windscreen, all we could see while we waited were specs of dust rising in rapid succession in a line across the tarmac ahead – the bullets on automatic fire striking it just five metres in front of the car – as the air was filled by a mighty *rat-a-tat-tat* from somewhere out there. More bullets were hitting a farm building just off the road, masonry dust flying across our view. Then there was an explosion behind, a mortar or heavy gun shell rammming into the embankment; in the mirror I could see earth and debris hurled across our retreat path. All I can recall of any conversation we might have had above the rumpus was an oddly restrained 'Oh Shit' from my passenger Gustinčić. This interminable moment, unfolding in slow motion, lasted the time it took to execute a U-turn on mental auto-pilot, ramming the gears, and to beat it towards the junction and the Bosnian roadblock. The other vehicles were by now scattered all over the place, turning or else screaming back through the checkpoint. The sound was all screeching and gunfire; the smell was burned tyre rubber, burned gearboxes and burned masonry as we made it round the junction and through the roadblock to safety.

During the flight, the back doors of the Land Rovers were kicked open and the soldiers were rapid-firing out at the hills. One of them overtook us, and the passenger, Major Jamie Sage of the Royal Engineers Field Squadron, turned to us with an extraordinary, doughty grimace – action at last. Back into Bosnian territory, the British gunners leaped from their Land Rovers and bunkered down in the ditches ready to continue the exchange. The officers then inspected the neat holes made in their vehicles by the direct hits. 'Most unsociable of them,' said Major Sage, 'to use light artillery as well as small arms fire.'

It is strange how fear plays no part until later. Until you are out of that bedlam, there is only the accelerator pedal, the gearstick and a steering wheel, and the vague idea that you are still there and still moving. It must be worse for the passengers. Only later did we recall that we had sixty litres of petrol stored in jerry cans in the car boot, which would have turned us into a mobile car bomb had we been hit. From then onwards, reporters tended to move around in their own armoured cars, changing completely the nature of our coverage of the war.

A road to Tuzla was secured a week later, by another route. Using an escort of Scimitar armour, a smaller, lighter version of the Warrior, the British secured entry into the city for a huge convoy, greeted by waving and cheering children who probably thought that the guns atop the Scimitars had come to fight the Serbs, not merely to protect the relief trucks. On the way back, however, the trucks and the journalists' cars behind them were shot at again.

The convoys to Tuzla continued to cross the mountains, the UN stubbornly refusing to examine the option of securing the mothballed airport at Tuzla to which a second air corridor could have been opened. At the highest levels, UN spokesmen insisted that the land routes were the only way to deliver aid – a railway from the coast through Mostar to Sarajevo was also discounted.

In December, the first mortar shells were fired into the British base at Tomislavgrad. On thirteen January, an HVO sniper shot dead lance-corporal Wayne Edwards from Wrexham as he stuck his head out from a Warrior during work on clearing the aid route through Gornij Vakuf, strategically vital to the British task, and contested by the Croats and the Bosnian Army. The first British casualty fell on the day that another 'peace plan' failed in Geneva.

By the end of November, UN observers had recorded more than one hundred violations of the much-heralded No-Fly-Zone by the Serbian air force. Impotent, the UN Security Council ordered a feasibility study for another plan: 'Safe Havens', used to try to rescue the Kurds in northern Iraq. The plan might help stave off what the UN's increasingly awkward Polish human rights envoy Tadeusz Mazowiecki was now describing as a risk of 'extermination' facing the Muslims, and ease the West's embarrassing dilemma over millions of refugees. If Muslims were 'safe' in their 'havens', then what was the obligation to accept them? However, Safe Havens would entail massive reinforcements of troops and a rethink of the UNPROFOR mandate.

The UNHCR was immediately cautious, with José Maria Mendiluce insisting on 'the need to distinguish between safe havens and ghettoes'. The Serbs were enthusiastic: the idea of having reduced the majority ethnic group in the country to the status of the stateless Kurds had considerable appeal, and 'Safe Havens' would be good places, acceptable to the international community in which to dump any Muslims left on Serbian territory. The Croats were mute, and did not need to become involved in the debate, since the international community was about to bestow on them a bounty that went beyond their wildest dreams.

Lord David Owen had written to John Major before being invited to replace Lord Carrington, saying there was a 'moral obligation' that the UN be given the option of military intervention if it was the 'only way to stop the carnage'. He later said that he had accepted the post only because it was clear that Vance was in no way going to 'aquiesce in ethnic cleansing'. As late as December 1992, he said that on ethnic cleansing 'no compromises are possible'.[1] To establish 'Safe Havens', he added, would be to 'make ourselves accomplices to this evil of ethnic cleansing'.[2]

At Geneva, Owen found little or no movement in talks between President Izetbegović and the two rebel leaders, and the UN was running out of ideas and interest. The man who had commanded the UN toops in Sarajevo for six months, General Adnan Abdelrazek, declared publicly: 'All our efforts here to save lives and restore utilities have completely failed.' The general, to Owen's annoyance, added his voice to the increasing clamour for military intervention, as the EC heads of state prepared for their next summit in Edinburgh.[3] The Americans were also using language that Lord Owen disliked intensely. In Little Rock, Arkansas, the triumphant President-Elect Bill Clinton said the time had come to 'turn on the heat' against the Serbs, although the complication of Croatia's ambitions seemed to have eluded his teenaged enthusiasm. The acting secretary of state Lawrence Eagleburger, who had been US ambassador to Belgrade and close to Milošević, toured Europe's capitals in December with Bosnia top of the agenda, telling reticent Europeans that Washington was ready to use military power to enforce the black joke of the derided No-Fly-Zone.

As Christmas approached, Eagleburger succeeded in breaking down British opposition to getting serious about the exclusion zone, and won clearance for Bosnian skies to be patrolled by NATO aircraft. Serbian planes violating the exclusion zone could be shot down, something which alarmed the demurring British, who secured a 'warning time' clause and stifled a further American proposal that allied planes be able to bomb Serbian air bases in pre-emptive strikes as well. Karadžić, spotting the listless link in the allied chain, wrote John Major a letter saying the shooting down of Serbian planes would constitute an act of war and would mean the end of safe passage for humanitarian convoys and endanger UNPROFOR troops on the ground, a conclusive argument that Major felt obliged to listen to. This was Serbian blackmail specially tailored for London, and blackmail which the Americans – who had assigned no soldiers – had little right to pontificate over. Karadžić's letter worked a treat.

Eagleburger emerged from the NATO Foreign Ministers meeting in Brussels on 17 December having presented his blueprint for a no-nonsense policy on Serbian bombers, admitting that 'there are differences among the allies'. Only Holland shared America's desire for a robust stand. British Foreign Secretary Douglas Hurd, aware of Karadžić's threat to John Major, said the exclusion zone could only be enforced if there were safety guarantees for humanitarian convoys and UNPROFOR. It was a piece of pettifoggery of course: Karadžić's letter was probably in his briefcase. Hurd instead placed his faith in forthcoming Serbian elections and 'a change of government or policy in Belgrade'. Hurd's opponent in the British Parliament, the interventionist Liberal leader Paddy Ashdown, now invoked the envy of his armchair-tied colleagues by being attacked outside

Travnik on his latest fact-finding mission, and was able to make the swashbuckling public statement that 'One mortar round is just like any other.'

The Serbs, panicking as usual in the face of American sabre-rattling, set about their own diplomatic initiative aimed primarily at Moscow. The plan was lucrative: a series of meetings in Belgrade and the Russian capital succeeded in testing the friendship between Moscow and the West, playing the Orthodox card and getting the Russians to plead for more time while supposedly well-intentioned Belgrade brought its wild Bosnian brothers to heel. Europe was unable to see the transparent guile of the Serbian–Russian tango. Fighters recruited and trained in Russia swelled the ranks of the Bosnian–Serb army and Russian MPs flocked to Belgrade to praise Serbia's defence of the faith. The emigré writer Edvard Liminov was taken to view Sarajevo from the siege lines and fired a few rounds into the city for the benefit of the television cameras.

The Serbs' close ties with Russia were extended to Greece, an EC member. Not only did the Orthodox axis ensure a diplomatic block to work in the Serbs' favour, but also made a mockery of sanctions, with Russia and Ukraine servicing their ally along the Danube, and Greece supplying the Serbs by road and rail, courtesy of its own rival, Macedonia, whose newly installed authorities (spurned by Greece) were always happy to take a cut. Ships were unloaded on the river in Belgrade for all to see, and the bizarre nighttime despatches of Greek goods by rail across the Macedonian–Serbian border, were only a little more covert.[4]

The Russian arrangement paid dividends during squabbling over the exclusion zone, with Moscow harassing the American project at every turn. The Greek alliance featured large in President Milošević's crude but effective re-election campaign: Belgrade TV was a cannonade of Milošević extolling the eternity of Greco–Serbian brotherhood and prancing about with Greek folk dancers. The result gave little credence to the touching optimism of the British foreign minister: Milošević won easily and there was a surge in votes for his extremist allies in the Chetnik 'Serbian Radical' party of Vojislav Sešelj and for the killer Captain Arkan, elected in Kosovo.

After securing formal agreement on the exclusion zone, Eagleburger went on to tell Owen that the US was ready to establish a war crimes tribunal. He even produced a list of defendants: General Mladic, Karadžić, Captain Arkan, Sešelj and Milošević. The outgoing Bush administration remained deeply divided, but for the moment the hawks seemed to have the upper hand. Mr Owen's response was that a 'War Criminal' label applied by Capitol Hill made no difference to the role of the accused as negotiating partners at his conference. Meanwhile, an irritant was reviving in another corner of what British diplomats were calling the 'flaky' quarters in Washington: officials earmarked for the new administration of President-Elect Clinton were advocating that the arms embargo should be selectively lifted to arm the Bosnian government. Not to be outdone, President Bush wrote a remarkable valedictory letter to Milošević during the last week of 1992, threatening that the US was ready to order unilateral air strikes against Serbian positions and within Serbia itself if UN forces in Bosnia were attacked.

A trio comprising Owen, Vance and Boutros Boutros Ghali made a pointed 'appeal' to the international community to stop threatening military intervention, saying that such threats jeopardised a solution at the forthcoming Geneva summit at which Owen and Vance were going to present a peace plan. Boutros Ghali even graced Sarajevo with a visit, and arrived to be greeted by jeering demonstrators and a placard reading: 'Please stop defending us your way. We are getting exterminated.' He placed such faith in the plan unveiled by Vance and Owen in January 1993 that if it collapsed he would have no alternative but to recommend military intervention to the Security Council.[5]

The Vance–Owen plan was this: Bosnia-Herzegovina would retain the outward form of a republic, but would be divided up into ten autonomous provinces, loosely bound and under a weak central government. The provinces would be ethnically based, Serb, Croat and Muslim, but would not have any 'international legal personality' which would enable them to 'enter into agreements with foreign states', that is to say Croat provinces could not accede to Zagreb nor Serbian provinces to Belgrade. The country was defined a 'decentralised state' made up of 'constituent peoples', with 'most government functions carried out by the provinces'. The new constitution would concede 'full freedom of movement' with 'internationally controlled highways' connecting the dismembered parts of the republic. The republic would be 'progressively de-militarised under UN/EC supervision'.

The plan was praised by its supporters as a workable compromise between the declared aims of the international community and what was politely called 'recognising the realities on the ground'. Its critics said it legitimised ethnic cleansing and cleared the way for more.

The Serbian spoils of war were acknowledged with restrained generosity. With thirty-four per cent of the population, Serbs were assigned half the territory, asked to concede areas of the Bosnian Krajina adjacent to the Bihać pocket and decimated eastern Bosnia. The losers, as usual, were the Muslims. With fourty-four per cent of the population, and the majority of these crammed as refugees into the central triangle or under siege, they were granted about twenty-four per cent of the country in dismembered segments and isolated pockets dependent on Serbian and Croatian goodwill for access to each other. In essence, the Muslims were to control Bihać, Zenica and Tuzla, plus stretches of countryside that linked them and an arm extending down through some of eastern Bosnia. Sarajevo would be divided into ten districts, three each plus an 'extra-territorial' centre.

The plan, for reasons best known to its architects, played fairy godmother to the Croats, whom it treated with illogical and gratuitous magnanimity. With seventeen per cent of the population, they were awarded some twenty-seven per cent of the land, most of it in a cohesive block conveniently adjacent to the border of Croatia proper. Vance and Owen endorsed the wilder claims of the 'Herzeg-Bosna' in its push northwards, giving the Croats not only Herzegovina, but country stretching deep into predominantly Muslim central Bosnia. The Ottoman city of Mostar, where you could cut the tension with a knife, was handed to the Croats on a plate. Jablanica, with its seventy per cent Muslim majority, was Croatian, as was 'cleansed' Prozor. Even the old Turkish Bosnian capital of Travnik was to come under the Croatian flag. One thing jumped out of the map like a jack-in-box in the face of anyone who knew their Balkan history: the terrain designated as Croat correlated almost exactly with the frontiers of the 'Banovina Croatia' of 1939 which Tudjman had susequently agreed with Milošević at the meeting back in 1991.

The plan got off to an inauspicious start at the most

The Vance-Owen plan

Serb
Croat
Muslim
Shared area

fanfared Geneva conference so far on 6 January 1993. Karadžić and Mladić rejected it. The Serbian republic of Bosnia-Herzegovina, they said, would be its own sovereign entity with the right to accede to Belgrade. The Serbs were not eager to give up territory they controlled and from which they could terrorise what they did not control. Karadžić was now being pushed by the groundswell of what he himself had created. His military commanders were adamant that the plan was unacceptable. Belgrade, however, was more nervous. Milošević and Ćosić were genuinely fearful that failure to accept could be followed by armed intervention, and indicated their willingness to fall in line. Lord Owen was threatening to impose the package by force, using air power,[6] to which Ćosić replied that his blood brothers in Bosnia faced either 'political and military capitulation or an attack by the mightiest powers on earth'.[7] Vance praised Milošević for having 'helped very considerably' to bring about a 'turnaround' in Serbian thinking. Milošević had arrived at Geneva as a war criminal and left as a peacemaker.

The Bosnian Serbs rejected the plan on 12 January, but then the bamboozler Karadžić returned to the table after a siesta to say he might agree to a compromise if he could win support from his Bosnia–Serb 'parliament' in Pale. The monkey-business was getting into gear, hanging Geneva on tenterhooks again. He even said he would resign if the 'parliament' rejected the plan. The Bosnian government remained uncommitted, and the Croats of course accepted. The Serbs were given six days to come up with a final reply.

Most observers saw the Serbs' deliberations over the plan as a mixture of cozening, cynicism and theatre. The Pale deputies accepted Vance–Owen, but said they were unhappy with the map, insisted on their right to form their own state and to secede from Bosnia, thus rejecting the plan's three main pillars. 'The Serbian people has shown its intention to make a separate state,' said their 'minister for the economy', Božidar Antić, nonsensically accepting the Vance–Owen plan. 'Ultimately any other solution is unworkable'.[8] General Mladić said he did not think the map needed to be agreed just yet, only the terms for military arrangements. The longer the boundaries won by violence could be debated and haggled over, the more frozen they became.

While the Serbs talked humbug to Vance and Owen, there was another rupture in the allied arc. President Clinton, unimpressed by the Vance–Owen plan, which he said rewarded ethnic cleansing, had called in a conclave of senior advisors to plot a different course of action: arming the Bosnian government and bombing the Serbs with American combat planes. The State Department lambasted the idea of 'ethnic cantons' and the partition of a nation state. The *New York Times* published a stinging editorial asking why a US president should have to cow-tow to the former leader of a failed British political party, insisting that: 'Clinton has a way out. He can insist on a better solution, one that has enforceable provisions for disarming the aggressors and assuring security to all the peoples of Bosnia who wish to return to their homes and rebuild their shattered country.'

Vance, Owen, the British and some of Clinton's own staff managed to win a grudging promise that the White House would not sabotage the plan provided that it was toughened up by acceptance of America's conditions on co-operating with it. These were: re-drawing the provincial boundaries, strengthening Sarajevo's authority, guarantees to the Kosovo Albanians, a war crimes commission and more ground troops. President Clinton said he would authorise troops to enforce the plan if it could be convincingly agreed. In return, the White House dropped its plan to supply the Bosnian Army and strike at Serbian military installations, for which the president was telephoned by John Major to say that he 'warmly welcomed' the volte-face. Secretary of State Warren Christopher despatched the United State's own envoy, Reginald Bartholemew, 'to ensure the survival of Bosnia as a state'.[9]

On 3 March, the UN Security Council said it pomised to take control of all Serbian heavy artillery as part of the Vance–Owen plan, and the Bosnian government in Sarajevo declared itself happy with its military, if not geographical, aspects, and signed. Lord Owen said he believed that 'a settlement . . . is possible in the next couple of days'.[10] He added that if the Serbs showed no 'readiness for settlement . . . we will have to take further action and it will have to be tough action'.[11]

All this while, the Vance–Owen plan had two supporters, unable to believe their luck: Mate Boban and Franjo Tudjman. The Serbs were not the only people in Bosnia who wanted to take what they could grab and acceed to a mother republic. But unlike the Serbs, the Croats needed a vehicle which would help them look as though they were annexing their corner of Bosnia with some legitimacy. Through its generosity to the Croats, the Vance–Owen plan gave Mate Boban and the HVO just the excuse they needed to take their brutish programme into top gear.

Chapter Seventeen

The Land Grab

By early February, the landscape up the green Lašva valley that cuts towards Travnik from the east was unrecognisable. A few weeks previously, the snows were melting into the dark lush soil of the hills that guided the River Lašva, and the peasants were tending to their winter supplies, grateful, like everyone else except the Serbian gunners, that it had been a mild winter. This had been some of the safest territory in Bosnia, behind the front lines where life was almost normal. Now, houses along the main road were burned out, the air was full of the inimitable and ugly stench of charred stone and roof rafters.

Down on the 'Ho Chi Minh trail' aid route, the next town north of Prozor was Gornij Vakuf, and was now almost impassable. A British base had been established on its outskirts but along its main street almost every house was either empty, burning or inhabited by nervous faces which peered out from behind the shutters after the latest ferocious exchange of gunfire had died down. Gornij Vakuf had become something between a ghost town and a battlefield. The fighting was ugly, shelling followed by house-to-house exchanges and heavy casualties for the sake of a few burned-out yards of rubble.

The warfare that shattered Gornij Vakuf and the Lašva valley was an unapologetic scramble for land as the HVO and the Bosnian Army reacted to the Vance–Owen plan by contesting frontiers which, while being wrangled over in

Geneva and New York, were more effectively established by violence on the ground. The Croats were fullfilling by force of arms that which Vance and Owen had promised them on paper, adding their own interpretation that an area designated as 'Croat' meant Croat only, and the here almost exclusively Muslim Government Army was trying to stop them. The word for 'thank you' in Serbo-Croat is 'Hvala'. By now a dry joke circulating among Muslims had it that HVO stood for '*Hvala* Vance–Owen'.

But aggressive columns within the Bosnian army were learning that the best form of defence is attack. As it became clearer that the West was not coming to aid the government or its cause, so pressure built up on the central Bosnian commanders to accept reality and resist Croatian expansion by securing what was in effect a Muslim ethnic frontier and retaliating in kind. At Busovăca in the Lašva valley it was the *Armija* which came down from the hills and 'cleaned' out the Croatians. This land grab would not be fought between two front lines, but between a plethora of fronts, each side carving out its jigsaw-pieces of land.

British and other UN or EC officers were drafted in to try to negotiate truces and to supervise the exchange of the 'prisoners' being kept in back sheds or small factories by both sides. In Busovăca, Muslim families had sheltered their Croatian neighbours from their own army as it came down from the hills, before having to hand them over for 'exchange'. The squalid small-town nature of the violence led to the rapid circulation of rumours which in turn fanned the flames of fighting. One infamous case was the tale of a Croatian taxi driver being hauled out of his car and having his throat cut. There had been a mortar attack on the accused village, with seven people killed, before the taxi driver telephoned his wife from Zenica to tell her he had decided to stay there overnight.[1]

The harum-scarum barracks in Travnik had been trans-figured. From the courtyard, the ransacked cars, bedraggled refugees, bonfires and washing lines had gone. Instead,

ranks of soldiers, male and female, were drilling across the
tarmac. Instructors were telling special female units how
to strip, clean and re-assemble machine guns. Along grass
banks at the back of the compound, men were running in
tight columns, diving, practising ambushes, preparing for
classic guerilla war. Even the latrine had been sanitised.
This was now the headquarters of the biggest and most
remarkable brigade in the Bosnian Army: the 17th or
Krajina Brigade, made up entirely of 'ethnically cleansed'
Bosnians and former inmates of concentration camps. All
of them had made the journey through Skender Vakuf,
Vitovlje, Smet and on foot across the battlefield.

Breakfast time was now an orderly and disciplined affair.
Men would wait their turn outside the massive canteen,
beckoned in when there was space to eat by a young soldier
with a red beret who was in Omarska seven months ago. In
the strange intimacy of the Bosnian war, you keep bumping
into people in different places at different times, and there,
in line for his meal, was Ibrahim Demirovíc whom I had
met behind barbed wire at Trnopolje camp back in August,
the boy who had spirited us away from the guards for a tour
around the stinking interior. His face was chubbier, his dark
straight hair longer, and we talked over breakfast of tea, soup
and bread. Ibrahim, after his initial questions about the rock
music scene in Europe, said he had got onto the convoy
over the mountains by squeezing in with the women and
children during the early 'releases' from the camp. Arriving
in Travnik he had been 'shall we say *encouraged*' to join in
the Krajina Brigade. 'They are actually sorting themselves
out here,' he judged, almost as though reluctant to admit
it. 'I would ideally like to get out, if I could. It's hard,
but it's necessary. I'm no soldier, but I'm willing to fight
and I belong here. These are the people who understand
what has happened; every soldier understands the others,
we share that experience, we've lost our families, we've
seen our homes burned, we've been in camps. We're the
lost people with nothing to lose.'

There is another boy with electric blond hair who is thirteen years old, called Sead. 'I'm from Jajce,' he says, 'I've lost my family and I am alone. I will either go back to Jajce, or I will die trying to get there.'

The deputy commander of the Krajiške Brigada was a man who appeared back then in February to be an unusually cordial figure for this cruel war. He smoked cigarettes through a carved Turkish cigarette-holder and seemed to have time on his hands. He was a shepherd from Skender Vakuf who had gone into military academy as a teenager and graduated to the rank of colonel. His name was Mehmet Alagić, and his convivial manner — especially courteous to the ladies — concealed his real self. Within six months, Alagić would become one of the central and hardest figures in the war. As the land-grab sliced up central Bosnia in February, Alagić already had a grand scheme worked out, one which he expounded, with the help of copious diagrams and generous amounts of šljivović, to anyone who took the time to call by. It concerned a consolidation of the 'Muslim triangle' in central Bosnia, a triangle which would link Tuzla in the north with Travnik in the west and run along a line via Prozor towards Jablanica and Mostar. It would be landlocked, but would depend for supplies on the opening of the Tuzla airport, the second largest military airstrip in the old Yugoslavia. Once consolidated, troops would be able to use the triangle as a base from which to strike out.

Up on the first floor of the now scrubbed barracks, over coffee and drinks, it all seemed like a bit of a pipedream. It meant taking on the infinitely better armed Croatians along the Lašva valley and towards Prozor, and holding onto the east bank of Mostar, where the Croats' heaviest armour was concentrated. In fact, it appeared that the plan would not stand a snowball's chance in hell. Colonel Alagić smiled and suggested that we meet up for dinner at a restaurant in a cavern dug into a mountain that was still open to those who knew about it. He had just outlined the Bosnian military strategy for the rest of the war, and one which would be pursued against all the odds, with remarkable tenacity, much of it directed by him. For Alagić, the triangle was a base for the re-conquest of Bosnia-Herzegovina and a way to get his men home. In the event, the men of the Krajina Brigade were carving the borders of what is probably doomed to become besieged 'Muslim' Bosnia.

There had been other changes within the army up the road in Zenica. The most stridently Muslim city in Bosnia, it was the command centre for the Government Army's Second Corps, under the grip of Enver Hasanović, and was becoming more pivotal to the running of the entire army as Sarajevo became isolated. Hasanović, an imperturbable, elusive man, was loyal to the government and its central ethos of multi-ethnic tolerance, but other units were emerging in Zenica, some under his authority, others not.

The 'Muslim Armed Forces' or MOS, were seen more and more around town, in the basement bars and keeping watch over the entrances to the blocks of flats on scrappy Zenica's industrial edges. These extremists and ruffians came under the army's command, but paid little attention to its politics – like young Ilhad Hadžisković, whose unit was based in a school where Westerners are not welcome.

'Islam,' said Ilhad, who had been an electrician, in a combative monotone 'is a religion, but with more than just a spiritual purpose. We have been betrayed by the West because we are Muslims. That is the only explanation for the West's tolerance of the crimes committed against us. This is now a revolutionary war against those who want to destroy us competely, our people, religion and culture. You in the West have allowed Bosnia to be butchered. Now we are fighting on all fronts only for the survival of the Muslim people, and for territory in which we can be safe, and it is a fight to the finish, against whoever.' A perfectly circular, red winter sun was setting behind the blocks of flats. There was something ugly about Ilhad's bellicose self-assurance. I was walking with a soldier from Travnik called Samir, who said:

'Those people are either the saving grace or the final end of Bosnia. It depends which way things go. At the moment they don't count for much, but that could change.'

But the boys in the MOS were models of rationalism compared to the real *Mujahadeen*, of whom there were now some 200 in Zenica and its surroundings, bobbing up occasionally on country roads. They really did frighten people, both locals and visitors, either with reason or just through reputation; these were the people who went around, with some of the local boys, telling Bosnians not to say 'good morning' but 'Allah salam alekum'. They didn't often smile after checking your papers. Mostly Afghans, Turks or Syrians, they were supposed to be formidable in battle although there was no evidence of this. They were feared by the Croats, disliked by most Bosnian Muslims and totally estranged from the political project of Bosnia-Herzegovina. 'They stick out like penguins in the desert,' said Samir. The *Mujahadeen* would play their role later. For the moment, the slightest rumour that they might be on their way was enough to make Croatians pack their bags and leave in the squalid tit-for-tat ethnic cleansing that was cutting central Bosnia into little ethnically pure pockets.

'Herzeg-Bosna' was meanwhile establishing itself as a nasty sort of place in which war had become big business and vast amounts of money were circulating. The 'Holy City' of Medjugorije and the border village of Široki Brijeg had become party towns. On Saturday night, Široki Brijeg was teeming with discotheques, cruising BMWs, pouting girls eyeing up loutish soldiers and men dressed in flashy Italian styles. In a reversal of roles since the old Yugoslav days, people now came up from what was the rich Dalmatian coast to have a good time among the clodhoppers on the Bosnian frontier, to pleasure-bathe in an economy flourishing on the sale of guns, drugs, 'duty-free' Western cigarettes and whisky, sex and stolen cars. The origin of the cars was barely disguised: most were Italian, stolen along

Italy's Adriatic coast, put on the ferry and driven up into Herzegovina where they would either be fitted with new 'Herzeg-Bosna' number plates or driven, like many other cars, without plates. Some of them still went around as self-declared cars from Ancona, Pescara or Rimini. In Medjugorije, a haulage juggernaut was parked in a front yard sporting the name of the Italian motorway services chain Autogrill, and the slogan 'Una piacevole sosta sull' autostrada' – a Pleasing Pause on the Motorway. It had brand new Mostar number plates.

Medjugorije had become a junction for the black market and a base for the imminent ethnic cleansing of the Mostar region, a sleazy and disagreeable combination. In the souvenir shops, statuettes of the Madonna were on sale in trays next to others full of Swastikas, Maltese Crosses and other Nazi regalia. The HVO put out a verbal warning that anyone found sheltering Muslims in the Holy City would have their homes blown up. Kiseljak was also thriving; as the port of entry into Sarajevo: 'Las Vegas' it was called in the capital. In May 1993, the Bosnian Army made a bid to break through the Serbian blocks on the Sarajevo–Kiseljak road, imploring the HVO to come at the Serbs from the other side and link up. The HVO didn't move; Kiseljak was happy with the way things were.

The fascist HOS had come under the command of the HVO, Croatian blood proving thicker than the politics of partition in the new war. The switch meant simply that former HOS roadblocks now flew the Croatian flag instead of their own Ustasha colours, that their thugs were now at the disposal of HVO command and that the uniforms of the official Zagreb-sponsored army were now often adorned by the heraldry of the Third Reich. The HOS-led attacks on the Muslim quarter of Novi Travnik were especially violent. Muslims were on the road into central Travnik throughout the days and nights of February and March, joining refugees from Serbian territory.

The Croatian stranglehold on aid was almost complete,

with HVO roadblocks refusing to allow convoys or distributors into specific areas of Mostar or smaller Muslim towns. During one week in January, 200 trucks of privately funded aid to Muslim areas were hijacked by the HVO troops in Čapljina and all their contents confiscated. The mountain roads were splattered with drivers from the Merhamet charity walking back to Tomislavgrad having been yanked out of their lorries and sent back at gunpoint.

In all areas designated as 'Croatian' by the Vance–Owen plan (except Travnik), the HVO issued ultimata to the Bosnian Army: surrender arms, place all soldiers under Croatian command or face the consequences. In the rural badlands of Herzegovina, the Muslim soldiers obeyed. But in Jablanica, seventy per cent Muslim, the army refused and the town was promptly shelled. On Fourth April, the authorities of 'Herzeg-Bosna' gave the Bosnian Government Army two weeks to lay down its arms and surrender its authority in all land designated as 'Croatian' by Vance–Owen, and for civilians to accept Croatian rule. The authorities would 'take matters into our own hands' if there were any failures to comply. The Croat idea was that in 'Muslim' areas, the HVO would do the same, but the few HVO units operating outside the Vance–Owen 'Croat' zone in Tuzla and the overwhelmingly Muslim towns were fighting in close alliance with the Government Army anyway. In Tuzla and Gradačac, and the front along the narrow Serbian corridor, they even came under a single command, and the commander of the Government Army in Tuzla was a Croat, Željko Knez.

But the Croats were not the only army engaged in a grab for land in the wake of the Vance–Owen plan. The Serbs now turned their attention to the pockets of government resistance in areas granted to the 'Muslims', on the assumption that towns which have been razed to the ground and emptied of people cannot be resurrected. While the Vance–Owen map was being finalised, the Serbs unleashed a torrent of bombardment and ethnic cleansing against the as yet unconquered pockets of eastern Bosnia. In doing so, they presented the West with its final chance to rescue a battered credibility in Bosnia, and put the name of a little light industrial market town before the eyes of the world: Srebrenica.

Interval

Travnik Voices – 2 – Spring 1993

In Travnik, many of the 185,000 refugees who have now passed through are starting to go mad. Salko Abaz, an intelligent enough man, is sitting on the floor where he always sits, and has sat for six months, in the high school: 'Chetniks on the hill, Ustasha down the road; if one doesn't get us, the other will,' he says in a monotone. 'I sometimes think we made a mistake leaving Prijedor. At night, there's always some jerk out there firing his gun. Most of the aid is hijacked by the local Mafia and sold to us. And we just sit here, no privacy, no room to think, no family life, wondering what to do next and hoping we don't end up like him over there' – and he cocks his head dismissively towards an old man in the corner, nodding rhythmically like a Hassidic Jew at prayer, and mumbling to himself, his mind apparently gone. A local psychiatrist, Helenja Dedić, is working with the itinerants, and among her patients is a woman in a headscarf at the back of the school who shuffles about, going through the motions of scattering seed on the ground. 'She thinks she is feeding her chickens,' says Helenja, 'she does it in here and on the streets around town.' Others hung onto their hopes and sanity, even after months of silence on whether their menfolk were alive or dead, like the women at the back of police commander Fahrudin Alihodžić's new offices. They ground their coffee and stared into mid-distance while one little girl, Aida, wrote and learned extraordinary poetry about the war and even about the concentration camps of which she had heard so much.

Travnik somehow succeeded in fending off the second war creeping up the valley and at times roaring at its gates. Fahrudin Alihodžić insisted that his miltary police units work in joint Croat–Muslim army patrols. The local HVO was in the hands of men who worked closely with the Government Army, and were refusing to implement Grude's policy. Croats in Travnik distrusted the Muslims but felt little affinity with the Herzegovinian fanatics, and at the head of their army had been the markedly moderate young Joko Pokrajčić, thirty years old and HVO commander at the crossroads of the war. 'My duty here is to protect the two victim peoples of this war,' he told me. 'And regardless of the pressures from both sides, I will take that line as long as I am still alive.' Within weeks, Pokrajčić was replaced.

But his successor Colonel Filip Filipović proved to be no more obliging to Mate Boban's project. One fine morning, as late as February 1993, we clambered up the slopes of Mount Vlašić to within 800 yards of the Serbian lines, their soldiers' silhouettes visible along the ridge. Colonel Filipović and the new Bosnian army commander Ahmed Kulenović were side by side as we crept under the brow of the hill to the outpost bunkers where a forward posse of seasoned Muslim and Croatian soldiers held the line a stone's throw from the Serbian guns. It was a reconnaissance trip to examine a crucial telecommunications aeriel which the Muslims and Croats were planning to capture together.

'We are being strangled by this second war,' said the Muslim Kulenović. 'We have no weapons, our supplies are blocked by the Croats. But here we cannot afford to divide. Look who's on the hill! We're personal friends and wish to remain allies. At least here we can tell each other that we don't trust each other!' Colonel Filipović spoke of 'fighting the common enemy. I am a military man. I do not take part in politics, and do not wish to.' Then he said, with unusual candour: 'Actually, I am walking on the edge of a knife.' The sortie up the mountain was probably one of the last of its kind in the history of central Bosnia's war. Filipović was removed within two weeks.

Emir Tica

Emir's bright face has dimmed over the past three months. He has seen the refugees decline into misery and try to move on, some successfully, others not. He has met a girl, although his duties stop him from seeing much of her. Emir's supplies – food, fuel, ammunition, uniforms, everything an army needs – come along roads now controlled by the Croats and since November his army's lifelines have been cut. The trucks for which Emir is responsible are seized and at the moment, he has a whole convoy of supplies impounded in Kiseljak, and will be lucky to get half of what he has paid for.

'What the Croats have done hurts me far more than what the Serbs are doing. To be the victim of a betrayal is worse than losing a fight. I want to get out, far from here. I've met this girl, but we never see each other. We talk on the phone about how we'll get married, leave Travnik and have twins. But this war is my life now. I realised that on the day that Jajce fell. I'll never forget that day as long as I live. I spent two days and two nights without sleeping, collecting people. I moved 40,000 in fourty-eight hours. I looked at them and began to doubt whether we as a people can survive.

'I don't know if Europe wants us to survive or not, but we are part of Europe. But not this Europe right now. I want to be part of honest Europe, of the Europe I have read about, ready to defend democracy. Not a Europe which stands back and allows the killing of 300,000 people and the rape of 40,000 women. Time moves. You really need a lot of time to kill 300,000 people. It hasn't happened in the last three days, it's happened over the past ten months.

I feel part of the Europe that would not wait for that to happen.

'It is becoming clear to me that we are completely alone. First the Serbs tried to wipe us out, now the Croats have started. Now we as a people are in danger of simply disappearing. When you ask me what am I fighting for, I now say that I have 300,000 reasons to fight, because 300,000 of my people, men, women and children, have been killed and killed brutally. They hadn't done anything. They were just living in their homes. Why? I don't know who can give me an answer.

'And so I become like an animal. Something has snapped in my head. I have never called myself a Muslim, but now I must feel like a Muslim, because the European Muslims are faced with obliteration. I know history, from books and movies. And I know that in the Nazi times they tried to destroy a people, the Jews. We are now starting to feel like the Jews must have felt in about 1940, when they realised it was for real. But we must survive – at least two of us. It is not a question of who will survive but that someone must survive. In order to kill a people, you must kill memory, you must destroy everything that belongs to that people. But if two people can stay alive, they can remember. The Jews can remember, and I expect they can understand what is happening here better than anyone else, and I know that they are praying for us.

'We start to feel like them because we become determined that those two who stay alive can talk about what happened to us, so that we as a people never forget what is now happening to us.'

Fahrudin Alihodžić

Fahrudin is shouting again. Back in November, he was shouting at one of his own men on a roadblock out of Travnik the day after the fall of Jajce, through which the processions of refugees were setting out along the road. The soldier had allowed through a man carrying a gun. 'You blockheaded idiot!' roared Fahrudin at the boy quaking in his muddy boots, 'Whatya do that for?! We're supposed to be disarming these morons! Not sending them sauntering off with their bloody pistols . . .' That was November; Fahrudin the commander, feared and admired by his men.

Now it is February and Fahrudin is shouting after an evening's work retrieving bodies of his men captured and killed on front lines at Visoko. He collapses into the chair of a friend's flat, spitting exasperated rage.

'I never knew who the Chetniks were. They must have worn a lot of deodorant, because I never knew they smelled so bad. Just to think I lived next door to them all those years. You should have seen the state of these men. I assumed it would be horrendous because some of them had been dead for a month. In fact, I didn't think we'd be able to carry them. But they were fairly well preserved, because it's so cold. When we carried the bodies to the truck, we saw that every single one had been mutilated; ears and noses cut off, and all their skulls fractured. Their teeth had been pulled out, and there were still fragments of teeth that had crumbled. My only consolation is to hope that my boys were dead when they did this. There were signs that some of them were alive, but I have to tell myself they were dead.

'There was one sixteen-year-old with his left side, arm, lungs and heart carved up. It couldn't have been a shell, it must have been an axe or something similar. I used to watch movies by Alfred Hitcock before this war, and enjoyed them, but Hitchcock was an amateur compared to what these Chetniks do in real life, to real people.

'My relationship with these boys was difficult at first, because we had all been driven out of our homes. We were all lost in a way. When we were preparing to go to the front, they could hardly wait to go and show their courage, they thought they were invincible. But when we took up our positions, a lot of them simply could not believe that this was really happening to them. They were brave at first until a shell tore one of the boys to pieces. He was a friend, we used to laugh and joke together. Many of them started shaking, almost crying. I said it was nothing, that we should carry on and a relative of mine, an experienced fighter, helped me calm them down. But when it was over, my relative and I went to pick up the remains of the young soldier who had been hit. That's when I realised that human life can be turned into nothing. I was terribly sad; I found the boot he was wearing still contained his foot and a piece of leg and I realised that this was the biggest part of his body that remained. We put the pieces in canvas and carried them back to the barracks. I have seen many ugly things, but that picture will never fade. Nor will I ever forget those boys chopped to pieces in Visoko, who thought this was all like a film where the ammunition is fake. This is no film from Vietnam, this a horrendous, macabre reality.

'At first the Krajina Brigade didn't have uniforms or weapons or anything. But we didn't want to give up. I was determined, and had good friends around me. Now the atmosphere in the units improves every day. We know now there isn't much hope of help from the rest of the world, and are ready to take our fate into our own hands, which makes us stronger. You have to be in the middle of an experience like this to know what war can be like and what life can be like, and what human beings can be like. It's all here, in its bravery and its bestiality. It is a war against an entire people, the Bosnian Muslim people. I really wouldn't mind if this was a war between armies, the Serbian army and Chetniks against the Bosnian Army. But it isn't. The saddest thing is that it is a war against the civilians.

'It is strange: there are a lot of people becoming religious overnight. This is not good at all. Religious faith should come gradually, not suddenly. It's an ugly thing for someone to start hating others because they are a Muslim, Catholic or Orthodox. I was never a believer, but I won't look down on any religion either. All I am interested in is putting an end to the killing of innocent people and the destruction of the places which we worked so hard to build together. And I am also fighting because my pride and honour as a free citizen has been hurt and insulted by this carnage. Because this war has changed me down to my soul. Before, I was just a lad. I am now a man who wants to create something, I am fighting to create something so that I can preserve it.'

Nura Čelič

Nura found a way to the Croatian coastal port of Split. Between them, Alihodžić, the local UNHCR and an enamoured American photographer managed to get papers to take her, her brother Samir, her mother and little sister, out of Travnik and down to the Adriatic.

But not to freedom. Their menfolk were dispersed all over: father was last seen in Sanski Most, one brother in a camp, another brother on the front lines in Travnik. Home is now a large dormitory in a converted school, crammed with bunk beds. A bossy Turkish charity worker barks orders at a fat man sitting with his feet in a plastic bucket of freezing cold water, despite the subzero temperature outside. 'We are going crazy in here,' says Nura's brother Samir, and his mother cries as she shows photographs of her husband and sons. The faces in the dormitory are prostrate and woebegone, except one, Nura's. She comes back from an evening appointment she has in a little room by the school entrance: her evening prayers.

This is something new for Nura, and she carefully folds and puts away a clean headscarf. Nura always has photographs to show, but the latest ones are different from all that table-top jollity in the Banja Luka cafes. These are professionally taken portraits and show Nura, against a pale blue background, her hair pinned back under her traditional Islamic scarf. She has three books: the Koran in Serbo–Croat, another entitled 'How A Good Muslim

Woman Should Dress', and the Koran in Arabic of which Nura cannot understand a single word. The latter is a gift from a young Palestinian, living in Amman and come to Split as a charity volunteer. 'He loves me,' says Nura, 'and maybe I love him too.' The Palestinian has asked her to marry him, and offered to take her to Amman to study and be his wife. Samir and her mother are disgusted.

We sit on the bunk beds to discuss the dilemma. 'You're *Bosnian*,' says her mother, 'What on earth are you thinking of, going to be an *Arab*?!? What about your father and brothers!?' Samir is gentler, but no less firm. 'Come on Nura, you never wore this stuff before. America maybe, but not Jordan. I'd go to America tomorrow, but we would not fit in an Arab country, you know that.'

Nura composes herself, clears her throat and embarks on a concise, resolute monologue.

'What do you want me to do? I have been pushed out of my home by soldiers. I have lost all my friends and some of my family and all my things. I have watched the town where I grew up burn. I have been driven over horrible mountains with guns pointing at me and walked through a battle to live for months in a gym. Now I'm here, and I'm supposed to be grateful, but the people don't like me, the police harrass us and we're locked in here at ten o'clock at night. I watch people go to the cafés, but I have no money to go myself.

'I look after children and work in the kitchens, but I do not believe in anything any more. I am twenty years old and there is nothing for me to live for any more. I have to believe in something, and to be somebody. I have been pushed into the arms of my religion.'

Chapter Eighteen

Srebrenica and Europe's Last Stand

*'The Bosnian Serbs need to realise they are not going
to gain what they have grabbed by force.'*
— Douglas Hurd, Foreign Secretary,
BBC, 23 May 1993

Through a twist of luck, military brilliance, ruthlessness
and endurance, four tiny but packed Muslim communities
in eastern Bosnia had withstood a year of Serbian siege,
despite having been cut off since the beginning of the
war. Arms had been smuggled into these redoubts by
shepherds and mules moving silently and by night through
Serbian territory, from Tuzla or Goražde. No one knows
how many were caught or killed. The summer of 1992
and even January 1993 had seen unexpected and vicious
sorties by the Bosnian Army out of Srebrenica into Serbian
territory, but they were short-lived, and by the time the
snows melted there was no logical military reason why
anybody in any of these four villages should still have been
alive. Reports reaching Tuzla and Sarajevo from ham radio
operators said that people were living underground or on
the streets, going out at night to find animals and plants
off which to live. Around the villages, hundreds more had
taken shelter in caves against the cold, rain and shelling. The
names of these pockets were Kamenica, Srebrenica, Cerska
and Žepa. Some 300,000 people were reported trapped in

the enclaves. Some were indigenous, but most had fled into them, and attempts by the UN to get convoys through had been repeatedly frustrated.

At the end of February, the Serbs decided to turn the screws. Troops and artillery were moved up to the ridges above all four towns, and they were pounded afresh, with a ferocity that witnesses said defied anything the war had hitherto seen. The first to fall was the smallest, Kamenica, which surrendered on St Valentine's Day and whose civilians fled through Serbian lines to swell the population of Srebrenica, though many of them were killed on the way.

For the first time, the Serbs untied their noose around the enclaves, to allow people who wished to flee for Tuzla to do so, at their peril. Families were reported wandering through battle zones, in search of shelter, their fate unseen by aid workers or journalists simply unable to reach them. One group of Muslim women and children was cast out over the mountains, straight into a minefield, where at least twenty were blown to pieces, according to survivors arriving in Tuzla. In all, said the UNHCR, 6,000 had fled down what the Serbs called the 'humanitarian corridor', but which the UNHCR re-christened the 'ethnic cleansing corridor'.

In mid-February, the UN tried to breach the Serbian stonewalling and get a convoy through to Cerska from Belgrade, a critical test of the humanitarian, rather than interventionist, solution in which the West had now invested its reputation. The convoy was stopped twenty miles from its destination. The Serbs said the reason was 'heavy fighting'; the UNHCR's José Maria Mendiluce replied: 'You just don't know how tired I am of listening to lies'.[1] The aid agencies had word that more than a hundred people, including thirty-two children, had died of starvation in Cerska. Doctors from Žepa sent word by radio that 350 babies and children had died during the first two months of the year, and the Bosnian government said that 2,000 had starved in all four pockets throughout the winter.

President Clinton then threw another idea into the ring: a plan to parachute aid packages from 10,000 feet. He met immediate opposition from his allies, concerned about Serbian sensitivity that the scheme could be a pretext for military involvement, despite a guarantee that the plan 'has no combat connotations at all'. For once, the Americans went ahead regardless, with aircraft from the Rhein–Main base in Germany dropping twenty-one tonnes of food on Cerska, in the 'MRE' (or 'Meals Ready to Eat') packs with names like 'French No. 14' that every soldier knows and reviles. A famous story reached Sarajevo about one package whose parachute failed to open and wrecked a man's back shed. His garden was turned into a mountain of 'Iodised Salt', 'Milk Caramels', dried 'Chicken Stew', 'Dried Peach Dessert' and powdered 'Cherry Drink'. Serbian snipers opened fire on villagers as they went out to the slopes above the villages to recover the packages, with many people killed. At first the Serbs got some of the food too, but the air drops continued with increasing success and accuracy, especially in Srebrenica and Žepa.

A voice that had become familiar to those huddling around radio sets in Sarajevo was that of Ismet Mustafić, a radio ham in Cerska. On the first day of March, the day after the food drop, that voice sounded unusually nervous. 'The Serbs are about to enter Cerska,' he reported. 'They have moved to the edge of town and have been bombing all night. Thousands are preparing to flee.' The following day, the radio sets reported that Cerska had fallen. The torment of Cerska and Srebrenica was a drama that unfolded down crackly radio receivers belonging to hams like Izet Karaman in Tuzla, who had rigged up his kit and tape recorders in the garage of his block of flats, the walls covered with signal numbers and names of people he had never met who were now speaking to the world via his equipment. The hidden war was apparently becoming hideous: relief workers left Belgrade in a convoy of ambulances to try to evacuate more than 1,000 sick and wounded people trapped as the Serbian militiamen moved into Ceska, but were blocked on their way. The Serb authorities told the convoys' organisers that the rescue could only go ahead if the UNHCR removed the entire Muslim population from the town[2] – the old ploy of getting relief agencies to do the ethnic cleansing. The ambulances turned back.

Some 1,500 people had scattered into the mountains and found their way to a bombed-out village called Konjević Polje, where they had tried to seek shelter but, said the UNHCR, 'they are being shelled and tear-gassed'. A convoy seeking to reach them was turned back. The UNHCR, in radio contact, said that tanks were moving down the streets of Cerska and there was 'plundering, killing and burning . . . People are begging to be taken out alive'.

Other terrified refugees set off over the mountains to Tuzla, arriving after some days with stories of living off 'hay, pumpkins, boiled pumpkins and half-boiled pumkins', as one man put it.[3] Some 20,000 people were now reported to be meandering around forest tracks and mined wilderness, and accounts among those reaching Tuzla told of indiscriminate killing in the snowbound forests as the Serbs opened fire on those in flight. They had walked past the frozen bodies of fellow villagers as they made their way by night, guided by soldiers of the Bosnian Army, through Serbian-held territory. 'We were all in tears,' said one woman, Hava Rizvanović, who had fallen in the snow, unconscious, during the journey before finally reaching an outpost Government-controlled village where 'the soldiers said it was okay for us to let the babies cry now'.[4]

UN Commander General Philippe Morillon finally won Serbian permission to head an armoured convoy through Konjević Polje and Cerska. He enjoyed three days of relative calm, the shells raining down after his departure, killing sixteen civilians in one explosion and blowing the legs off two children, according to a report by a subsequent British army convoy, which was forced to retreat from Konjević Polje, unable to evacuate sick and wounded civilians. The

British convoy had been trapped by villagers blocking its way out for fear that the bombardment would become even heavier when it went – as had happened after Morillon's departure. British troops said they had seen corpses littering the streets and two women were killed in front of the aid workers. The soldiers said that women were trying to run down the street out of town clutching blankets, and being fired upon by tanks and snipers. Major Martin Waters of the British task force said it was 'obviously well-aimed fire, deliberately avoiding the UN vehicles and obviously directed at the groups of women and children'. The numbers now trapped in Konjević Polje were now put at 20,000 and the village fell some days later, its civilian survivors driven on once again, this time into Srebrenica.

A British doctor, Simon Mardell of the World Health Organisation, reported conditions in Srebrenica, where 80,000 were now trapped, to be 'indescribably appalling'. The doctor had been accommodated in a house occupied by five families, and five of the people living in it had been killed during his four-day stay. People were staying alive, said the doctor, by eating leaves, acorns, and grinding down the hard centres of corn cobs to make cakes with the powder. People were sleeping on the streets, trying to make fires to stay warm, and amputations were being carried out without anaesthetic. Dogs were feeding off corpses. Thousands of people had been reported fleeing Srebrenica, heading for Tuzla, but few were arriving; people were simply disappearing in flight, in the minefields and snowbound forests. The Bosnian journalist Haris Nezirović returned from the town to report that: 'Facing starvation, the people of Srebrenica have been reduced to an animal-like struggle for survival . . . They have walked into enemy fire or fields full of land mines. Now, they scramble for meals dropped by the United States planes, fighting and even killing for the precious packages. Every day, new arrivals stream into a town already packed as tight as a new box of matches . . .'[5]

On 12 March General Morillon first arrived in Srebrenica

by armoured car to what was by all accounts a tumultuous and disbelieving welcome. Flabbergasted by what he saw, he sent a radio message to say that he would stay until aid was allowed through. Something had obviously snapped in the general's mind; his usual lofty, cynical language changed to compassionate anger. Within a week, the main road through Srebrenica was re-named 'General Morillon Street'.

After being obstructed, searched and hampered for nine days by soldiers of the Yugoslav army in Serbia proper (which denied a role in the war), a UN aid convoy finally got through, the crowds weeping tears of deranged joy as trucks entered the town. The UN team established early that the danger from shelling was even greater than the nutritional problems. 'The real humanitarian problem is 120 mm shells,' said one report, 'There are so many displaced people on the street here, that every shell will kill civilians. They can't miss.'[6] Morillon had negotiated a delicate treaty: the evacuation of sick and wounded women and children by air would be allowed, and the gradual evactuation by road of those not 'militarily capable' would be considered, if 10,000 Serbs in Tuzla were transported in the opposite direction. The UNHCR warned that the deal would open an escape route down which Muslims would flee, leaving the Serbian guns to batter what was left of Srebrenica into submission. But Morillon struck the deal, and persuaded the authorities in Tuzla to go along with it.

Day one of the airlift, 24 March, showed the helicopter crews exactly how serious the Serbs were about the plan: before and after their arrival, the landing pad at Srebrenica's soccer pitch was shelled, two civilians waiting to board were killed and two Canadian troopers injured. The Tuzla airstrip at the other end of the air corridor was also hit. 'This is the ultimate in despicable behaviour,' fumed the British brigadier in command, Roddy Cordy-Simpson. He scorned Belgrade's protestations that the obstacles were the work of breakaway gangs, saying the tactics formed part of 'a calculated policy of ethnic cleansing.' Some tearful Serbs left Tuzla, but the airlift was called off. Three days later, trucks arrived to bring out the first women and children by road. The scramble to board them and ride back to Tuzla, during which six people were crushed to death, was a wretched episode. Tony Birtley of ABC television was one of only two reporters to witness it; he sent his despatch by radio to the *Daily Telegraph*:

'The hunched shape slowly trudged through the snow and ice as dawn broke in the besieged town of Srebrenica. On its back was a large bundle, and attached to one hand the small figure of a child trying hard to keep its feet. As the figure approached I could see it was a woman breathing more heavily with each step. Soon more black shapes followed until there was an endless stream of panting, heaving bodies. This was the start of "evacuation day".

'Soon there were literally thousands hurrying towards the nineteen United Nations trucks which on Sunday night had brought 160 tons of desperately needed food and medicines and would soon depart for the Muslim-held town of Tuzla. The UN did have a plan. The day before, they had carefully selected 900 . . . who were to win a coveted place on the convoy to safety and freedom. Each of the chosen had a number written in magic marker on a hand. It was well intended but in the end meaningless.

'By the time the mass of people reached the lorries they were already full. In the middle of the night hundreds boarded the vehicles and waited . . . Armed police tried in vain to get them off . . . The shouting, the screams, the cries for help became deafening as people surged forward when they saw the final truck being filled. Women fought to get on, and in the end, in desperation, weeping uncontrollably, handed their babies and young children to those already on board.'[7]

By the time Mrs Hanifa Hajdarovié arrived in Tuzla, her five-year-old daughter Senija and her baby son Senad had both died aboard their truck. 'There was a jolt, I was knocked down and my children were crushed,' she said. In addition to the six bodies recovered at Tuzla, two more had died in the scrum to board at the other end. Other people said they had paid hundreds of Deutschmarks to a military extortion racket to secure a place on the trucks. The UN suspended its plans for the overland evacuation.[8]

The Serbian onslaught was deemed sufficient to get the UN to try to enforce the No-Fly-Zone, although the British denied the project her aircraft. Taking heart from Britain's irresolute approach, Karadžić called the plan a 'catastrophic error' which would lead to an escalation of the conflict. As the parliament in Pale rejected the Vance–Owen map, US Secretary of State Warren Christopher replied that if Pale continued to resist, his administration would push for a lifting of the embargo on the Bosnian government and facilitate a supply of weapons to the besieged enclaves. Christopher said he accepted the fighting would escalate, but that arming the government troops would 'level the playing field'. Owen retorted that it would simply 'level the killing field'.

The embargo was by now the single most crippling factor in the neutralisation of the Government Army and the inability of the Muslims to defend themselves. In the three-sided war, two of the combatants involved were, absurdly, pleading that the world continue to deny them arms. The reasons were two: one, the embargo froze the chronic disadvantage of the Government Army, and two, the Muslims, unlike their enemies, were virtually cut out of the international arms bazaar, landlocked and hemmed in by their enemies. Such an arrangement could not but facilitate and hasten the carve-up, and the West concurred. Some supplies were reaching the Muslims, however. The Serbs were selling ammunition to both the Muslims and Croats at exorbitant prices when and where it suited them tactically. There was also a perverse smuggling route along which guns paid for by the Muslims using money from Turkey and the Arab countries would arrive at the Croatian port of Rijeka, where the Croats would take a half cut. Another half of what was left would be commandeered by the HVO as the guns made their way up country, leaving the Bosnians with a quarter of what they had paid for, by agreement – there was no alternative. The irony was that the Bosnian Army had paid for much of the weaponry being aimed at it.

The proposal to end the embargo to the army had been tantalisingly advanced and withdrawn throughout the war, and now the United States tried once again to 'level the field'. The British, French and Russians were appalled, along with Karadžić who said he did not want to co-operate with those seeking to 'punish the Serbian people'.

Meanwhile, the UN advanced an ambitious scheme: a mass evacuation from Srebrenica in daily convoys which would bring 15,000 people to Tuzla. Even President Izetbegović acknowledged that the situation was so desperate that arguments over co-operation with ethnic cleansing had to be set aside. The UNHCR said they were faced with a straight choice: moving people or exposing them to massacre. But the first convoy of trucks was turned back empty, turned away this time by the people who had been defending the civilians for a year, the Bosnian army. The military authorities decreed to the fury of the UNHCR that the removal of the population would ensure the collapse of what was left of the town. In the days that followed, three more aid convoys were turned back by the Serbs, and the whole relief effort reached the brink of collapse. The world was losing interest; only 20 per cent of the 38,000 tonnes of food budgeted for April had been procured, and there was little sign that even this amount was going to get through.

The Serbs' response was a day's shelling of Srebrenica, 1 April, which left seventy-seven dead, including fifteen children. The bombardment started at one end of town, moved up the High Street and stopped twenty minutes later. 'There is blood everywhere,' said a radio operator reaching Tuzla, 'a massacre in the town centre.' A Canadian UN official, Louis Gentile, saw the attack, and said later:

'It was clearly intended to kill as many civilians as possible. People were throwing bodies onto ox-carts or anything that would move, throwing them onto wheelbarrows. I say bodies, though some were still alive and others were not. Some did not really look like people any more. There were parts of bodies . . . I saw two children who did not seem to have any faces left.' 'The Serbs will just carry on,' said their deputy military commander Manojlo Milovanović on Belgrade radio. 'And if NATO has any oil to spare it can chase its own tail in the skies of Bosnia-Herzegovina.'

The attack provoked another forthright speech from Lady Thatcher: 'You cannot go on feeding these people and then leaving them to be massacred,' she said. 'The first thing is to see that the Bosnian Muslims are armed. Everyone has a right to self-defence . . . I am ashamed of the European Community, that this is happening at the heart of Europe . . . We have been like accomplices to massacre.'[9] British Defence Minister Malcolm Rifkind was supported by a grey chorus of men (who all owed their careers to Lady Thatcher) when he dismissed her remarks as 'emotional nonsense'.

On 15 April, a voice came down the ham radio from Srebrenica to Tuzla: 'I don't know how much longer we can resist. We beg you to do something, whatever you can. In the name of God, do something.' Belgrade television was reporting Serbian troops and tanks entering the outskirts of Srebrenica and the surrender of Bosnian forces in the surrounding villages. Lord Owen, suddenly steeling his position, proposed the 'selective bombing' of Bosnian Serb supply lines from Serbia proper 'which are fuelling this war.' 'Srebrenica is burning,' said the voice on the radio. UN reinforcement teams were prevented from entering the town by the Bosnians, then by the Serbs. For the first time, General Mladić met with the commander of the Bosnian army, Sefer Halilović, in Sarajevo to negotiate the surrender. UN troops began the collection of weapons – 'Everything from knives to armoured cars,' insisted Mladić – and General Morillon said he had 'saved Srebrenica'.

The allies floundered like headless chickens. John Major called for 'swift, tough, new measures' but did not say which. The whimsical ebb and flow of the United States position had gone into backtrack mode again: President Clinton said he was 'considering air strikes' but that a brief ceasefire had 'eased the situation'. Greece closed its airspace to Turkish planes patrolling the exclusion zone and Belgium found itself spearheading the interventionist lobby. Lord Owen said the Serbs had become 'Cocky, confident and think they can get their Greater Serbia. They believe the West will not intervene.' In the panic at UN headquarters, Srebrenica was declared Bosnia's first 'Safe Haven'. Within days, hundreds of shells had landed in the town centre.

The incoherent disorder within the alliance – blowing hot, then cold – was jolted by a revolt on Capitol Hill. Madeleine Albright, the foursquare US ambassador to the UN, insisted that America initiate unilateral air strikes. Memoranda from twelve state department officers accused the administration of 'capitulation to Serbian aggression and genocide', and urged lifting the embargo on the Bosnian Army. They were backed by the national security adviser Tony Lake and the leaders of both Democrats and Republicans in the Senate backed Ms Albright's call for air strikes. President Clinton now accepted that 'America should act and should lead' from now on, although he would not act unilaterally. 'Ethnic cleansing is the kind of inhumanity the Holocaust took to the nth degree. You have to stand up against it,' he said, adding that he was ready to start 'stronger action' within days.

The joint chiefs of staff chairman Colin Powell flew to Brussels to co-ordinate plans with NATO allies. The Pentagon had assembled an air armada of one hundred fighters and bombers, now heading for the Adriatic and German bases. Also on the American agenda: arms to the Bosnians and 'Safe Zones' protected by allied air power. The Serbs' bluff was being called; the West's moment of truth was just around the corner. In London, even

Rifkind was preparing reporters for a policy shift, saying the international community found the Serbs' behaviour 'intolerable, and will be obliged to respond'; threatening that air strikes would be 'an important and powerful signal to the Serbians'.[10] Ministers were admitting privately that military intervention was on the way.[11] Royal Air Force planes were on standby and emergency evacuation plans were being drawn up for the Cheshire Regiment. The Serbs sensed a different atmosphere from the usual mutable hullabaloo, and panicked: Srebrenica was quickly recognised as a 'Safe Haven'. President Milošević implored the Bosnia–Serbian 'parliament' to accept the Vance–Owen plan.

The climbdown by the weathercock alliance was a gradual one. The Proteus Clinton delayed pushing the button 'for a week'. Britain said it would use its security council veto to neutralise any attempt by the US to clear arms supplies to the Bosnian Muslims. The Americans were persuaded to give the Serbs one more chance: a sudden summit in the Serb-friendly capital of Athens at which Karadžić would be invited to sign the Vance–Owen plan, which he did with the Greek prime minister's fountain pen subsequently offered and accepted as a gift. Everyone at the diplomatic and media circus in Athens, kissed by the Aegean spring, knew that that the Serbs' and the Croats' ambitions had not shifted a millimetre. But what mattered in Athens were appearances. Milôsević had persuaded Karadžić to put his signature to a document that bound the Bosnian Serbs to return swathes of 'cleansed' land to the Muslims and to live with them and the Croats in a federation. It was a naked piece of jiggery-pokery, and the West bought it hook, line and sinker. 'The bombers have had their day', proclaimed Lord Owen, 'this is the start of what I suspect will be an irreversible process towards peace.' Bill Clinton was less impressed: 'We will judge intentions by actions,' he said. The Serbs insisted on one further hurdle: endorsement by the Pale 'parliament'. If their approval was not forthcoming, promised Karadžić for the second time, he would resign. Milošević, hailed as the peacemaker of Athens, was confident.

But a grotesque tragi-comedy began. Within two days, the enclave of Žepa in what Vance–Owen designated as 'Muslim' eastern Bosnia was in flames, following an artillery barrage. UN field officers reported 30,000 trapped people looking for cover in caves and forests to escape the onslaught. And in a final act of scorn, the 'parliament' in Pale ruled that only a 'referendum' by citizens of the 'Serbian Republic of Bosnia' could return a democratic verdict on Lord Owen's plan. 'We are ready to die to defend the principles of democracy,' puffed the 'defence minister' Dušan Kovačević.

Bill Clinton looked nervous and unconvinced as he tried to rally the allies for quick and decisive action in the face of such effrontery: 'America has made its position clear and will do its part,' he said. The strike at the Serbs was still ready for lift off; all that could stop it now was for Europe to crumble or for Milošević to pull another hologram rabbit out of his trick top hat. As it happened, both followed, in quick pursuit of one another. Milošević came up with probably the most transparently ridiculous but lucrative of all his meretricious ruses to date: he said he would blockade his Bosnian–Serb kin, switch off their supply lines across the Drina and throttle their war. Lord Owen and the British, unable or unwilling to see through this banal cozenage, reached out to grab at the lifeline thrown by Milošević which once again swung them off the hook.

Meanwhile, five more 'Safe Areas' were established under the tutelage of UN troops, in addition to Sebrenica: Sarajevo, Bihác, Tuzla, Goražde and Žepa. Quite what it meant to be a 'Safe Area' (as opposed to a Kurdish 'Safe Haven') no one quite knew; this purely academic detail would have to be learned through experience, as would the imaginary arrangements for Milošević's 'blockade'. Within two weeks, border traffic was rumbling as normal: armoured trucks, troops, fuel and food, off to war. Karadžić was still in place, and General Mladíc had barred UN convoys from entering the 'Safe Area' of Žepa, against which he now mobilised.

Radio operators reported 200 dead in the fusillage against Žepa, with the Serbs bringing troops up by helicopter from inside Serbia – a combination of circumstances which flouted just about every deal in which the West had placed its faith: air exclusion zone, border blockade and Safe Areas, all in one go. The Americans said again they would start arming the Muslims and mount air strikes 'within the next few days' if the attacks continued. The thinking in the White House was to go in quickly, train and help the Muslims to defend themselves, and pull quickly out again.[12] It was, said Clinton, 'a very specific, clearly defined strategy' with 'very clear tactical objectives'. But then the young president said he would wait again, this time for the Bosnian Serbs' 'referendum'. He admitted he had been forced by overt European and Russian pressure to back down, a novel position for a US president to be in. Douglas Hurd somehow thought he had detected 'a change in attitude' among the Serbs, and Owen convinced himself of 'signs that the Serbian leadership is no longer trying to ride the dangerous tiger of nationalism'.

The Atlantic alliance was riven. Warren Christopher said he found nothing but 'indifference, timidity, self-delusion and hypocrisy' on his last tour of European capitals. But it was the indelible Senator Joseph Biden of the Foreign Relations Committee who made the obvious and irresistible historical comparison which had been spoken a million times on the ground in Bosnia: 'The president,' he said, 'has sought to bring the allies into participation in a well-conceived western response. They are refusing, and I foresee grave consequences not simply for Bosnia but for the entire western alliance. They have shown the same vision and the same principles that gave us the immortal image of Neville Chamberlain's umbrella. I cannot even begin to express my anger,' concluded Biden, 'at a European policy which is asking us to participate in what amounts to a codification of the Serbian victory,' Chamberlain and Appeasement, fifty-five years on. Unattributably, other American officials preferred a more modern term than Appeasers: 'Wimps'.

On the same day as the senator's speech, 10 May, the UN convoy reached Žepa, with Ukrainian and French soldiers set to establish the Safe Area. The soldiers were aghast at what they found. A week ago there had been 10,000 people crammed into schools, houses and onto pavements. No one had known what to make of the subsequent radio reports that 'thousands' had fled into the forests and caves to escape the bombardment. UN officials in New York and Zagreb had played down the panic, and told reporters about the problems of exaggeration by the Bosnian authorities. But now the troops found fifty people left in town, most of them elderly, mad or wounded, cowering in cellars. There were bodies on the streets, bodies in what was left of the mosque. Ten thousand people had disappeared.

To nobody's surprise, 98 per cent of the Bosnian Serbs voted 'No' to the Vance-Owen plan. Here was the climactic moment when Washington and Europe were either going to show their mettle or walk away. The outcome was even more miserable than could have been expected. A plan was cobbled together in Washington by the US, Britain, Russia, France and Spain. It was in effect a new map of Bosnia in which the 'Safe Areas' had been restructured as a new Muslim state. Not only had another opportunity to be serious with the Serbs been lost, but lost with far-reaching and irreversible implications. Moreover, it had been agreed to by the mercurial Clinton, who quietly caved in rather than risk isolation in the final hour. The armed carve-up of Bosnia now stood on the brink of international blessing, with the inconvenient Muslims consigned to disconnected ghettoes into which they had been bundled by the gunmen after a year's free reign. Mr Hurd celebrated what he called 'quite a coming together among the allies'.[13]

It was a cruel betrayal packaged as a new initiative. The

decision to send more troops to defend the 'Safe Areas' was marked by a savage bombardment of Goražde, with two hamlets captured and razed to the ground. UN monitors were denied access to the Goražde pocket and in Sarajevo eleven were killed by a mortar attack while playing a game of soccer. Next day, fifty more in Goražde were killed by rockets. Six hundred people had died in the town during the two weeks' negotiating since the Athens summit. Europe had made its last stand.

The logic of the War of Maps, and of Europe's role, drove towards its inevitable conclusion at Geneva on 16 June 1993. Just over two years after their first meeting in Spring 1991, Tudjman and Milošević appeared, hot, shiny and beaming, to announce a 'breakthrough agreement'. They had found the basis for a deal on the partition of Bosnia into ethnic mini-states. On the day of the announcement, the UN finally reached Goražde to find that ninety-one people had been killed that morning. The plan was endorsed by Lord Owen and later by the EC Foreign Ministers. Bosnia's foreign minister Haris Silajdžić called the deal 'an injustice that disgraces us all', but Lord Owen dismissed his objections as 'nonsense'.

In the meantime, war in the central Bosnian countryside had spiralled into anarchy.

Chapter Nineteen

Massacre and Revenge

If the Serbs had won almost all they needed with the Srebrenica debacle, the Croats still had business to settle with the Muslims before their task was completed. Business in what was still the designated capital of 'Herzeg-Bosna', Mostar, and business in central Bosnia. In the words of the *Guardian*'s Ian Traynor, this is what British soldiers found when they arrived at the Muslim village of Ahinići, near their Vitez base, after the HVO had been through on the night of 16 April:

'Not a single Muslim house has been spared. Methodically and systematically, the hit squad went around the village blowing up at least 50 homes. "It was a band of 15 to 20 gunmen high on šljivovic. They went through the village house-to-house, lobbing grenades through the windows and shooting people as they rushed out of the burning houses," said Lieutenant Mark Jones of the 9/12th Lancers. "We found bodies inside houses, outside houses and in sheds. With one man, they had worked their way up his body, they shot both his knees, then his groin, then his chest and finished him off with a bullet in his head" . . .

'Elsewhere in the region, the 700 British troops fighting their own probably hopeless battle to stem the frenzy of violence that has erupted in and around their base at Vitez have encountered shocking sights. Soldiers tell of seeing civilians gunned down in cold blood, of finding a young boy clutching his puppy, both shot at close range, of women who were shot clinging to their babies. "Whole families have been killed. My men have seen children shot in their mothers' arms," said Colonel Bob Stewart, commanding officer of the Cheshire Regiment.'[1]

Colonel Stewart and a team of EC monitors were followed by Martin Bell from the BBC when they came upon the ugliest sight in Ahinići: a cellar containing the charred bodies of three women and two girls who had been trapped and burned alive. A man and a boy were dead on the stairs by the front door. 'Swine!' fumed the enraged Stewart, surmising that the men of the household had sent their womenfolk into the cellar for protection while they tried to defend the home from the ground floor. On Bell's film, a carload of HVO soldiers, mocking Stewart's wrath, tells him that he needs HVO permission to visit the village. 'I don't need the permission of the bloody HVO, I'm the United Nations!' he rails, 'I want to tell you this is an absolute disgrace! Whole families have been massacred here; who is responsible for this?' And the roughnecks drive off, laughing at the Colonel's ire. 'The Croats,' Stewart turned to Martin Bell, furious, 'realise what they have done in this valley. These are all Muslim villages that are burning here, and I'm sure they have not done it to themselves.'[2]

The arrival of spring had opened a new killing season in central Bosnia. Ahinići was the culmination to date of a Croatian push that had deliberately accelerated fast during the weeks that the eyes of the world were fixed on Srebrenica. If there was method in the madness unleashed by the HVO, it was to finalise the hold on aid routes and secure territories allocated as 'Croatian' under the Vance–Owen plan. Two days before the bloodbath started, the HVO issued another ultimatum that all Muslims in areas assigned to the Croats by the plan submit to the HVO. The defence minister of Croatia proper, Gojko Šusak, arrived in Travnik and demanded that the Croatian flag be hoisted. The systematic ethnic cleansing of the Vitez area, where a Muslim pocket was surrounded by a predominantly Croatian population, followed Šusak's visit, and was announced by the explosion of a car bomb outside a mosque, destroying half a street and killing at least seven people.

In the 'mop-up' operation that followed, HVO squads moved into the Muslim quarter killing at random for seventy-six hours and leaving a trail of bodies, including women and children, caked in the mud. During the fighting, 150 terrified Muslims flocked to the British base for shelter in tents which the soldiers erected, and another 300 came to live in five houses adjacent to the schoolhouse. The Muslim town of Zenica was subjected to an artillery pounding for the first time in the war.

There was retribution in the Muslim villages, where Croatian minorities were set upon and driven out, 700 from a village near Zenica, their houses then burned although the British and the head of the EC monitors, Jean-Pierre Thiebault, said they found no evidence of civilians being killed – yet. The expelled Croats were reported trying to cross the mountains to Vitez. The death toll in two days was put at 200, the majority of them Muslims. The British spent their nights roaming the hillside lanes in Warriors retrieving bodies and picking up the wounded under sniper fire. 'There have not been many dead combatants,' said an army spokesman, 'most of the dead are civilians.' One officer found ten bodies of peasants, including women and children, in a field near Ahinići, murdered with particular brutality. 'The Croats,' said one soldier, 'are crazy. They are very thorough in their ethnic cleansing. When they go into a village, they just shoot at anything that moves. In one village, they even shot the chickens, one by one, with a bullet to the head.'[3]

The army supervised a burial in the orchard behind the Vitez mosque: 'They have torn up the blossoming apple trees to dig a huge pit,' wrote Robert Fox in the *Telegraph*, 'the anonymous grave of ninety-six Muslim victims of the fighting . . . Across the street was a huge Islamic banner in

green and white, emblazoned with the green crescent . . .
As the business of transferring the Muslim bodies began, it
started to rain. The cadavers, mangled and decomposing,
were loaded from an abattoir truck onto the grass under
the white apple blossom beside the mosque. Young girls
were frozen in agony; women mutilated beyond recognition. "There is a small one, decapitated," said one of the
impromptu morticians.'4 In return, the Bosnian army had
handed over the bodies of four Croat militiamen.

Riding on the wave of violence, President Tudjman
toured parts of Bosnia-Herzegovina, flanked by Defence
Minister Šusak. The president laid the blame for the fighting
at the feet of the Muslims who, he said, were massacring
Croatian villages. Tudjman said the Bosnian Croats were
entitled to assert their right to union with the mother
country; 'Croatia's interest,' he promised, 'is a Bosnia-
Herzegovina arranged so that Croatian people within it
are sovereign, and that on their land there is no authority
but sole Croatian authority.'

That weekend, the rotation of the Cheshire Regiment
began, with their replacement by the incoming Prince of
Wales' own Yorkshire Regiment, straight into the mayhem,
but toughened by expectations of the worst. By now
there were Bosnian soldiers running around the region
wearing badges of the Cheshire Regiment on their uniform.
This would not be the case with the newcomers, who
would prove more detached and less stitched into the
tragedy unfolding around them. But theirs was a baptism
of fire. At Kiseljak, a Bosnian army police unit hijacked
a patrol of British troops while they were consulting
their map, and took their weapons at gunpoint. But this
was tame stuff compared to what would happen to a
convoy of buses approaching Vitez five days later – the
Convoy of Joy.

The sprawling convoy of 521 trucks had been organised
by the mayor of Tuzla, a joint Muslim and Croatian initiative
bringing fuel, food and medicine to the million people in the

area. It was not operating under the UNHCR umbrella, but had been accompanied by British patrols along some of the route. Between Novi Travnik and Vitez, the convoy's way was blocked by Croatian women on the road. It was a trap; soldiers from the HVO suddenly emerged, dragged eight civilian drivers from their vehicles and summarily executed them, the killers urged on by screaming women. Others were beaten senseless. Stranded along six miles of road, the convoy was a prisoner to the insanity of the mob gathering round it; thirty drivers were taken. British patrols trying to reach it had been stopped by HVO roadblocks; only later did a party of Warriors smash its way through to the scene to stay with the convoy throughout a night of looting by Croat villagers.

At first light, the head of the convoy decided to run the gauntlet, but as it arrived in the village of Nova Bila, the cab of one truck was pumped with gunfire and the driver killed. Women appeared, and started picking their way through the contents of the lorry with the driver's body still slumped in the cab, until journalists arrived, were spat at and punched, and the whole company then dispersed by the arrival of British Warriors.[5] The bulk of the stranded convoy was still being attacked and a driver bleeding to death, while British re-inforcements were trapped by women drinking coffee and children dancing in the road.[6] The British eventually got the convoy moving and retaliated only when mortar rounds were fired at the escort; two of the HVO highwaymen were killed.

The news from Ahinići, Srebrenica and Washington carried an implicit message to the now exclusively Muslim Bosnian army in the region: fight or die, fight hard and if necessary fight dirty. The retaliation began at the cross-roads of the war, in Travnik. Mehmet Alagíc, the deputy commander of the 17th Krajina Brigade, had undergone a metamorphosis: he was now commander of what had been re-named the 'Bosnian Krajina Command Group', by which was meant that the whole Travnik army came under

'Refugee' command. The men with nothing to lose had taken over the area's defences. Alagić's face had hardened; he still had time to discuss his plans and talk about the war, but it was sober stuff now, no smalltalk. The Croatian offensive had cut Travnik off from the aid routes. Commanders said they had supplies for only a few days, and if the Croatian ring was not broken by the UN convoy escorts, they would break it from the inside.

The HVO had been spoiling for fight in Travnik since Defence Minister Šušak's visit and the Vitez fighting. For three days, Croatian snipers fired into the town centre, picking off civilians, refugees and soldiers. There was artillery fire from the neighbouring Croatian villages and the Croat headquarters above the town at Jankovići. The flat of the officer running the Bosnian army radio, Nadja Ridjic, was raided and ransacked. The HVO hijacked a back-road arms convoy to desperate Srebrenica. By nightfall of 8 June, Croatian guns had finally closed the road linking Travnik to Zenica and the 'Muslim Triangle', and left the town surrounded. Alagić waited three days, then ordered the Krajina soldiers to strike. Within seventy-six hours of sporadic house-to-house fighting, the HVO had surrendered and been driven out of town. Its fighters, with 3,000 civilians, took flight over Mount Vlašić and into the arms of the Serbs for shelter. The choice of refuge was less ironic that it seemed: UN officers and observers reported that the Serbs had agreed to accommodate and allow the redeployment of the HVO in return for access to military positions it had held at Travnik's gates. The Serbs were brilliantly playing one side off against the other, for much of the artillery and ammunition unexpectedly produced by the Bosnian Army had been sold to them by the Serbs at giddy prices over Mount Vlašić.

Travnik, the ancient capital that had epitomised the Bosnian dream, ruled by a dual authority during some of the worst Croat–Muslim fighting, was now more of a Muslim town than ever before, and there was something sad and ugly about this, although people were on the streets again for the first time in months. The *Armija*'s offensive continued, linking up isolated pockets cut off from one another and re-opening the road to Zenica. For the first time in the war against the Croats, the 'Muslims' were the aggressors. The Croatian hamlets in the hills above the town fell one by one, the HVO retreated, taking with it hundreds of terrified refugees, streaming east towards Vitez. So far, the UN had found no evidence of atrocities against civilians, but they were not long in coming. The Bosnian Army in the region was now a militia with multiple faces. Alagić's Krajina Brigade Group were tight and disciplined fighting units with orders to engage soldiers but to leave civilians and churches alone, which they were credited by the British observers as having done. But the same could not be said for other units becoming increasingly potent in Travnik and in Zenica: the swelling Muslim armed forces or MOS, and the feared *Mujahadeen*, who treated the Croats little better than their Muslim brethren had been treated elsewhere.

If there was a chance to glimpse the ugly side of what any new 'Muslim Republic' might look like, these people were it. In the scrappy steel town Zenica, teenaged girls were sunbathing along the riverbank one July afternoon, giggling and tanning their legs and shoulders. The posse of five boys that came strutting up to them had not come to chat the girls up and offer them cigarettes, but to tell them to cover up those legs and shoulders, for this kind of thing was not considered decent in Zenica any more. After they had gone, the girls did actually manage another, even louder giggle. But the eldest of them, Ermina, was not really amused. 'I've never seen anything like it,' she said. 'Where do they think they are, Iran?' Later in the summer, the Imam of Zenica was kidnapped by a squad of MOS fighters for refusing to toe their extremist line at the local mosque. The first attacks on Serbs and Croats in the city were being reported, including an assault on a Catholic priest whose church offices were ransacked while he and his staff were tied up and beaten. Non-Muslims were desperate to leave as the Muslim thuggery grew worse, and within a week there was killing on both sides as the HVO was subjugated and chased out of town.

The fundamentalists, from both Bosnia and from Turkey, Afghanistan and the Muslim Sandžak area of rump Yugoslavia, collected into what became the 7th Muslim Brigade of the army. It was men from this division who were accused of killing the first Croatian civilians, at Guča Gora near Travnik. Among their more insidious pieces of handiwork was the desecration of an 800-year-old monastery in the forests above the town. Nuns, monks and 180 Croatians had taken refuge there as the Muslim offensive surrounded the village, and were rescued by the British. After their departure, stained glass was smashed, dynamite placed around the walls and graffiti sprayed on the walls: '*Casa del diavolo*' – 'House of the Devil' in Italian. Alagić sent up a team to remove the explosives and organise local Muslim women to wash off the graffiti. There was another stand-off in the village of Metrovići when the *Mujahadeen* rounded up 240 Croat civilians in a schoolhouse and had threatened to slaughter them when a group of *Armija* guards arrived and sent the bearded visitors away.

These forces were a liability, politically antipathetic to the Bosnian Army's cause, and, of more immediate concern, their presence meant that hundreds of military police who should have been fighting had to patrol the gained territory. The dilemma, however, was that the fundamentalists were often winning the territory in the first place. The head of the UN Centre for Human Rights, Payan Akhavan, said astutely in June: 'The Muslims have refrained from systematic ethnic cleansing because they realise that it means an end of a multi-ethnic state. But that element of self-restraint is disappearing, because they realise that they have to defend and take territory. They are losing faith in the possibility of a multi-ethnic existence, and we could now see Muslim atrocities'.[7]

The forecast came horribly true in September 1993, with the first brazen massacre by the Muslim side, at Uzdel, near Prozor. The HVO retreated from the village, the MOS from Jablanica entered it, the HVO counter-attacked and as they fled the Muslims slew the remaining thirty-five citizens in cold blood. Croatian television, which had studiously ignored the HVO massacres, showed pictures of the slain innocent villagers lying in the humble buildings, including an elderly couple clasping one another by the hand. Between Jablanica and Prozor, becoming one of the most ferocious fronts in Bosnia, the Muslims were now doing the burning.

All across the central fronts, the fighting was following the lines of Mehmet Alagić's 'Muslim Triangle'. His army was now a classic and ruthless guerilla organisation, equipped with only small arms, but running fighting patrols at night, deep behind their enemy's heavy guns and inside his territory, to wreak bloody revenge on soldiers and occasionally killing civilians too. Sometimes, they would withdraw, their night's work done; other times they would dig in, harrass and face the counter-offensive. That is how Uzdel was massacred.

By mid-summer, the central Bosnian front, or mesh of fronts, had become a rabid madhouse, a yard-for-yard battle for razed territory and what may one day become the Muslim–Croat border. Arms from Croatia and busloads of uncongenial military trippers were chugging up from Split and the Croatian coast to join in the killing caper. Stretches of the aid route to Vitez had become battlefields, with all traffic dependent on an escort shuttle service by British Warrior and Scimitar armour. The two sides were fighting each other to a standstill, taking hefty losses in and around Gornij Vakuf, where travellers ran a gauntlet of gunfire. The main road through Gornij, littered with shell casing and the wrecks of cars blown off course, was an unavoidable chicane on what was by now the only open land route into both central Bosnia and Sarajevo. It was also the border between the Government and HVO lines, flanked by wrecked houses, deserted but for the fighters and the occasional inhabitant, somehow hanging on – a woman was drying washing on a balcony one morning.

Relations between the British and the HVO hit a nadir, especially after a gang of Croatian gunners blasted wanton fire into the British Tomislavgrad base, Camp Redoubt. By the end of August, the official number of Croats killed by the British was eighteen, but any mention of that figure invoked an embarrassed cough from senior officers and a defiant, secretive grin from the lower ranks. 'You don't think we'd take that shit lying down do you?' said one private, brewing up tea en route. There was particular bitterness over the killing by an HVO sniper of a treasured interpreter employed by the British – she was a Serb. Life in the Vitez base had changed. The schoolhouse outside which sentries once helped children mend bicycles was now a sandbag fortress with a pill-box entrance and the canteen served mountains of delicious high-energy army/school 'scoff' with freshly fried chips or roast potatoes and jam sponge puddings smothered in custard and sweet Carnation milk accompanied by tea from aluminium urns. Bob Stewart's 'Sit. Reps' had been replaced by formal, detailed and expansive briefings. For several weeks in July, the hill right above the barracks and above so-called 'Press Alley', where the BBC had pitched camp, was occupied by a sniper flying a flag with a green crescent. He would amuse himself by firing rounds over the heads of either soldiers or journalists, and once it became clear that he was either a terrible shot or aiming to miss, he became so much part of the furniture that people would happily sunbathe or read in the shade of the BBC's garden directly along his sightline. Late in August, the HVO 'took him out', after which he and his flag were almost missed by 'Press Alley'.

A strange twist emerged in the Croats' ethnic cleansing programme: they started doing it to their own people. Thousands of Croatians from central Bosnia were being told by the HVO to pack up and leave for Herzegovina.

While Croats were rightly desperate to get out of Zenica and the Travnik–Vitez hinterland, many from quieter parts were equivocal about the move. The uprooted Ćorošić family had come south and were practising saying *Tisuca* for 'thousand' and not the central Bosnian word *hiljada*, which in Herzegovina was associated with Muslims and Serbs. 'We are grateful for the hospitality and help here,' said Săsa Ćorošić, 'but it will take some getting used to. It might have been too dangerous to stay at home, but our minds were made up for us. The HVO said the *Mujahadeen* were coming and that decided it. It is a relief to be amongst my own people, but creating "Herzeg-Bosna" in the way it was done did cause trouble for Croats in Central Bosnia.'

The day the HVO left Travnik, General Života Panić, commander of the Yugoslav army and a devout Serb nationalist, said that the 'best military solution' to the Bosnian crisis was now an alliance between the Serbs and Croats against the Muslims. Within twenty-four hours

of his remark, the Croatian guns trained on Travnik had joined the ranks of Serbian artillery. The unholy alliance was materialising too in the hills above the besieged town of Maglaj, where Croats who had fought alongside Muslims for a year simply switched sides to help the Serbs amputate the night ammunition runs from Travnik to Maglaj. The same happened at neighbouring Žepče, which fell early in July, after UN observers reported the Serbs and Croats joining together to build pontoon bridges to establish their supply routes. At Konjic, Serbian trucks were transporting Croatian troops, and the first civilian buses resumed between Croat and Serbian zones. Sources among all the international observer groups reported the two erstwhile enemies striking deals over towns along the borders between their respective slices of territory. The HVO and the Serbs jointly proclaimed 'the end of hostilities on the Neretva valley', which would enable both sides to concentrate on squeezing Mostar's Muslims north into a miserable landlocked state if not kill them off. Serbian tanks were given free passage through Croatian Kiseljak and on 30 June, the UN reported that there was now not a single front line between Serbian and Croatian forces within Bosnia.

For the Serbs and the Croats – at each others' throats in Croatia proper – to be brothers in arms in Bosnia was confusing but completely logical. The stage was all set for the final betrayal by the international community in Geneva.

Chapter Twenty

Meanwhile, the Diplomats: The Final Betrayal

The usually circumspect and gingerly Slobodan Milošević looked more puckish tonight. Even Franjo Tudjman let a stilted, prudent grin pass across his normally unresponsive features. These men had struck another deal. They were going to work together, they said. They were going to make 'changes' to the Vance–Owen plan which would take account of the 'realities'. Radovan Karadžić was cock of the walk; his burly frame breezed past the attendant crush of cameras with an affected swank. Even Mate Boban, who never exactly set the heather on fire, was queening it. President Izetbegović had left; he walked out of the talks that had just ended.

On 16 June, in Geneva, the reading of the last rites for Bosnia-Herzegovina began. The presidents from Zagreb and Belgrade who had professed their distance from the Bosnian cauldron were going to draw their own draft map of Bosnia which could consolidate everything their armies had done since the first shot rang out in Sarajevo, and the first torch was lit in Prozor. Moreover, they were going to do so with a writ and licence from the men who, time and time again, had vowed that Bosnia-Herzegovina would not be divided, that 'neighbour states' would never be allowed to partition the republic. The proud quartet had won themselves an ethnic cleansing charter, underwritten by the New World Order. 'There won't be anywhere near the sort of settlement that I would have ideally liked,' admitted Lord Owen. 'But I am a realist and we have to live with what is happening, what has happened, on the ground.'

Izetbegović's next stop was Copenhagen, where the foreign ministers of the European Community were meeting. He implored the managers of European foreign policy: if Europe would not defend Bosnia, then could it allow his government to buy arms while it still had some land left to defend with them. The ministers shuffled out to face the press and their Danish host Niels Helveg Petersen said briefly: 'We told the Bosnian delegation that in our view it would not be a good idea to lift the arms embargo.' The Danish president of the EC council added the pledge that the community 'would do all in its power to help the Muslims to obtain a just settlement',[1] whatever that meant.

Milošević and Tudjman drew up the rough map of three ethnic states – 'republics' – and showed the mediators in Geneva. Karadžić, also promoted from war criminal to hoity-toity statesman, invited 'the Muslims' to join in 'for the sake of peace and stability in the region'. John Sweeney of the *Observer* was there: 'One way of describing the negotiations is that last week in Switzerland a mass-murdering tyrant, his paler shadow and an English Lord whose political following at its last outing won fewer votes than the Monster Raving Loony Party, sat down to carve up a nation state . . . "Don't mention the ethnic cleansing!" would be Basil Fawlty's cry at Geneva if, as some would prefer, he was Lord Owen's co-chairman rather than Thorvald Stoltenberg.'[2] By now Cyrus Vance had stepped down and the Norwegian Stoltenberg had taken his place.

Izetbegović and his deputy, Ejup Ganić, had stayed away because they outwardly regarded partition as a betrayal. But their position was not shared by all of the collective Bosnian presidency. The remaining 'Seven Dwarfs' as they are called in Sarajevo, went to Geneva and then met in Zagreb to discuss the plan: three Serbs, three Croats and, more important, one Muslim on whom the international mediators now pinned their hopes. Owen had found his man in Fikret Abdić, the canny King of Bihać. And with him the revolt against Izetbegović began.

In search of at least one Muslim signature for partition, Owen now held a series of meetings with Abdić, a convicted fraud whom everyone in Bihać called 'Babo' – Daddy. Seedy, shrewd and sociable, Abdić entertained visitors with gusto throughout the war at his home in Velika Kladuša, lying in some of Bosnia's most lyrical countryside inside the Bihać pocket. Abdić had been among the richest entrepreneurs in communist Yugoslavia, as director of the Agrokomerc food distribution combine, one of the biggest companies in the Balkans. He was imprisoned in 1987 for a deal made possible by the Yugoslav state bonds system, under which Abdić's Agrokomerc issued £200 million worth of promissory notes without backing. Abdić went to jail as a local hero.

Now Mr Abdić had waged an exceptional war. He had managed to keep part of Bihać fed (the part that had hard currency) by trading with the Croats and with the Serbs too, across the front lines, with whoever had anything to buy or sell. He was acclaimed in Zagreb, was in regular contact with Tudjman and spent much of his time at the busy Croatian port of Rijeka. Abdić was now also praised in a Belgrade military magazine for advocating an end to the war, having accused Izetbegović of betraying Bosnia's interests. He had still not set foot in Sarajevo, presumably because had he done so he would have been lynched. In the week that Lord Owen threw his weight behind Abdić, the Austrian police put out a warrant for his arrest on charges of defrauding Muslim refugees. Relatives of refugees in Austria, Germany and Switzerland had been asked to pay a total of £5.6 million in order to get their kin out of Bosnia or else transferred from one refugee camp to another. The money was paid into accounts belonging to Agrokomerc. Mr Abdić has denied the charges.

The open rebellion came later. In October 1993, Abdić

relegated the carve-up to farce by declaring the Bihać Pocket 'The Republic of Western Bosnia', for which he said he had secured a sea corridor through the Serbian-occupied Krajina and through Croatia to Rijeka. Abdić represented both his own naked opportunism, and a genuine exhaustion with a war the Muslims had lost. By declaring potentially the fourth 'republic' in Bosnia, Abdić ignited the first intra-Muslim fighting, between his supporters and the army corps in Bihać which remained loyal to Izetbegović.

After Geneva, the pressure came at Izetbegović from all sides; from within weary Sarajevo, from Lord Owen, who urged 'necessary compromise' and from the battlefield. The Serbo–Croat allies were pounding Maglaj to pieces. UNPROFOR bases had been blockaded by soldiers from all three sides, and aid was at a standstill; Hurd warned that the humanitarian effort may have to be withdrawn. The UNHCR, attacking the paltry donations by rich member

states, said that two million faced starvation during winter unless the knot was untied. Three of the 'Safe Areas', Srebrenica, Goražde and Žepa, were under incessant fire, blockaded and untenable and the Serbs began a bloody push against the outskirts of the capital.

The Bosnian presidency said it would accept a 'federation' of mini-states, and Izetbegović agreed to come to Geneva to examine the detailed map that Owen and Stoltenberg were preparing on the basis of Tudjman's and Milošević's draft. But the talks were sent spinning into sudden disarray by events on the ground and in Washington. The Serbs had taken a crucial vantage point overlooking Sarajevo and President Clinton had burst unexpectedly back onto the stage, threatening imminent air strikes against their positions. Moreover, he had this time secured an endorsement to go ahead from NATO high command in Brussels. Six months ago, the Bosnian capital's heart would have palpitated at such bravado. But not this time, for Sarajevo was now dying from within.

Chapter Twenty-One

Serbian End Games: Sarajevo

Every catchpenny gesture by the Americans and the world played hard on Sarajevo's hopes and fears. Every mention of arms or air strikes made hearts pound reluctantly, and gave rise to unwilling hope yet again – only to send it diving, each time into deeper chasms. But by the summer of 1993, the Bosnian capital had become almost deaf to good news. Something had snapped; whatever it was that had enabled the city to endure, that had steeled its will to survive, had fractured. And what cracked it was not shells or sniper fire, but water and wattage.

'Damned if you Do, Damned if you Don't' was doomed Bosnia's motto. It underpinned the political dilemma: if Izetbegović signed for partition, it was a surrender; people did not want to live in an unsafe 'Safe Haven' on the floor of a school managed by a crowded, economically crippled landlocked Muslim state. If he did not sign, the merciless war went on. And in July, the Serbs found a way of translating Hobson's choice into something more insidiously immediate.

They proclaimed a grotesque diktat: you let us repair the electricity supply to our Vogošća arms factory on the edge of town, and then you can have your water and electricity back. You let us recommence production at one of the biggest munitions works in the former Yugoslavia, and we will re-connect the utilities necessary to keep the overloaded hospital going and to pump the water needed to keep life afloat and avoid epidemics. No arms factory, no electricity or water. The Serbs were doing what all sides in the war said they would refrain from doing: denying the basic means of life as a weapon of war.

The severance of electric power to the factory at Vogošća, north of the city, was one of the few spectacular successes scored by the defending army in recent months. Much of the factory was built underground, and it was the manufacturing line for deadly 240mm Orkan shells that rapid-fire from multiple rocket launchers, with whose potency Sarajevo was only too familiar. It produced mortar bombs and some 500 shells a day. The Bosnians had now secured positions from which they could snipe at any Serbian or UN engineering team trying to fix the power line. Major Nicolas Studer, French head of the UN engineering team, pointed to a map showing the minute details of the utilities network, and concluded: 'Bosnia-Herzegovina has made the difficult choice of preventing the operation of the munitions factory. If Bosnia-Herzegovina is not supported in its decision by the international community, or if any of the warring parties do not change their mind, then the international community must accept the slow death of the town.'

Gordana Knežević, deputy editor of *Oslobodjenje*, called it 'a clear strategy: to strangle the city until it becomes so desperate, it commits suicide. They don't need to take Sarajevo, they just need us to kill ourselves with fear and prison psychosis.' The paper itself was now so short of fuel that it was printing only a few copies, and news disseminated by magic marker headlines scrawled on paper billboards around town. At the grim mercy of the ultimatum, Sarajevo's End Game was under way.

Some people thought it had begun when two lovers, Admira Ismić, a Muslim girl, and Boško Brčkić, a Serbian boy, were killed by a sniper while trying to cross a bridge and escape, the Romeo and Juliet of Sarajevo whose entwined bodies lay where they had fallen for four days while each

side haggled over which had the right to them. Each side
blamed the other; 'I don't care who killed them,' said the
dead girl's father, 'I just want their bodies so we can bury
them.'[1] He never got them, the Serbs did. Others thought
the End Game had begun when some lads went to play
a game of football and were targeted by a mortar bomb;
eleven were killed.

But now the whole city was imploding, using up its last
sparse reserves of drinking water. The Serbs were holding
up a whole convoy of fuel at their checkpoint out at Ilidza.
The doctors at the main Koševo hospital were working
without electricity, treating acute injuries from shrapnel,
still coming in at sixty a day, and unable to wash their
hands in clean running water between operations. The
doctors and nurses had to join the rest of a city carrying
plastic canisters about, trying to find the few water pumps
that tapped into underground river sources, or else gathered
in clusters around some of the pipes carrying the drops left
in reservoirs on the western edge of town.

Out in the water queues, Fuad, twenty-six, joined a throng
taking water from a pipeline over the Miljacka river, along
which the remains from the idle Bačero pumping station
were still trickling through. 'There is no right choice for
them to make,' he said, 'there is no right or wrong in
this city any more, only wrong.' An elderly man called
Branko clambered with difficulty along the pipeline to
fill his container: 'What kind of choice is that?' he said,
'between death and death.' Behind him in line was Berina,
aged sixteen: 'Of course it is dangerous to come here, but
we have to. We have no option. Water is life and we have
to try and live. We know they could kill us at any time.'

Berina took her water and lived, but her fears were
justified. Next day, the unseen gunners sent their message
to those who still need to drink and wash, arms factory
or none. People were lining up for what was left of water
coming out of the pump in the pummelled promontory
suburb of Dobrinja, clutching their plastic containers, when

the mortar came in. The slaughter recalled the bread queue massacre of fourteen months ago: twelve died and fifteen were wounded in the broad silvery daylight of a summer shower. An hour later, the street was still strewn with corpses covered with sheets of canvas. The blood had mixed in with the rain, and was being washed down the sewerage gratings with corporation brooms by municipality workers in blue tunics. The ghosts of the stricken queue were still there: a neat row of hastily abandoned plastic containers, in a long, perfect arc along the tarmac polished by rain. In the hospital, doctors were trying to treat the wounded and amputate limbs without water, anaesthetic or power. That same afternoon, the Serbian SDS party was celebrating its third anniversary in Pale, with a special lunch featuring cognac and strawberry tart.

The funerals were next day, and the press were turned away. Dobrinja had had its fill of trying to persuade the world to take pity by making itself a spectacle. Six months ago, that would not have happened. Despite its will to survive, the city bore the anarchic marks of the end of the line. Thieves and criminal gangs were profiting from the misery and taking over everyday life. The Sarajevo Mafia had joined ranks with rogue sections of the UN forces to combine their black market business acumen. The Ukrainians were dealing in cigarettes and, it was alleged, heroin.[2] Incongruous, powerful German cars with local plates would pull up outside the UN headquarters, driven by flashy men accompanied by well-ornamented and manicured women. In a downtown bar favoured by visitors, Coca Cola made under licence in France (most troops in Sarajevo were French) was now twenty Deutschmarks a can. The barman explained that the cans came into town at two Marks each but that he paid fifteen and was obliged to charge twenty. There were stories about Deutschmarks levied to secure hospital beds. Sarajevo hospitality remained undefeated, and it became difficult to know what to do when pressingly invited into people's homes and offered supper which consisted of a shared lump of feta cheese that had cost your host three months' pay. To eat it was to devour a slice of their life; to refuse was dire insult. However, the market was fuller than usual, with people selling either their last possessions or a couple of lettuces they had presumably managed to grow with advice from 'war recipe' tips on local radio. Women found that a good way to feed themselves, their families or children was to sell their bodies to the soldiers. For those who had been prostitutes before the war, the competition got tougher as sex became a means by which a young mother could keep her children alive. Soldiers will be soldiers, and there was hard currency flowing around town, the only currency that mattered.

The weak were going to the wall first.

Old Sejda's eyes are leaden as she tries, through her chronic speech defect, to explain how she came to be in the dank, bullet-spattered kindergarten now turned into what is euphemistically called the Sarajevo 'City Psychiatric Hospital', tucked under the barrels of Serbian guns 500 yards away. 'There was a lot of shelling around the old hosptial,' she starts to explain. 'Chetniks came and said they would kill us if we stayed. And so we started to walk into Sarajevo together, and they put us here. I don't sleep or eat; just expectation, waiting for the bombing, until the bombing comes again . . .'

Most of the fifty chronic psychiatric patients in the kindergarten have lost or been separated from their families, although some still have kin in Sarajevo, like young Jugoslav, whose mother came to visit him three days ago. But she was shot dead by a sniper as she approached the boarded up entrance to the building. Jugoslav is in no mood or state to discuss his mother's death today.

The patients, of all ages, sleep on the floor of a classroom decorated with pictures of Bugs Bunny. There is wooden hoarding on the windows shattered by blast. The chairs, tables and lavatories are all infant-sized; the few 'comforts'

are all in minature; this is a godforsaken, surreal Lilliput
Bedlam under constant fire, above a maze of scrappy streets
which bear all the scars of sisteen months' bombardment.
You don't need binoculars to see the Serbian positions
nowadays. 'These are no conditions for a human being to
live,' says the doctor, Ferid Mujanović. 'We have a little bit
of food, but nothing else.'

The patients, in various degrees of derangement, had
been, as old Sejda said, in a hospital now under Serbian
control over the other side of the hill until the bizarre
wartime 'cuckoo's nest' exodus on foot into Sarajevo.
'The departure was hurried,' says Dr Mujanović. 'The
hospital was occupied and the patients told to go. They
were wandering along the roads into town. Some found
the main hospital, others were picked up by the police
and they were all brought here.' Now the patients are
forever trying to wander home, strolling out towards the
front lines, vaguely aware of the directions they need to
follow. Zefir almost made it. 'He tried to get to his family
at Iljaš, thirty kilometres away', says the doctor. 'Somehow,
he crossed no man's land and the battlelines, and was picked
up way into the Serbs' territory. I expect they could see
he was mad, so they brought him back the same way.
Apparently, he gave the Chetnik a good kick up the arse
when they stopped him!'

Of late, the patients seem better equipped than the staff
to cope with the End Game. 'They certainly know what is
going on, but I'm not sure if they feel the emotional effects,'
says the doctor, who is himself listless and heavy-hearted.
'On the other hand, they are more closed into themselves
than we are, they don't know what has happened to their
families or children, and they imagine the very worst. And
yet some of *their* symptoms have improved with the war,
unlike us, who have become nervous wrecks. It's us who
are the patients now, really, and the whole city is the
madhouse.'

Across the Sarajevo valley is the Mjidevica Street school

for mentally handicapped children. They suffer variously from Down's Syndrome, epilepsy, hyper-activity and severe learning difficulties, shell shock and confusion. These children think their parents are alive; they last saw them when they were being dropped off as boarders in January 1992, before they were trapped by war. They may or may not be right; most are probably wrong. Either way they are the orphans of riven Bosnia. They come from Foča, Bijeljina, Goražde, Maglaj, Srebrenica – 'In a way they are orphans because this is their family now,' says their teacher Merlida.

As the war began in April last year, Hazir, fifteen, from Maglaj tried to make his way home. 'I got as far as Zenica on the train,' he says proudly, 'I wanted to find my mummy and daddy, but the police said I had to come back because there was bombing in Maglaj.' Two days after Hazir returned, Sarajevo was surrounded. 'It's very frightening,' he says, 'but we go to sleep in the cellar when the bombs come.' The recent news from Maglaj was deliberately kept from Hazir; it was being torn to shreds by the Serbo–Croat guns. Aziz, fourteen and with severe speech and sight problems, was almost lucky. His parents tried to come and get him just as the siege was beginning. 'I was told they were here,' he enthuses even now, 'but the Yugoslav army stopped them at the barricades and wouldn't let them come this side of town. They *did* come to see me, but they weren't allowed to.' They left without their son, back to Odžak, which was soon subjugated by the Serbs and its Muslim inhabitants killed, set in flight or imprisoned at the infamous camps in nearby Brčko. 'I think my Mum and Dad must have run away when the Chetniks came,' says Aziz. 'There is a world-famous factory in Odžak, where my Dad worked.'

The childrens' attempts to get home increase as the End Game progresses. 'They do not understand,' says Merlida, 'that there are places they simply cannot go.' Marijo was one of the more determined wanderers at the start of the war, forever trying to cross the siege lines. 'He stopped trying during the worst shelling,' says Merlida, 'he was too terrified like all of us. But now he is used to the explosions, and has started again. He was injured recently, and even escaped from the hospital. The police found him at Sedrenik, right on the front lines.'

The school has taken seven direct hits and is repeatedly smitten with shrapnel and sniper fire. 'We staff are ready to face death here,' says Anna, one of an extraordinary team who stay on, working and sleeping, for three Deutschmarks a month, 'but the children do not understand this any more, that they could die, although they did in the beginning. When they go out to play, they ask, "What if I get killed? What will happen then?"'

'We are not getting food or help,' says Merlida. 'There were many uncertainties before, but the children were not hungry before that. And now we have to get all our water from the river and wait for these talks with the Chetniks about electricity. It's like being a hostage. Now, the cut in aid is so serious that if the blockades aren't broken we will have no food to give the children. We are tired of this war, tired of the cellar. If the children could leave, to somewhere we were happy with, we would leave our husbands and go with them.'

Little Zorica from Doboj – now in Serbian hands and 'cleansed' – puts her head around the door. She wants to say something to the visitors, but is too shy to start. 'Do you get frightened?' 'Yes.' 'What do you want to do when you grow up?' 'When I grow up I want to go back to Doboj.'

The day before the water-queue massacre, there was a social occasion at General Morillon's residence: lunch and a farewell address. There was orange juice, caviar, cakes and French Ricard Pastis. It was Morillon's last day in Sarajevo before his recall to France, and he began with a declaration in melodramatic tones which recalled either De Gaulle or an overblown performance of Shakespeare's Mark Antony. '*La Peur*,' he exhaled, and repeated it for good measure, '*La Peur*'. 'Fear. This is a city of Fear.' But the address was not all hot air. Srebrenica had undoubtedly changed Morrilon since his pompous arrival; there was a valedictory swipe at the plans to partition Bosnia into ethnic mini-states. 'There can be no solution which separates the three peoples,' he boomed, 'because there are not three borders, there are millions of borders. The inevitable consequence of such a policy will be to wrench hundreds of thousands of civilians from their roots, and the creation of a new Gaza strip here, with the result of continuing, intensifying and prolonging the present fighting for years.'

The dilemma over partition – 'Damned If You Sign, Damned If You Don't' – underpinned the End Game. There was a graffiti up in town: 'Sign, Alija, Even For a Back Yard'. The riven presidency had agreed on a 'federation' rather than a 'confederation'. There were rumours that Izetbegović – who might have preferred to lead a mixed Bosnia but always propounded a form of Muslim nationalism – was now ready to agree to partition, and a deal which would give the Muslims 30 per cent of the land, disjointed into 'Safe Havens', and a corridor to the sea. But in public he continued to refuse. Izetbegović's hands were tied by his own side. His deputy Ejup Ganić was the most hardline member of the presidency, insisting that: 'Partition is not an option for us. Agreeing to partition is like allowing someone to come into your house, move into more than half the rooms, steal your furniture, rape and kill your daughters and then ask you to sign on the dotted line. We just cannot do that.'[3] The Sarajevo Croat Stjepan Kljuić believed that 'If the Muslims accept the cantons, it would be a loss for all time. They would be landlocked, and open to blackmail for ever.'

Those who wanted to sign kept their heads down. Their constituency was among the exhausted people on the street, like a soldier who said: 'For me now, victory is staying alive, defeat is being killed.' The debate reached the ubiquitous water queues. Leila, holding her canister, said: 'I don't see the point of continuing. We have no chance, no food, no running water. The world will not give us anything and I am not prepared to die for idiotic ideals.' Her neighbour Šejla, also with plastic canister, was angered by this: 'I would fight on. If I had a gun I would fight and die for Bosnia-Herzegovina.' Leila sighed. 'It's exactly because you would die that we should sign.'

Sarajevo was now more cut off from the rest of the war than at any time, capital of a state across which atrocity was now the workaday currency of warfare, now failing to muster headlines in a world tiring of brutality in Bosnia. But for some in Sarajevo, the idea of Bosnia refused to die, not for reasons of sentimentality or the need to talk sky-pie, but in dread of the alternative. There were still people like Bojan Zec, the young graduate who had returned from Edinburgh:

'Federation, confederation; they are trying to find a word for something they can agree on; you can call it Monty Python's Flying Circus if you like, it's partition; racial partition into ethnically pure states. This is what has made things fall apart. We survived the winter quite well. It is when confronted by these options for racial states that things fall apart in this town.

'I have never understood the terms in which the West has described this war, desperately avoiding the obvious. There is a new fascism emerging in Europe, and this is its sharpest expression. You talk about fascism in Berlin or France, but not, for some reason, when confronted by Bosnia: camps, rape, population control, extermination. Fascism is an overused, and wrongly used word, but what is it if not this? We are resisting fascism and you refuse to see it that way.

'Partition means this: we will have Serbian fascism rewarded, and Croatian fascism rewarded, and out of that can only come Muslim fascism. It is already getting harder for the Serbs and Croats in the free territory. Soon, anyone called Milan Mihajlović [a typical Serbian name] will be a traitor. I have a terrible vision of this place in five years' time, though I hope I'm wrong: two fascisms, tolerated and rewarded by the West, producing a third one in response.

'The Serbian and Croatian fascists have never suceeded in extinguishing Bosnia except, logically, by creating police states, and that is exactly what they have done. I am real Bosnia, I suppose. My father's a Serb, my mother a Muslim and my grandfather on my father's side was Jewish. Bosnia has never had ethnically clean towns. Sarajevo has never had ethnically clean suburbs or even blocks of flats. But now the new fascism has created such areas, and that is why people start to feel that the war is close to an end.

'Some see partition as defeat, others see it as getting out of Hell. The reason to continue fighting is that we have paid an enormous price. What's the point in stopping now, the guys in central Bosnia are winning, let's get what we can. The reasons to give up are fairly similar. There has been too much loss. Too many killed, the infrastructure devastated. If we stop now we might be able to build something out of what we have, if we carry on, all we can see is bloodshed.

'But if you sign, what are you going to say to the people in Mostar, who are outside the "Havens"? The dilemma is that the price of peace is fascism. I am afraid there is no time now for illusion. The masks are off, they have cracked apart. It is all too brutal now.'

By the summer of 1993, Sarajevo's tradition of tolerance was being shattered by emergent sectarian Muslim nationalism in both the Army and the political leadership. Some Serbs and Croats who had remained loyal to the Government and stayed felt insecure and ostracised. The Army's deputy commander Jovan Divjak, a Serb, remained in position, but said privately that he did not expect to retain it in an increasingly intolerant and ungrateful atmosphere.

The general decay was ripping the army apart. The main command was still loyal to President Izetbegović, but the ranks were fragmenting. And no one in town was safe from Caco's boys.

Mušan 'Caco' Topalević is commander of the 2,500-strong 10th Mountain Brigade, fighting up on some of the most convulsive front lines at Mount Trebević. No one has ever interviewed Caco for he tends not to be seen, unlike his men who come into the town centre and press-gang idle or 'professionally' engaged men they may find into front-line duty. Caco was a mediocre musician in a rock band called Narodna Muzika (People's Music) and has developed, say those who know him, a mix of passion for the Bosnian cause and hatred for the intelligentsia. Legend has it that he saw one of his men fall into a fire because he was so tired after both digging trenches and fighting, so he decided to press people like Zaim Sidran into service. Zaim was an English student who had done a month's fighting, stopped after an ankle wound and managed to lie low. 'I was in café when they came and suddenly ordered four of us to leave for the front – immediately. They told us not to worry about clothes or food. I was up there six nights, digging and carrying sandbags, and lost a friend in a mortar attack.' Grander people than Sadija were caught in Caco's net, like Vladimir Bilić, head of Sarajevo TV and Telecommunications, or the celebrated musician Vedran Smajlović whose deep, sorrowful timbre had become Sarajevo's anthem to those who had heard him. Caco is especially wary of the 'Serbian fifth column' inside Sarajevo, and Serbs are particularly likely to be sent digging.

As Sarajevo's tolerance of the 'loyal' Serbs came under strain, the row over the fifth column nearly sparked open conflict within the army. A Serb in the army was rumoured to have shot one of his comrades and disarmed another two so that an enemy unit could take over a mountain position. Caco's men responded by kidnapping some forty Serbian soldiers, including the son of deputy commander Jovan Divjak, whom they beat up. For some reason, the former hardline commander of the entire army, Sefer Halilović, was somehow indicted in the imbroglio and quite out of the blue a rocket was fired at his flat, killing his pregnant wife and his brother. People gathered to inspect the damaged apartment, across the road from Radio Zid, and tried to work out the conceivable trajectory of an acrobatic enemy missile. No, it was impossible: this was an 'inside job'.

Attentions were quickly disracted from such small time depression in early August by the news that the Serbs had taken Trnovo to the south and thereby cut off the supply trail to Gorazde. Not only that, but General Mladić and his troops were moving on Mount Igman, over which ran the only non-UN supply route for ammunition into the capital. This was during the last waltz at Geneva, and it was this that spurred the USA to decide the time had come to strike at the Serbian positons with the best military technology that the world could offer. The Serbs sent a clear message to the negotiations by moving up Mount Igman on the eve of the Geneva expiry date for President Izetbegović to agree to partition. And Mladić sent an even clearer message to the UN by personally co-ordinating the operation by helicopter in the now strictly enforced exclusion zone. The Serbs took the mountain on 4 August. 'I'm here,' said Mladić to the EC monitors who came to take a look, 'and I'm staying.'

There was diplomatic consternation, NATO warplanes ripped into position, ready for the attack, all of which General Mladić fended off with a promise, barely fulfilled, to pull back off the mountain if the UN guaranteed to hold it themselves rather than allow 'other forces' to re-occupy it. It was a brilliant move: although the French Foreign Legion and the Serbs had been shooting heartily at each other for some time, they had one thing in common: oppositon to air strikes. And by bringing French troops up into the mountains among his own lines, Mladić not only took the wind out of President Clinton's sails, but read NATO's mind: so long as there were UN troops on the ridges, air strikes were out. Within a week, the issue was buried by the beautiful stare of little Irma Hadžimuratović, the child who would have died had her face not graced the world's newspapers, provoking her flamboyant rescue by the Royal Air Force. The airlift of injured children and adults was one of those symbolic moments that caused as much anger at its tokenism as it did joy to those who benefited.

In Sarajevo, the army of the End Game fought on along its claustrophobic, fearsome fronts and trenches built for hand-to-hand defensive fighting. To reach the intimidating line at Bistrik, the road winds up the hilly southern outskirts until it reaches the little bunker where the 1st Mountain Brigade had been based for fifteen months. Here, even the slightest 'provocation' by the defence lines can set things alight. Just as we arrive, a mortar drives into a house next door, injuring a woman who has to leave her two children, one with heart disease, while our driver Hasan, without being asked, takes her to the hospital. 'Just as well he was here,' grunted one of the soldiers, 'we've no fuel and if he hadn't, we'd have had to carry her into town, and she probably wouldn't have made it. There is a water pump up here, that's why they're shelling.' Most of the rough-and-ready boys in the accursed checkmate on this front line had worked at the Volkswagen factory at Vogošća, as did most of the Serbs over the brow of the hill.

'It's strange; the godfather of my child is a Serb, and he's probably fighting over there,' ponders young Jasmin, the deputy commander, with a pistol in his belt. 'We get to talk to them occasionally and I have asked a couple of times about him. The whole thing is mad. We're thirty yards away from them, we even call each other by our names. They ask us about individuals we know and whether they are alive. We were all friends before war; at this time of year, we'd be planning to go to the seaside. One of our men here was killed by his cousin because he refused to join the Chetniks.'

We are sitting in a little room turned into a dug-out by rows of planks leaning diagonally against the rafters – the battlements. The men just accept the shelling and wait for darkness. It is a stalemate; warfare up here is Sisyphean labour. 'The line hasn't moved since the beginning of the war,' continues Jasmin. 'They tried to break through six times and we took them out as they came down the hill. But there is no way to stop it, since they have all the shells. When we fight ground-to-ground, we win, but we don't have artillery, and therefore can never win conclusively. It's not war, it's just torture, psychological and physical, until we scream and surrender. They don't really want to come down the hill any more because we always kill more of them that they do us. We have more guts because we are defending what it ours, not trying to destroy something, and because we have the women and children on this side of the line. So all they do is fire mortars and heavy guns. Only the Romanian and Russian mercenaries; they do come down the hill. Sometimes, the local boys call at us to be careful because the Russians have come up to the front.

The men's commander, Suad, was thirty-one years old, and had nightmares at the start of the war about former friends trying to kill him; 'Only thing is it wasn't a dream,' he says, 'it was true. People who were like my own family, whom I adored, leaving town and joining in those cattle up there, killing my friends and their friends. It completely fucked me up. What it did was it taught me to hate, which I had not done before. Now, we have no choice, we have to fight to the end. All we have left is courage, the knowledge of what will happen to us if we don't succeed in defending this line and our town, and our hatred of their hatred, which really is past my understanding. We have to go on, even if all we end up with is a city of invalids and lunatics.

'Every man here has changed in his own way. Did you see that man in there sitting on the table? [There was a strange soldier with a baseball cap on.] Well, he's stark staring mad, gaga, crack-brained. Every so often they just go potty. A year ago, I was driving a van around because I didn't have any money. Now I'm responsible for these men and this line and I could go cuckoo at any moment. I've become like an animal who has to survive; one mistake, and we are dead.

'I'm no philosopher, I'm just here to fight against those

insects up there. But I do know that we think more deeply about all this than the Chetniks do. A baby from here died today because there is no electricity at the hospital. I think pretty hard about that sort of thing whenever I get a moment to myself.'

Senada Krešo works for the government but speaks as a friend; her apartment is a confluence of endless conversation about the war and Senada is invariably the only one in the company who is never in jeans. Recently, a shell went straight through her flat and dug itself into the kitchen wall. Luckily her elderly mother was in the bathroom, and luckily it didn't explode. Senada believes that the debate within the government she works for is cosmetic; that it is already all over:

'They call it federation, confederation, united republics of Bosnia or whatever; some call it defeat, I call it betrayal. A betrayal by the world and by the government. We trusted. We were not cynical like the others. We were naive, and because we were right and we were attacked, we thought the world would do something, trusting in the UN and all those conventions. Meanwhile, 300,000 civilians were killed. Looking back, we should have seen that we were doomed from the moment President Bush called it "a *humanitarian* nightmare". How stupid of us not to realise: not a political nightmare or a military nightmare, but a *humanitarian* nightmare. And even that they cured with the wrong medicine.

'I suspect that there are people in this city who will not be too upset about being part of a "Muslim" state. But for me that is the end. The UN troops will keep giving us food packets to stay alive, but it won't really be living, just as we can't call it living now. "The humanitarian nightmare"; there'll be no economy, we'll be living on "humanitarian" aid for ten years now. It's still prison, whoever the warder is. I have a good friend who is dead now, and sometimes I envy her.'

Chapter Twenty-Two

Croatian End Games: Mostar and the Camps

The Croatian soldiers came to Husnija's door at nine in the morning on 4 July ask if she had any men in the house. Only her husband, she replied, who is an invalid, and can only walk with sticks. But they got him out of bed nevertheless, and put him on the trucks along with every other Muslim man in Čapljina, south of Mostar, and took him away. In Mostar and its surrounding villages, the Croatians had launched their most savage wave of ethnic purges to date as they embarked on a final push to realise a racially pure 'Herzeg-Bosna' in advance of any outcome in Geneva. 'Men in uniforms, with automatic weapons,' mumbled Husnija, her eyes full of tears, 'they took him to the camps; there is no news and we hear they are moving them on.'

Čapljina was left a terrifying, sealed-off town. It's mayor is Pero Marković, who declined to receive us and had recently advocated proposals for a 'breeding programme' for Muslims which would restrict Muslim women having children. He called the Muslim refugees in town 'a Bohemian group, breeding anti-social, anti-authoritarian individuals'. Under the Vance–Owen plan, the Croats had Markoević lined up for the governorship of province number eight. We got into town by driving a beat-up old car with Croatian plates and pretending to read low-grade Croat newspapers with our feet sticking out of the car window, spitting and chewing gum – the kind of deportment that gets you waved through HVO roadblocks without problems. In town, there was an inhospitable, menacing silence; few people were on the streets except the usual uncouth heavies from the HVO. The smell of charred stone was hanging in the air, shops and houses recently dynamited, and an ambience strongly reminiscent of Prijedor and Banja Luka on the eve of the hurricane of Serbian killing and deportations last year. Four foreign aid workers had been arrested and detained in Čapljina and a CNN crew had been uncovered, detained and had its equipment confiscated that day. An old man walking down the street by a park said he was going to check his son's apartment to see if it was still there. Both his boys had been taken; his eyes filled and he crossed the road: 'I cannot talk,' he said. We elected to move with caution, starting from the mosque. A woman, also too nervous to speak, ushered us up a back stairway to the Imam's house, through which other women passed to narrate their stories.

'I am the only Muslim male under seventy left in the town because I am a religious official,' said Imam Hassan Palić. The seizure of the men of Čapljina began in June after all telephone lines were cut and roadblocks thrown up around the town. Suddenly, on 4 July, there was a blitz, a mustering of several thousand, leaving only the terrified womenfolk and children. An elderly woman comes in, and declaims: 'Look, I am not going to cry in front of you, or tear my hair out. Just this: they took my four sons. We went to the camp to ask what had happened to them, they said they had killed my second son and put stinging nettles on his grave, as an insult.' This lady said that women were now starting to disappear too. And she had two names of places where the men were being kept: Gabela and Dretelj.

'They are now going round the town taking everything we have,' said Husnija, 'My friend tried to hide her money in her knickers, but they searched her and of course soon found it and pulled it out.' A third woman, aged twenty-eight, came in and told us to stop talking, and stay on quietly, because a group of soldiers was patrolling the street below, and if we were found talking . . . 'I don't know, anything could happen.'

'My husband is a football player,' she whispered, 'he was just kicking a ball around in the stadium with our son when they took him. That was just after the Bosnian Army launched an offensive. Every time the *Armija* wins any victory, they take it out on us. They have been blowing up shops and houses every night for weeks now, and one night, suddenly, they destroyed ten.

'But we fought with these people against the Chetniks. Our men were in the HVO and some were fighting on the front lines when they came for them. We accepted the Croatian flag, we realised we were never going to be part of Bosnia even if we wanted to. And now this. Now they have turned on us, we have lost our men, we don't know where they are, and there is no appeal, no law here any more.'

The Imam then said we had better leave his house, for everybody's sake. 'I have seen all this before,' he said as a parting word, 'on television, from Prijedor.' Indeed, the wheel of the war had turned full circle. Here we were again. Houses and shops bombed, men disappeared, women in tears, troopers stomping the streets, sneaking out of town in fright, and word of concentration camps.

There was a frosty reception at Mate Boban's head-quarters in Grude, now moved from the hotel to a packing factory. No, Mr Boban was not available. And no, it would not be possible to visit either Dretelj or Gabela because they were, said Boban's Canadian spokesman, 'in a declared military action zone' (even though Dretelj is ten miles from the nearest Muslim–Croat exchanges on the Mostar front, and Gabela was a further six miles away, almost on the border with Croatia proper). We said we were quite happy to risk it. 'It's a sealed area. The area around Čapljina is closed by the HVO, you can't get in.' We said we had just been to Čapljina; 'Oh'.

The prisoners in all camps were 'soldiers captured in

battle', said the spokesman, changing tack and trying a bare-faced lie. Muslim men from Čapljina, Stolac, west Mostar – the side of town under Croatian control – and a host of other villages were being 'gathered', said the Canadian, 'for our own security, in case they take up arms against us.' It was an exact repetition of what the Serbs had said in Prijedor.

Another word for 'security' in this context is racial purity, and in this the Zagreb government was happy to oblige, offering to assist in the mass deportation of Muslim men from the area. In a joint aproach to the UNHCR, the Croatian government and its puppet in Grude proposed the setting up of a transit depot in the Herzegovinian town of Ljubuški, where 10,000 Muslim men festering in unseen camps could be concentrated before being deported to third countries, if places could be found. Mate Granić, the Croatian foreign minister, promised his government's co-operation, saying that the appropriate 10,000 transit visas would be arranged. The UNCHR said the scheme was 'abhorrent', its officers 'horrified' at being invited yet again to facilitate racial purges. It was not only we who were refused entry into Dretelj and Gabela. The Red Cross and the UNHCR had for weeks been trying, and had been refused.

Six weeks later, UNHCR officials and journalists in the Muslim-held town of Jablanica saw the first men to be 'released' from the camps. They were skeletal and malnourished. The men had been stripped naked at the Croat outpost positions and sent running down a rocky track towards the Government Army lines, fired upon as they did so. Prisoners said they had been mentally subjugated as well as beaten, forced to sing fascist Ustasha songs. The UN officials had also dealt with teenagers in conditions of severe trauma, some of them as young as thirteen years old. 'They spoke,' said one official, 'in an awful, flat monotone' when submitting their testimony. Some prisoners said they had been forced to have anal sex with each other and with animals. In all, the UN teams estimated that 45–55,000 Muslims had now been 'cleansed' from their homes around Mostar between June and September.

At one camp, said the witnesses, the guards had opened fire into sheds full of prisoners. That was Dretelj; and on 7 September 1992, two months after our first request at Mate Boban's office, we finally made it through the gates of the Dretelj concentration camp.

Their huge burning eyes, cropped heads and shrivelled, sickly torsos emerged only as one became accustomed to the darkness: hundreds of men, some of them gaunt and horribly thin, crammed like factory farm beasts into the stinking, putrid spaces of two large underground storage hangars built into the hillside on the edge of Čapljina. This infernal tunnel had been their hideous home for ten weeks now. The murky hangars are two of the six sheds that make up the Dretelj camp at the former Yugoslav army installation, now run the by HVO police. This was the first access achieved by the press since it was re-opened at the beginning of July.

Talking to the prisoners was not easy: men leaned forward from the huddles that gathered around us to whisper snatches of recollection or fear, or else took us back into the murky shadows to speak in hasty fragments of testimony: 'I'm afraid to speak; I'm afraid they'll beat me,' said one man as though trying to talk with his eyes, running a finger across his throat.

At the back of the hangars, the walls were pockmarked with bullet-holes; the bullets had obviously been fired through its pierced metal doors. Prisoners talked about Croatian guards coming up to the hangar doors after drinking sessions and singing as they fired into their quarters, particularly over a period of three days in July. Estimates of the numbers of dead on these occasions ranged from three to ten. A young prisoner supplied the name of one of those killed: his friend Emir Refik; then he lay back on his filthy blanket, squashed up against this comrades, tucked his palms under his head and continued to fix his stare on the dark ceiling. After the shootings, said another prisoner with the skin of his chest sinking back between its bones, 'a man had bullets in his leg for three days before he could get any help.' Many others were wounded, and there were accounts of routine beatings. 'They would beat us every day,' said a prisoner cowering in the obscured corner of one of the hangars.

The men were kept in these two hangars, effectively giant human pens, black as pitch apart from a sickly light bulb. In July, said the prisoners furtively, the doors were shut as a matter of course. During one stretch, apart from a single meal a day, the men in the underground hangars saw no daylight for fifteen days. And for one period of seventy-six hours they had been left without food or water, totally incarcarated in the dark, steaming heat and in their own excreta. 'We had to drink our urine to survive,' said one prisoner, in a whispered aside from the interpreter.

When the camp was first established, there had been no sanitation facilities whatsoever, neither in the overground sheds or the hangars. In the sheds, a man called Senad said that for the first month, the doors were locked, and excreta had to be 'picked up off the floor and thrown out of the window'. The shed had been 'infested with lice and other bugs,' he said.

In the two hangars and in the four sheds above ground, there was insufficient room for all the men to sleep fully streched at the same time. In the overground sheds particularly, they were packed tight on the floor, crouching, sometimes on filthy blankets, with what few belongings they had hanging in plastic bags from the beams above because there was no room on the floor. The men were in varying states of trauma and decay. Some had obviously been admitted more recently, as little as a day ago, and were in manifestly better condition. Others had hollow cheeks, blank, neutral eyes, bad skin rashes and barely shared the surprise of the healthier prisoners when we walked in.

The prisoners were told by the camp commander Tomo Šakota that they could speak freely, but interviews had to be conducted through an interpreter; conversation in English or in German was quickly and angrily stopped, and no photographs were allowed. Men would draw us aside, and talk in whispers. During the early days of their internment, says one boy from Sarajevo, who had been held in two camps before, 'they did everything, just imagine for yourself – everything'.

The 1,428 prisoners turned out to be some of the Muslim men rounded up off the streets and from their homes at Čapljina, Mostar and Stolac. Many had served in the HVO, in its war against the Serbs, and some had been interned directly from the front lines. 'We fought with these people and died with them,' said one prisoner. Not one of these men has any idea whether his family, womenfolk or children are dead or alive, or where on earth they might be. (We found out later, on the day we went to besieged Mostar.) For me, there was a terrible aura of *déjà vu* and of a ghastly wheel coming full circle, for the camp was the same Yugoslav army installation as the one we found in August 1992, when it was run by the HOS and Major Hrsto, and used to keep Serbian prisoners at the outset of the war. That day, the hangars were concealed from us, their doors slammed shut.

Access to the now far worse conditions at Dretelj was this time authorised by the commander of the HVO, General Slobodan Praljak, to the angry surprise of the guards when we arrived, and to the rumoured irritation of Mr Boban, who had refused to see us and had not been consulted. We suspected General Praljak's motives might have had something to do with concern in Zagreb over the offence the Croatian camps had caused internationally, with Croatia proper still trying to score democratic brownie points in the West. On the day before our visit, a Croatian newspaper published a letter to Boban from Tudjman urging him to 'take all measures to obey international humanitarian laws' in detention camps. A team from the Red Cross had finally gained access to the camp the day before us, nine weeks after its first request.

But one prisoner said that '120 men have not been registered by the Red Cross. They were taken away before the Red Cross arrived, we don't know where, and then brought back when they had left.' Our enquiries later showed that these were either men too thin for the Red Cross to be allowed to see, or boys in their early teens.

The prisoners at Dretelj agreed that most of the more serious brutalities, beatings and murders, as well as the worst conditions, had been dealt out during the early weeks of the camp's opening. The arrival of Commander Šakota seemed to have ended the worst of the killing and torture, although one prisoner managed to say in English that things had only got better 'three days ago', before the arrival of the Red Cross. A prisoner called Emir who had been admitted on Monday, and was allowed to do work duty cutting wood, said a man had been beaten to death with wooden planks the night before our visit.

The heavy steel doors of the hangars were at least open, with some men crowding around the entrances to bathe in the daylight and gawp at our arrival; others, resigned, preferred to surrender to the darkness, staring into the gloom as though they were blind. We asked those by the entrance why they did not go out into the compound. 'We're not really allowed out of here,' said one, scornful at what was clearly a presentation job for the benefit of our visit and that of the Red Cross.

The systematic beating and what one prisoner called 'every kind of torture' seemed to have eased or stopped only very recently. In the first hangar, a man managed to say in English: 'It is very dangerous to speak in here; there is very tight security. Just in the last three days there has been some change, that's all.' Commandeer Šakota admitted that he had been telephoned by the Croatian foreign minister Mate Granić from Zagreb only two days ago (with the Red Cross visit scheduled) and 'given the order that I had to make these peoples' lives a little easier'.

In the second hangar, one man rose, gave his name and place of origin (one of the very few to do so) and said he wished to declare how much better conditions were since the commander took over. There were nearly fisticuffs as other prisoners jeered him down. There was a bizarre moment when Commander Šakota did say that 'I feel sorry for these men, and no one would be more pleased than me if they could be re-united with their families', and the prisoners applauded. As ever with these reluctantly conceded prison visits, a theatrical game of power, terror and deception is played, and it is hard to work out what truths lie behind the desperate but muted stares that follow you. The beefy guards who patrolled the site and the hangar entrance, swinging their machine guns, either snarled or else smiled unpleasantly to themselves as we made our way round, and found the applause episode markedly funny.

The tour had begun with a visit to the 'medical centre', a shed where men were packed onto primitive beds, shared between two or three inmates, in differing stages of decay, tended by three Muslim doctors. They lay in a leaden silence, with hollow stares, some very thin and others with eyes glazed over with fluids, curled up under scanty, dirty blankets. One man was so ill he could not sit up. Doctor Hasan Redjić from Stolac said that most of his patients were suffering from chronic malnutrition, and he had also had to treat 'broken ribs'. Wary of the supervision of the conversation, the doctors said that many others had died from 'natural causes', and prisoners gestured to signify intense heat and starvation.

Past the overground sheds, the daily lunchtime drill was in progress. It was a humiliating, spiteful business: men were lining up at the entrances to their huts in groups of ten, and being forced to jog in single file to quickly gulp a watery dish of rice and sauce from metal bowls, which they did crouching in a huddle in front of a hefty guard sitting in an old chair. Their meal completed, they would then line up again and proceed to a tank of water, wash the bowls, and then in another line take them to a spot where they were laid out on the ground, ready for the next group of ten to begin. Back in the sheds, a disc jocky called Ethem Redžić said that 'we are just ordinary folk in here, and all we want to do now is to leave, no matter where'.

As we left the camp, on a lonely road out of Čapljina, a car with official HVO number plates pulled up alongside, crashed into the side of our car and tried to push us off the road. It had come from the direction of the camp.

The following day, members of the 'Herzeg-Bosna' government were speedily despatched for a chaotic press conference at which officials managed to simultaneously admit that the pressures of 'security' had led to breaches of the Geneva Convention, but also to insist that conditions in the hangars met international humanitarian standards. A spokesman for Mr Boban, Barislav Pušić, said that 'The hangars meet international standards. If Yugoslav soldiers can sleep in them, then why can't Muslim soldiers now?' (the hangars had been used to keep fuel trucks). However, an HVO spokesman, Kresimir Zubak, conceded that some points of the Geneva convention had been breached because of the hasty detention programme and the lack of facilities. (Much play was made of Muslim camps where Croats were detained. These existed, on a much smaller scale, and conditions were harsh, but incomparable; prisoners were usually housed in schools or kept under house arrest.)

The upshot was for the Croatians to subject the relief agencies to exactly the same grotesque blackmail as that deployed by the Serbs after the discovery of their camps: the men would either have to be left in conditions which violated every international standard, or else the agencies would have to take them, thereby helping the bully boys in the racial clearance of their territory. Certainly, there was no question of the men going back home, or being assured the slightest guarantee of safety if they did. Home for these prisoners had been taken away, just as it had been taken from those detainees killed by the Serbs when they returned 'home' from Trnopolje last year. Inmates are at the time of writing are being 'released' from Dretelj, and taken to an island off the coast of yet another island, Korčula, in the Adriatic, held by the Croatian authorities pending their expulsion (Zagreb calls it 're-settlement') to either third countries or back into 'Muslim' territory if nowhere else could be found.

Dretelj, it emerged, is one of a network of camps, only three of which were admitted to exist and to the rest of which the UNHCR and Red Cross had been, at the time of writing, denied access. One village, Gradska, has been sealed off by HVO roadblocks and has been found by UN police to contain only ten remaining residents.

At the centre of this wave of ethnic cleansing was what the Croatians regarded as their prize: Mostar, the city 'Herzeg-Bosna' claimed as its capital, but in which the Muslims had been the biggest population group before the war. The final Croatian assault had begun on 9 May with a night-long barrage of mortar and rocket fire which set the Muslim quarters of town on fire. The mass deportation of Muslims from the sealed-off west bank followed, with the UN observers that could get in seeing hundreds of men, women and children kicked, bused and marched out of town every day to factories, a stadium and the local heliport. Like the Serbs, the Croats ordered Muslims to hang white flags from their homes. The men were sent to the concentration camps, while the grotesque harvest of women and children, from the west bank in Mostar and the villages around, continued from May onwards. Their menfolk gone, they were rounded up at gunpoint, bused up to the front lines and sent, with shots fired over their heads, marching across the bridges and the fighting lines, into the tiny Muslim enclave on the east bank of Mostar itself. There, they would swell the population bracing itself for what would become the most savage and pitiless siege of the entire war. Spokesmen in Grude denied that any women or children were being removed from their homes; 'truth' in the putative 'Herzeg-Bosna' was of no greater value now than 'truth' in Banja Luka.

EC monitors and UN civilian police reported that the siege lines building up around Mostar were being mounted by tanks, artillery and men from the army of Croatia proper as well as the HVO. 'Spanbatt', the battery of Spanish troops from the so-called Protection Force promptly abandoned its base in town; they ran away. The more reliable British army had for months been trying to assume responsibility for Mostar, but the Spanish had refused to hand it over, confident of their capacity to do the job.

For ten weeks, the Croatians allowed no food, aid or medicines into eastern Mostar. At the end of August, a convoy finally made it, after giving generously to the besiegers of the town as a condition of entry, and having been obstructed for days by the HVO and demonstrating Croatian women and children blocking its way. The convoy was greeted on the east bank by ecstatic and desperate crowds. The UN found two thirds of the buildings too badly damaged to be inhabited, and warned of starvation 'within days' if a supply line was not secured. It was then trapped for three days by crowds who knew that the minute it left, the siege would resume its full glory , which of course it did when the UN finally pulled out.

Mostar, September 1993

The Croatian guns across the river are laying the old centre of Mostar in the dust of its own ancient stone. The siege has become a prolonged, relentless torture by sniper fire, shell fire, tank fire. The tearing out of life in the once mighty Ottoman city is without cease or mercy, its crammed and terrified people suffocated by claustrophobia, fear and the callous ferocity of an assault which is levelling its buildings, literally, to the ground.

East Mostar is surrounded, trapped, concussed and comfortless. To the west, the Croatian assault lines are ranged along the riverbank, 200 yards away, across the venerable old Turkish bridge, delivering their barrage. On the ridges to the north and south, newly arrived tanks from the Croatian army are bunkered down, blasting what is left of the enclave to smithereens. On the hills to the east are the ranks of Serbian artillery, adding their own dutiful dose of death to the mayhem. And General Winter is also advancing with every petrifying day.

The population of the bombarded pocket is still swelled daily by wretched deportees bullied out of their homes in the surrounding towns and on the west side of the city by squads of Croatian gunmen, and herded across the front lines to be caged into this nightmare. They are almost all women and children whose menfolk have been incarcerated in the Croatian camps; others are themselves former inmates of those camps, 'released' naked and skeletal into Jablanica and then making the two-day hike to Mostar to join in the defence of the city, if they can be made fit enough. The headcount in East Mostar when the siege began in May was 10,000. The number is now 55,000 and rising. Some 400 people have died over the past weeks in the makeshift 'hospital' alone, plus God knows how many in the pulverised outskirts, where the dead are hard to find and harder to retrieve and bury.

It is impossible to imagine any place at any time during these two cruel Balkan wars to compare with the concentrated claustrophobia of east Mostar. 'It is far worse than Sarajevo ever was,' says a doctor who was one of the leading brain surgeons in the old Yugoslavia. He walked the perilous track for four days from Sarajevo after seventeen months endeavour in the capital, to live and work in east Mostar's crowded subterranean 'hospital'. He asks that his name not be used in order to protect his family which has fled to Croatia. 'There are conditions here which make this more serious than anything I have seen so far, the sheer concentration of wounded people, women, children and released prisoners make it impossible to endure while the war goes on like this. The difference is that the Serbs know they could not possibly rid Sarajevo of 380,000 people; but these people are determined to take, cleanse and claim Mostar, and do believe they can kill or expel 55,000 Muslims.' This man was due to return to work in one of the best-equipped hospitals in the world, in Chicago, when the war began; dissecting and rebuilding grey matter. Now he treats the cleaved flesh of shrapnel and sniper victims.

The outpost to the north is a nest of mauled blocks of flats which people now call Beirut, where the elderly live day and night in the cellars beneath the towers of smashed glass and concrete. Beirut is now almost cut off from the centre of the pocket, because there is too much open ground across which to sprint through the sniper fire for those trying to reach or leave the estate. Young Adnan, sitting on the wall in the town centre, will have to sleep there tonight. He comes from Beirut and is marooned from his underground home; he cannot consider attempting the dash since shrapnel cut into his legs after an explosion last week. Cautious soldiers from the Government Army advise that 'you'd have to be Linford Christie to make it alive', managing a weary smile. Two girls are bringing up burned furniture from a ravaged house down towards the river, preparing to make a new home in the already packed old centre. 'They are from Beirut,' says Adnan, resignedly. 'Quite a lot of people are moving down to town to be like sardines in this tin. But what happens when the Ustasha come across the bridge and really start to cook us?' He waves his crutches around the points of the compass: 'Fascists to the north, south, west and east. We are a Muslim sardine sandwich for the fascists to eat.'

To the south, a dusty track runs into town through the flailed suburban hamlet of Blagaj. This was the route we took into Mostar: past the Croatian artillery dug into the houses from which their troops have burned out the Muslims, and across the no man's land of the airport runway. Up the rugged tracks into Blagaj stagger huddles of deported itinerants, all women and children, the latest to be wrenched from home; their menfolk are in the camps, and they are cast over the fighting lines and corralled into the Mostar enclosure. En route, they were trying to find homes in the few buildings that had not been lashed to shreds, and to join those who waved a pathetic greeting to the sight of foreign armoured cars from the world outside.

The mutilated centre of the Mostar stockade focuses on a single main street. Every building has taken several direct hits, and most have been incinerated into uninhabitable charred masonry. Crowds of faces gather at the windows of those still occupied, to peep out when the shells slam in and shake the ground. One single block to the west is the river, and the splendid high-arched Turkish bridge, 420 years old this year. A survivor of wars and twenty earthquakes, it is still loved, and now, poignantly draped in a shield of suspended car tyres to protect it from what might be its last and final enemy, the Croatian guns. There is of course no running water in east Mostar, and people still go down to the river to collect infested refreshment, if they dare. A few days before we arrived, a mother and her two children tried to do so and were killed by an anti-aircraft missile fired straight at them. Immediately across the bridge is the only Government Army outpost on the west side, a forward promontary, somehow defended, on the ground of what was the old Turkish market or Souk, a lovely row of shops kept open by the rogues who owned them throughout the worst of the Serbian siege. But the Souk now comes up as far as your knees, bludgeoned literally to nothing. Back where the old bridge joins the east bank, there is also nothing but rubble and the odd scarred, isolated stone wall still stubbornly standing.

The harsh rattle of machine guns, the *crack-crack* of the snipers' high-velocity rifles, and the loud, dull hammer blow of the shells refuse to relent for more than a few minutes at a time. They are continuous and impenitent, sending people scurrying for the probably useless cover of a wall or doorway. The Croatian tactics are those tried and tested by the Serbs at Srebrenica and elsewhere: indiscriminate shelling of civilians, sniping at civilians, little stomach for hand-to-hand combat but an infinite supply of artillery and ammunition, and the denial of food, medicine and water as a weapon of war. Not dissimilar, in fact, to what was dealt out on a smaller scale to the Croats themselves at their shrine of Vukovar, but this time at a closer, more ruthless range and inflicted on a larger, swelling population. This time, the infernal cacophony of the exploding ordnance is completed by another torturous sound: a barrage of Croatian patriotic and fascist Ustasha songs – laced with a bit of loud rock and roll – blaring out from specially constructed hi-fi speakers lining the Croatian banks opposite. Apart from any intimidatory message, there is the simple signal: we have electricity, you don't.

On the thrashed masonry of the old centre's street corners, the sad flag of defeated Bosnia is stencilled, along with painted signs reading: *'Pazi! Snajper non-stop'*. It barely needs a translation, except to say that *'Pazi'* means 'Danger'. Every intersection that affords a sightline to the Croatian snipers is a shooting gallery across which old people, soldiers, women and children sprint for dear life as the bullets cut the air above and around them. At one point, not even Linford Christie would make it, and so the main street is forced to divert into a warren of crushed houses, rubble and former stairways – and also the kitchen of the Segetelo family, through which between 350 and 500 people pass each day.

Mrs Segelato is the local hairdresser, and still takes customers beside the sink – price: two cigarettes for a cut – snipping at their locks as the endless procession wanders to and fro along the dark brick hallway, past the kitchen table and out into the rubble. 'It's better that they come through here than get killed in the street,' she says, styling the head of a lady. 'We get to know people, everyone knows us now, and we like to think that we have made a little house of peace here.' 'We've taken three direct hits,' says her husband Hasan, who built a special doorway in a wall to facilitate the new highway, 'like a 120 mm shell just outside the other day. Whether it's because they know about this arrangement, or just co-incidence, I don't know.' Little Sabina, who is eight, quite likes the coming and going, but not enough to avoid reflecting that 'all I want is to play at school and draw with my friends'. In the back room, three teenagers sit and talk. It should be a scene from their normal lives, with their coloured leather thongs around their wrists and the boys' hair in pony tails. Ilhan, Selma and Samir are their names; 'Life has frozen,' says Selma, a pretty sixteen year-old, crouching on the floor, 'there is nothing to do but to sit here, to be terrified, to wonder if it is real and wait for the end.'

Let no one say that people become 'accustomed' to shelling. The people passing through this kitchen and passageway do so with an uneasy trudge as though waiting for the axe to fall, only just managing a sad acknowledgement with their dead eyes and taut, frightened faces. For no labyrinthine passages can offer protection against the shelling. The morgue is brimful and stinking, there is no refrigeration and there are no body bags. The dead are buried in parks at night; funerals are nocturnal and as silent as possible so that the snipers can neither see nor hear them. The last appeals to Allah or to personal memories, made as the bodies are lowered, are whispered, not spoken. Twenty-three were killed on the day we arrived.

For those who are hit but who live on, there is east Mostar's godforsaken – if throroughly impressive – 'hospital' in an old health authority office built by the Hapsburgs. Down, down, past the anxious waiting relatives and soldiers with their girls eager for news, into the cellars lined with the rough beds where doctors and young nurses equipped with next to nothing mount their round-the-clock struggle against death, pain and desperation.

Little Arijana's dark eyes stare out with a stab of apprehension from her beautiful, lacerated face. She is eleven years old and confused beyond reason. Half her head is shaven, and the locks of a little girl flow down the other shoulder. Shrapnel was removed from her brain and her left leg amputated after a tank shell exploded near where she was playing. Then her stomach swelled, and it emerged that more bits of flying, burning metal had dug their way in there too. Arijana's was one of the 800 operations performed by the tireless surgeons, using what equipment they can muster. Since the convoy, at least there is anaesthetic; before it came, there wasn't any. The wards are underground, full of horribly injured men, women and children, and the latest severely wounded arrival lies bloodily on the operating table – for all to behold, for there is no privacy here – an old man hit by one of the mortars that fell that morning.

'It is inconceivable that we could survive the winter,' says Dr Dragan Milavić, taking us up to the evacuated and empty second floor of the building, where the roof now dives to the floor and a carpet of rubble. 'We have taken fifty direct hits,' he says, 'including ten tank shells in the last fortnight which destroyed most of our medicines. The hospital is clearly marked, and the Croatians know exactly what they are aiming at.' Pathetically, men are busy sawing planks of wood, and setting about building a new roof from the inside in anticipation of the cold weather. 'Sometimes, we send people up to try to replace the tiles, but the snipers just open fire on them.

'We have treated 3,000 people so far, and can barely cope. Now we can only expect all kinds of infections, respiratory problems and epidemics which would be far more serious than the shelling. People are malnourished, we have problems with water, there are no flushing lavatories, no electricity or regular supplies. In addition to that, there is trauma and daily fear, and a sharp increase in suicide. My concern is that people, in desperation, will simply break out with their bare hands.'

Suicide moves in where hope has fled. Outside the entrance to the Government Army's bunker headquarters, a tearful woman called Asmira is waiting to see the commander. Her husband, whose photograph she brandishes painfully, was one of his bodyguards until, unable to feed his wife and children any more, he put a hand grenade to his mouth, pulled out the pin and blew his own head off. Asmira cries; she wonders if there is any way she might take the children and leave. 'Where to?' says the soldier at the door, 'and how?'

There are others in the little crowd by the sandbagged doorway who have come in the more likely direction — into, not out of, east Mostar — like Jasmina, who was bundled over from the west side just three days ago and is still looking for somewhere to sleep. 'We knew the Croats would come for us in the end,' she says, 'we must have been among the last left in our neighbourhood. And of course they did, shouting "Out! Out!" and "Don't Carry Anything!" They said we had to go because we were "filthy Muslims" and "gypsies". They put us on a bus without seats, nineteen of us, but kept back the young ladies, at least the pretty ones. I don't want to say what I think they were going to do with them, but I think I can guess. As we got on the bus, trucks were already arriving and they were ready to load up the things from our houses. The bus took us to the river and then they sent us across the lovely old bridge.' The group is scattered by the first of three tank and mortar shells that come punching into the nearby flats, sending us diving for cover.

Deep down in the bunker is General Arif Pašeljic, by now one of the central figures of the war, having stayed in his post since the day we last met when the HVO came and took his radio transmitter from the old headquarters on the western side. 'This is a sudden, urban war we are fighting now,' he stressed, 'and we are having to improvise and create new tactics.' The defence should in theory have crumbled a long time ago, but there have even been moments of unexpected success as the army sends out its fighting patrols to strike way behind Croatian lines. The strategic significance of Mostar is that it lies along the Bosnia's route to the sea, a corridor the army wishes to force by fighting if it cannot get it at the negotiating table. Ammunition comes in on horseback or is carried along the single feasible mountain track into Mostar from Jablanica, a two-day hike under constant shell and sniper fire from the Croats as they try to cut off this precarious umbilical lifeline. If the Croats don't the snow will.

The general sees two motives for the ferocity of the siege, one political, one economic. 'They want this to be the capital of the state they have carved, which entails ethnic cleansing or killing all the Muslims because of their ideology. We cannot accept this. Mostar must remain a free, open and mixed city, or else it cannot exist. But on top of this, they need the Neretva valley for its resources, and the hydro-electric plants that power the coast. At the moment, we still control the energy sources in this country, and they don't want half of Dalmatia's electricity supply to be in our hands.'

From the general's bunker in Mostar comes the clearest statement of Bosnia's desperate position as the warring parties prepare to sit down in Geneva for what some are saying will be the beginning of the end of the War of Maps. 'At the beginning, when you and I met in the old headquarters, yes, we insisted that we were fighting for a unified, multi-ethnic Bosnia, because we were fighting in alliance with the Croats and there was the possibility of victory together against the aggressor, as we had proved here in Mostar. Then it became clear that the Croatians were pursuing other aims; we were betrayed and needed to take stock politically as well as militarily of what was being done to us. We had a knife in our back, and now we are fighting for the basic survival and existence of the Muslim people.

'We would now accept a just settlement of divided territory for all the three warring peoples, and with access to the sea. But if the Serbs and the Croats claim for their states all that they have conquered, and in the particular way they have conquered it, that we cannot accept. In that case, we shall seize territory as well. We must have links open to Sarajevo and Jablanica; if we don't we are surrounded, cut off, helpless and dead. The substance of the war is now to secure a fair territory for the Muslim people, and for any other nationalities who want to live with us and are welcome to do so. If we do not get a just settlement, there will be a major offensive, and a final battle for Mostar, the Neretva valley and the corridor to the coast.'

At the time of writing, that battle is between massive fire power and unrelenting brutality on the Croat side, blunted by military incompetence; and guerrilla ingenuity, sharpened by the capacity for the blind violence of the trapped wild animal on the Muslim side. No sane analyst could foresee anything other than the total destruction and surrender of east Mostar, but then war is a strange thing.

Under the partition plans, Mostar is a divided city under an EC tutelage. But Mate Boban said on the day we left the city: 'No one will divide Mostar and no one will have Croatia's coast' (although a sector of it falls within Bosina-Herzegovina). UN observers have seen what the Croats are doing to support his words: columns of tanks digging in all around the valley to grind east Mostar, now the new symbol of Bosnia's war, into further submission until its life is torn to shreds and it can endure no more. There is no longer any pretence: every UN and EC observer reports the tanks to belong to the army of Croatia proper; this is armed annexation from Zagreb to complete the War of Maps, and the squeals of its government are no different from the play-acting by Slobodan Milošević.

Others in east Mostar have more immediate and urgent aims. 'Don't even speak to me about the winter,' says Safet Krkic who runs the local branch of the Islamic charity

Merhemet. 'I daren't think about more than one problem at a time. There is no food, that is all I can think about; 35,000 people eating one scrappy meal a day in fifteen public kitchens, that is all I can think about. We have problems with water, the city is dying and people are very, very hungry.'

Outside the commander's bunker, the shells have come, done their damage and stopped for the moment, and our little huddle emerges from hiding to re-group outside the sandbagged entrance. One man has just trudged in having been 'released' from the Croatian camp at the heliport and walked down from Jablanica. 'This is just a larger prison camp, I know,' he admits. 'But in a way I feel free here, and good to be here. I can say what I want. I can listen to what I want. I can tune into Voice of America if I want. Over there, I am told what to say, what to listen to and what to think. At least we can all die together in a free prison.'

Interval

Travnik Voices – 3 – Summer 1993

In Travnik, some things have changed completely, some things have stayed the same.

This is what has not changed: on the night of 19 July, a small huddle of people emerged out of the gloom along the road into Turbe on the edge of town, at the end of what was now a shorter walk from the advanced Serbian front line. One year on, and they were still coming, dazed by not just days or weeks but months and months of fear and loss.

'We had to work ten hours a day in the factory; there was no pay. We were slaves, really,' said Ismet Smoljan from Doboj, who had come via Banja Luka and had been on that now well-trodden road. 'Then they said they wanted us to go, if we could pay 150 Deutschmarks for a ticket, or 100 for the children. They said they didn't want us any more, put us on buses and brought us here. They seemed bored by the idea of beating us up and didn't even hit us very hard. A man just called me a filthy gypsy, took my money and kicked me onto the bus. It is terrible back there, terrible.'

This time it was not Emir Tica's buses which picked them up and took them to Travnik, but the British army, although they were not allowed up to the front line. The thing that has changed in Travnik is that it is now more or less a Muslim town. There are more people on the streets than at any time during the war, but few of them are Croats or Serbs; it is not the same Travnik. The other big difference is that people don't complain any more. Sympathy is neither required nor welcome. The betrayal is complete, the pride and ruthlessness of the fight is all that is left; there are plenty of hard-luck stories to tell, but no one tells them any more. There's no point.

Merhmet Alagić

Alagić is now the military 'Muhktar' of Travnik. He is now purposeful and solemn. If the affable, hospitable, uncle-ish man is still there, he has been tailored to the requirements of the hour. The talk in Geneva is of partition and of signing agreements. Alagić is rarely in his office, he tends to spend time at the front, but when he is around, the talk is of fighting on regardless.

'I am in command of men who have all lost their homes, who have mostly lost their families, and who have nothing further to lose. I love them and they respect me. They are fighting for only one thing: to go home. I will not surrender their war to President Izetbegović or any other political authority. We shall fight on whatever he signs. Tens of thousands of my men and neighbours have died. They died in the camps, or were exectuted in cold blood, or died fighting. To sign for partition, or to accept a Muslim state in which we live as beggars on the floors of schools would be to lie to the dead. They were not fighting for a Muslim state, they were fighting for Bosnia-Herzegovina and they were fighting to go home. I will not lie to the dead. That is why we shall carry on the war.'

And if the command at Zenica tells you to stop, on Sarajevo's orders? 'The phone lines are very bad around here,' he replies.

Emir Tica

Emir is thin and pale, his skin has yellowed and his eyes are sorrowful, but he still manages a smile. He is writing a book. It is not a diary or history of what has happened before him; each chapter features a different girl whom Emir knows, has known or been in love with, and the book sees the war through her imagined eyes, or else through his own dreams.

'We feel better now. We know we're on our own, that no one cares, that we have been betrayed, that Europe is not coming and never intended to. If only we had known that at the beginning, what a different war it would have been! All the things we have done in the past few weeks we would have been doing from the beginning. With the men we have, who knows, we might even have won the war. Now we have been taught not to trust anyone but ourselves.

'No, I don't think I will leave Travnik after all. I've changed my mind. If I have a part to play, then I will stay here. I must try to work it out for myself, I am confused. If we are still free agents, and free to fight on, then I will stay. But if I find out that there is some great game going on, that we are being used by someone, that this is all some experiment to see what happens in modern war, then I would go. But if I have a role, I'll stay.

'I don't think about the future any more. There are these questions: will I survive? will I stay normal? But I don't think about them any more. Before the war I was planning to get married. Before the war it was important to me to have a family, a wife and children. Some day maybe. There is no future in my head any more.'

Fahrudin Alihodžic

Fahrudin has been transferred, and is now running the military police in Turbe, spending all his time on the front lines and rarely back in town. He fell out with the commanders and with Alagić. But he likes to recall how, during the push against the HVO, he sat on the bonnet of his car with a machine gun: 'Me and the car: we made a good tank in those days.'

'There are some bad people in this town, and good people in this town. People doing deals, people I don't like. But that's enough of that. It's not like it was in the early days.

'But the reasons for fighting are the same. Always the same: the innocent ones, the weak ones, the ones who can't fight for themselves. I may have changed, and learned how to hate, but that hasn't changed. I still the love the weak and normal people most of all, though I love the brave people too. We knew at the beginning that the innocents would suffer most, and that is what this war is all about. And now it's clearer than ever: last week a shell landed right at the entrance to the gym where the refugees are living. Aimed, of course. I was there, I saw the refugees covered in blood, four of them killed. I helped the wounded. It's my job to deal with the bodies. All we can do now is to try to keep people alive, defend the elderly, our women and kids and the refugees, and to wait for the end, knowing that we are on our own.

'But I have lost so many of my friends now. You remember those lads who used to hang around that office in the barracks where you used to sleep? They're mostly dead now. And the young kid in the café who was so scared at first? Him too. And it gets very lonely. I want us all to be together again, sitting in the same room, talking – that is my only dream. Most days now, I go up to the graveyard and I sit among the graves of my boys, the ones I fought with, and the ones who died in front of me and whose bodies I carried back. I sit there for hours, until it gets dark. That way, at least we're all together.'

Afterword

The End of Hope

> *'Deep under turfy grass and heavy clay*
> *They laid her body, and the child.*
> *Poor victims of a swift mischance were they,*
> *Adown death's trapdoor suddenly beguiled.*
> *I, weeping not, as others, but heart-wild,*
> *Affirmed to Heaven that even love's fierce flame*
> *Must fail beneath the chill of this cold shame.'*
> — Wilfred Owen

17 November 1993

The 427-year history of Mostar's mighty bridge has ended; it collapsed into the River Neretva last week, victim of continued pounding by the Croatian artillery — a symbolic victory for the Croats which caused ripples of discomfort in Zagreb. The bridge was one of the marvels of Ottoman Bosnia, and seemed to span the divide between West and East. Next day, two little children were shot by Croat snipers while playing in a street on the Muslim side of the river, but this time there was little or no newspaper coverage.

Moderate Croatians who tried to keep the peace in the central Bosnian town of Vares, surrounded by Muslims and Serbs but taking refugees from all sides, were ousted by a coup. HVO heavies took over, and responded to the effective Muslim siege by moving into the village of

Stupni Do and massacring all the civilians. Two weeks later, with the Muslims advancing, the Croats suddenly evacuated Vares, 15,000 people going over to the Serbs, and soldiers from the Muslim armed forces moved into town, looting. The flag they raised in the schoolyard bore not the lilies of Bosnia but the green crescent.

Six children died, three immediately, in a single burst of Serbian shelling into Sarajevo last week. The power of the underworld gangs has broken out into open warfare within the imploding city. And the first snow has fallen already, threatening the precarious aid routes that remain, and raising the prospect of tens of thousands of people being cut off and dying from cold and hunger in what this time promises to be a less merciful winter. With 2.3 million people now refugees, the war has exploded out of control.

With President Izetbegović and his team boycotting the initial carve-up negotiations in Geneva at the end of July, Owen and Stoltenberg found themselves dealing on the Muslims' behalf to etch their state into the Tudjman–Milošević partition draft. The mediators produced their map which gave 52 per cent of Bosnia to the Serbs, 18 per cent to the Croats and 30 per cent to the Muslims. The Sarajevo area would come under UN tutelage, and Mostar under the EC. The Croats were angry that they had been denied the extended 'Herzeg-Bosna' after all, and insisted on being the sole authority in Mostar. Mate Boban accepted on condition of border changes in central Bosnia and control of Mostar. Karadžić told his militants that although some territory had to be conceded, the principle of Serbian statehood was the thing that mattered, and had been won. The Muslims were to be granted some lost land, but their republic was divided between a main chunk and four pockets, with a road linking Gorazde to Zepa. It looked like blobs of ink. Central Bosnia presented an almost surreal mesh of roads, some for use by Croats, others by Muslims; people of different ethnic groups would be taking different routes to get from one place to another.

Eventually, late in August and under extreme pressure, Izetbegović recommended that his government accept partition. But he and vice-president Ganić said they could accept the plan itself only if the Serbs conceded another 4 per cent of land, the most savagely 'cleansed' regions around Sanski Most and Foca, and if the Muslims were granted an outlet, even by tunnel, to the sea. With the former demand unacceptable to the Serbs, and the latter to the Croats, the acceptance in principle was a rejection in practice. Karadžić warned that unless the plan was accepted as a *fait accompli*, the country would instead be shared between the Serbs and Croats only, using their superior fire power and probably formalising the alliance at work in the field (an alliance made all the more ironic by the fact that fighting had broken out again between the old rivals in the Croatian Krajina).

While the US blamed Serb and Croat intransigence for the failure to agree, Lord Owen sounded an unpleasant harmony with Karadžić, warning that Bosnia might be 'cut in two' if the Muslims did not sign. The victims were being browbeaten into accepting the new order.

In mid-September, the Bosnian government did agree to a clause formalising the disappearance of Bosnia-Herzegovina, entitling the eventual Serbian and Croatian 'republics' to accede to their respective mother countries, in acknowledgement of their annexation. In return, the rump 'Muslim' republic would be allowed to inherit Bosnia's international status. In Sarajevo, 53 out of 349 Bosnian MPs voted to accept the plan, 260 to accept it if the conditions were met, and 78 to reject it. In October, Izetbegović proposed that the disputed territory be put under UN authority, but the Serbs said they would not consider further concessions. Attempting to break the *impasse*, the mediators have now started talking about lifting sanctions on Siberia.

And that is how things have stuck, as Bosnia's war becomes

worse than war; the war in which the worst always happens, and happens to the innocent, a story of the betrayal of the weak and of its victims, both on the battlefields and along the corridors of international powerbrokery.

Bosnia presented the new Europe and the New World Order with the first serious test of moral and political fibre – a test that they have miserably failed. The cost of Bosnia's war and of that failure has been hundreds and thousands of brutally taken lives, millions of lost homes and also a forfeit of principle which, rather than inaugurate an era premised upon the notions of justice and human rights, seems instead to bury such an epoch. Those of us who grew up in the generation that followed the defeat of the Third Reich, who travelled hopefully and who believed that the bullies of history need not triumph, are left, after Bosnia, with the example of our parents' war and the guiding principles of our continent, as well as Bosnia, apparently betrayed.

Every diplomatic initiative, usually from the United States, to intervene effectively and halt the crushing of Bosnia's stillborn democracy and the country's Muslim population was filibustered and negated by the European Community (especially Britain) and by Russia. Troops were instead deployed to steward what was regarded as a humanitarian, not a political, crisis, and professional soldiers obliged to work with ingenuity and bravery within the perilous and frustrating straightjacket of that halting, partial brief.

By its failure to act decisively, and by sponsoring the carve-up of Bosnia by racial population control through extreme violence, the international community has written a new book of rules for the volatile new Europe: rules under which the motives of those perpetrating the Bosnian carnage can be tolerated and accommodated, and their achievements rewarded and recognised as the basis for new national frontiers. The constitution of the New World Order, just two years after President Bush coined the phrase with the liberation of Kuwait, has been turned into a bullies' charter.

The Bosnian Serbs and Croats, backed by their respective parent regimes in Belgrade and Zagreb, have been granted the full spoils of their violence. The armed dismemberment of a new, sovereign, recognised state, and the annexation and racial purging of most of it, was accepted and later even encouraged by the West. The 'mediators' representing the EC and UN at first treated the aggressor and victim as equals, but ended up by going even further: endorsing the ambitions of the warlords against what was left of the resistance. And the rewards for the brutality of the Warriors of Maps eventually but inevitably brutalised their victim.

Not only did the international community decline to defend Bosnia's government, unity and victim population, but it denied that government and population the means of defending itself. As a result, Bosnia's war was not a war between armies. It was a war by men of arms against civilians, mostly Muslim civilians defended by no more than a collection of desperate, landlocked guerrilla militias. In the First World War, nine out of ten victims wore military uniform. In Bosnia's war, 85 per cent of those killed, let alone the displaced, the bereaved and the wounded, wear T-shirts, headscarves, old suits, skirts, childrens' clothes or sneakers.

On the ground, Bosnia's war is where the worst always happens. You hope something cannot be true, but you fear it might be, and it is. You hope that the next stage in the grotesque and tragic logic of the war will be averted, but you hope in vain.

Appendix

Genocide in our Lifetime

Mohammed Curac, Mayor of Travnik, said some weeks prior to an attempt to kill him by blowing up his car: 'Look at the way this war is being conducted: it has become city-cidal, culture-cidal, history-cidal, memory-cidal, dignity-cidal, economicidal – in short, genocidal. Our parents' generation bore witness to the Holocaust against the Jews. That was on a different scale. I think this is what genocide looks like in our lifetime.'

In January 1993, the Chief Rabbi of British Jewry, Jonathan Sacks, added his cogent voice to the call for military intervention in Bosnia, saying: 'There are some crimes which, because they are crimes against humanity, implicate us all, and we are sometimes morally responsible for what we fail to prevent as well as for what we do. I wonder if future generations could ever forgive us if we, who have lived through the century of the Holocaust, did not rise up and prevent the beginnings of a second Holocaust.'

Among the declared ambitions of modern Europe is to make sure that nothing like the Nazi persecutions should ever be repeated. But the characteristics of genocide, its tone, its dictionary definition, its component parts, can be revived without a second Auschwitz or Dachau. And some of those characteristics have undoubtedly hallmarked the crushing of Bosnia's Muslims in the eighteen months since April 1992, setting Bosnia's war apart from other recent wars, like Vietnam, the Gulf, Central America and Lebanon.

Europe is not now menaced by a grand and lunatic quest for supremacy like Hitler's, but it is fragmenting into a plethora of fiercely harboured ethnic identities. And genocide in this Europe will be a more localised, parish-pump, grubby business – but genocide nevertheless.

The Bosnian government has established a war crimes commission under the leadership of a lawyer, Mirsad Tokaca, who argues that what has happened to Bosnia's Muslims meets the various internationally recognised definitions of genocide. He cites mass ethnic cleansing, the murders in the camps and mass rape. 'We know we cannot solve anything,' he says, 'we are here only to get facts, documents and testimonies, to prepare data for an international court, if there ever is one.'

One important facet of genocide, though less costly in human terms than the main tranches of Tokaca's submissions, can be seen by anyone who drives through the towns from which Muslims have been 'cleansed' by the Serbs: the obliteration of historical identity and memory, and of an entire culture, as expressed in architecture, in religious buildings or historical records. All this has gone, systematically destroyed. Nowhere is the destruction more clearly measurable than in the fate of the mosques in towns that have come into exclusively Serbian hands. The same happened, on a smaller scale, to the Roman Catholic churches of the Croats, whose destruction was a trademark of Serbian aggression in Croatia during the first war.

Among the Croatian Catholic shrines wrecked in Bosnia was the Franciscan monastery near Jajce, badly damaged during the siege and ransacked after the surrender. In Derventa, Catholic churches were set upon with just as much savagery as the mosques, that of St John the Baptist blown to bits. The churches were burned and wholly destroyed at Modrica, Vidovice and many others. The monastery at Gura Goca near Travnik was defiled by Muslim extremists.

Jewish shrines have suffered too: the old temple in Sarajevo, which survived the Nazi occupation and was converted into a cultural centre, has been converted by a Serbian squadron into an artillery and sniping position, with reports that artefacts have been desecrated. The Jewish cemetery at Kovačići outside the city, an important necropolis five centuries old, has also been turned into a military position and is badly damaged.

But the principal cultural pogroms have been inflicted on the symbols of Muslim history. More than 800 Bosnian mosques have been either completely or partially destroyed by the Serbs and latterly the Croats. Libraries have disappeared altogether, and cemeteries paved over. Some of the lost buildings were among the finest examples of Ottoman architecture in the Balkans. In the libraries, the documentary history of the Ottoman empire in the Balkans has been eradicated. Here, for the record, are just a few of the monuments to a culture which have been consigned to memory.

One of the finest of all was the Ferhadija Džamija mosque in Banja Luka, built in 1583 and finally dynamited to pieces early in 1993. The remaining members of the Muslim community asked if they might be allowed to preserve the pieces in the hope that one day another mosque might be rebuilt with them. They were denied, the site cleared and the masonry taken to the municipal rubbish dumps.

The oldest mosque in Bosnia no longer exists: this was the Emin Turhan Bey Mosque at Ustikolina, built in 1448/9. The other fifteenth-century mosque in perfect condition at Ćelebići was also smashed to smithereens. The site of one of the loveliest old mosques in Foča is now a car park. All the mosques in Foča have been destroyed, notably the Sultan Bayazid Imperial Mosque and the Aladza, built in 1501 and 1550 respectively and among Bosnia's earliest, wrecked by explosives and fire. Five other mosques in Foča dated from the sixteenth or seventeenth centuries. Sixteen mosques in Zvornik have been wrecked, with the remains of that at Kula Grad, along with its graveyard, levelled by bulldozers.

In Višegrad, the Imperial Mosque was burned down and a 'Serbian Cultural Centre' has already been built on the site. At Rogatica, the sixteenth-century Semsudin Mosque was pounded by tank shells before being burned, and the Islamic religious community buildings burned, including a library and archives. The mosque in Modrica was used jokily as a makeshift slaughterhouse for pigs, before being converted into a prison for Muslim captives and then destroyed. The main mosque at Bjeljina was desecrated, looted and covered with graffiti with a Serbian flag flown from the minaret and was allegedly used to keep and execute prisoners before being demolished. That at Čaparde was turned into a barracks, and the minaret used as a snipers' nest, until it was blown up during a retreat from the town.

Šipovo's mosques had been destroyed by Chetnik irregulars during the 1940s, were rebuilt in the 1950s and ransacked again in 1992. Newer mosques were also erased, notably the large one in Sanski Most, built in the oriental style, opened in 1985 and blown away by explosives seven years later. The mosque and graveyard at Kozarac were, unsurprisingly, entirely dismantled. Mostar's seventeenth-century Coše Jahja Mosque was levelled to the ground, and others have sustained heavy damage during both Serbian and Croatian bombardments, including the lovely Koski Mehmed Pasha Mosque of 1618 which is a ruin. The Great White Mosque in Brčko was last heard of as having been turned into a café. Reports reached Sarajevo that the brand new mosque at Hanifići had been set on fire with forty-three people locked inside it. The Imam was said to have been ordered to dig their grave, and was then shot.

In Sarajevo itself, the deepest wound was the destruction of the Institute for Oriental Studies, done away with by a cascade of inflammable rockets on 17 May 1992. The library, founded in 1950, boasted a catalogue of thousands of documents and manuscripts, almost all of which have been incinerated, bar a few salvaged by staff and journalists as keepsakes. Most of the important historical and literary documentation of Ottoman Bosnia was there and disappeared in a single day. There were manuscripts from all over the Orient, in Arabic, Turkish, Persian and Serbo-Croat, making up one of the major libraries in Eastern Europe. There were musical scores, grammars, poetry books and philosophical, political and economic tracts. Some 7,000 documents of the history of Bosnia and elsewhere from the sixteenth to the nineteenth century were kept there, including original *Berats* (Sultan's Edicts), land ownership certificates, charts and maps – in effect, the tangible history of Ottoman Bosnia.

Mr Tokaca the lawyer sat in Sarajevo this summer, preparing his evidence for the promised international war crimes tribunal which still shows no sign of materialising. At the same time, he watched the extremist Muslim 'nationalists' in his own city (and indeed in his own offices) accumulate power and entrench their positions while the intelligentsia prepared to leave at the first possible opportunity. Serbs and Croats were becoming uncomfortable, and being deposed from jobs for the first time since the siege began. 'People,' he says, 'have been corrupted. There has been a change in aims, and a change in the methods of our war. Genocide produces extremes, and we will have to go to the extreme too. I dare not even think about that. If that happens, it is war without end.'

A rump Bosnia in the form of a Muslim state, probably an ugly political creature, will be born out of the war in order to accommodate the victories of the other two factions and the sentence of the 'international community'. The first generation to grow up in this bereft, crowded, mono-ethnic state will know only too much about how it came to be, and about the suffering which their parents – who never wanted or asked to live in such a place – went through at its inception. The country into which they should by rights have been born, Bosnia-Herzegovina, will have ceased to exist, shattered and blown asunder.

This next generation will grow up seeped in the recent history and memory of that destruction, with goodness knows what outcome. But they will never see an Ottoman minaret and may never see a Bogomil tomb. The tangible, visible and rich history of their people and its strange hybrid culture down the centuries, of their curious and inimitable place at a fulcrum between the Orient and Western Europe, will have been decimated. And that is the underlying purpose of genocide, on whatever scale, and of warfare of a particular, singular and intolerable kind.

It has, however, been both tolerated and rewarded.

Notes

1 What is Bosnia-Herzegovina?

1 Prince Dmitri Obolensky – *The Bogomils* (Cambridge, 1948)
2 Mustafa Imamovic – *Agriculture in Bosnia-Herzegovina* (Re-printed, Sarajevo, 1992)

2 Bosnia's End Game: the Players

1 Interviewed by Peter Millar, *The Sunday Times*, 4 July 1993
2 A lucid account of the Chetniks' miasma of alliances and emneties can be found in Fred Singleton – *'History of the Yugoslav Peoples'* (Cambridge, 1985)
3 Quoted in the *Independent*, 20 May 1993
4 M. Imamović and R. Mahmutčehajić – *Bosnia and the Bosnians Vol IV* (Re-printed Sarajevo, 1991)
5 Balkan Research Centre, London (Serbian)
6 Quoted by Steve Crawshaw, *Independent*, 29 August 1992

3 Sarajevo, the War Begins

1 Quote by Colin Smith, *Observer*, 14 June 92
2 Quoted by Tim Judah, *The Times*, 3 March 92
3 Quoted by Ian Traynor, *Guardian*, 4 March 92
4 Quoted by Maggie O'Kane, *Guardian*, 29 May 92
5 Quoted by Yigal Chazan, *Guardian*, 28 May 92
6 Reuters 12 July 92

4 *The First Ethnic Cleansing*

1 Quoted by Derek Brown, *Guardian*, 21 September 91
2 Marcus Tanner, *Independent*, 6 April 92
3 Maggie O'Kane, *Guardian*, 20 August 92
4 Quoted by Yigal Chazan, *Guardian*, 18 April 92
5 Andrej Gustincic, Reuters.
6 Ian Traynor, *Guardian*, 17 October 92
7 Quoted by Maggie O'Kane, *Guardian*, 29 July 92
8 Roy Gutman, New York *Newsday*, 4 August 92

5 *The Camps, Echoes of the Reich*

1 The team that uncovered the Omarska and Trnopolje camps was made up of the Guardian and two ITN television crews, including reporters Penny Marshall and Ian Williams
2 Ian Traynor, *Guardian*, 10 October 1992
3 First interviewed by John Mullin, *Guardian*, 7 August 1992.
4 Ian Traynor, *Guardian*, 29 September 1992

6 *Meanwhile, the Diplomats: The World Wakes up*

1 Quoted in *Guardian*, 7 August 92
2 Letter to Paddy Ashdown, 4 August 92
3 Quoted in *Financial Times*, 8 July 92
4 Quoted by Martin Walker, *Guardian* 1 July 92
5 Quoted by Hella Pick, *Guardian*, 30 June 92
6 *Independent*, 8 July 92
7 *Herald Tribune*, 8 July 92
8 Quoted by Michael Binyon, *The Times*, 10 July 92
9 Quoted by Hella Pick, *Guardian*, 11 July 92
10 Leader by Leslie H. Gelb, *New York Times*, 10 August 92
11 Quoted by Simon Tisdall, *Guardian*, 6 August 92
12 Lady Thatcher was writing in the *New York Times*, 6 August 92
13 Quoted in the *Independent*, 11 August 92
14 Quoted in the *Independent*, 10 August 92
15 *Guardian*, 11 August 92

9 *Meanwhile, the Diplomats: Promises, Promises*

1 Patrick Wintour, *Guardian*, 13 August 1992
2 Quoted by Hella Pick, *Guardian*, 26 August 1992
3 Quoted by Ian Traynor, *Guardian*, 8 August 1992
4 *New York Times*, 28 September 1992
5 Hella Pick, *Guardian*, 7 October 1992
6 Ian Traynor, *Guardian*, 18 November 1992

10 *'Top Guns' – a People under Siege*

1 Kurt Schork, Reuters, 18 August 1992
2 *Daily Telegraph* 19 August, 1992
3 Tim Judah, *The Times*, 28 September, 1992
4 The *New York Times*, 19 September, 1992
5 *Daily Telegraph* 28 September 1992

11 *Sarajevo, from Siege to Torture*

1 Quoted by John Burns, *New York Times*, 11 June 1992
2 Quoted by John Sweeney, *Observer*, 23 August 1992
3 Quoted by Robert Fox, *Daily Telegraph*, 9 December 1992
4 Reports by John F Burns, *New York Times*, and recording property of government of Bosnia-Herzegovina.

12 *Rape – 'Reward against the Innocent'*

1 Maggie O'Kane, *Guardian*, 19 March 1993

14 *Blackshirts and the Rule of Madness*

1 Robert Fox, *Daily Telegraph*, 19 June 1992
2 Kurt Schork, Reuters, 31 August 1992

16 *Meanwhile the Diplomats: A Foreign Field that is Forever England*

1 Interviewed by Hella Pick, *Guardian*, 5 December 1992
2 Ibid.

3 Ian Traynor, *Guardian*, 7 December 1992
4 Operations witnessed by John Landay, UPI
5 Hella Pick, *Guardian*, 2 January 1993
6 Quoted by Tim Judah, *The Times*, 7 January 1993
7 Quoted by Ian Traynor, *Guardian*, 7 January 1993
8 Alec Russell, *Daily Telegraph*, 21 January 1993
9 *Daily Telegraph*, 11 February 1993
10 *The Times*, 4 March 1993
11 Quoted in the *Guardian*, 26 March 1993

17   *The Land Grab*

1 Robert Fox, *Daily Telegraph*, 29 January 1993

18   *Srebrenica and Europe's Last Stand*

1 Quoted by Ian Traynor, *Guardian*, 15 February 93
2 Quoted by Yigal Chazan, *Guardian*, 3 March 93
3 Quoted by Adrian Brown, *Daily Telegraph*, 4 March 93
4 Quoted by Patrick Bishop, *Daily Telegraph*, 9 March 93
5 Slobodna Bosna ('Free Bosnia')/Associated Press, 7 April 93
6 Quoted in the *Guardian*, 20 March 93
7 *Daily Telegraph*, 30 March 93
8 Michael Montgomery, *Daily Telegraph*, 1 April 93
9 BBC TV, 13 April 93
10 Quoted by Martin Walker, *Guardian*, 24 April 93
11 *The Sunday Times*, 18 April 93
12 Ann Devroy, *Washington Post*, 10 May 93
13 *The Times*, 23 May 93

19   *Massacre and Revenge*

1 Ian Traynor, *Guardian*, 22 April 1993
2 BBC TV, 22 April 1993
3 Quoted by Ian Traynor, *Guardian*, 21 April 1993
4 Robert Fox, *Daily Telegraph*, 28 April 1993
5 Bill Frost, *The Times*, 12 June 1993
6 Maggie O'Kane, Chris Stephen and David Fairhall, *Guardian*,
   12 June 1993
7 Quoted by Ian Traynor, *Guardian*, 17 June 1993

20 *Meanwhile, the Diplomats: The Final Betrayal*

1 Quoted by John Palmer, *Guardian*, 22 June 93
2 *Observer*, 27 June 93

21 *Serbian End Games – Sarajevo*

1 Kurt Schork, Reuters, 24 May 93
2 Maggie O'Kane, *Guardian*, and Alan Little, BBC, August 93
3 Quoted by Ian Black, *Guardian*, 9 July 93

Index